The Fantastical Art of Jim Pitts

Volume One

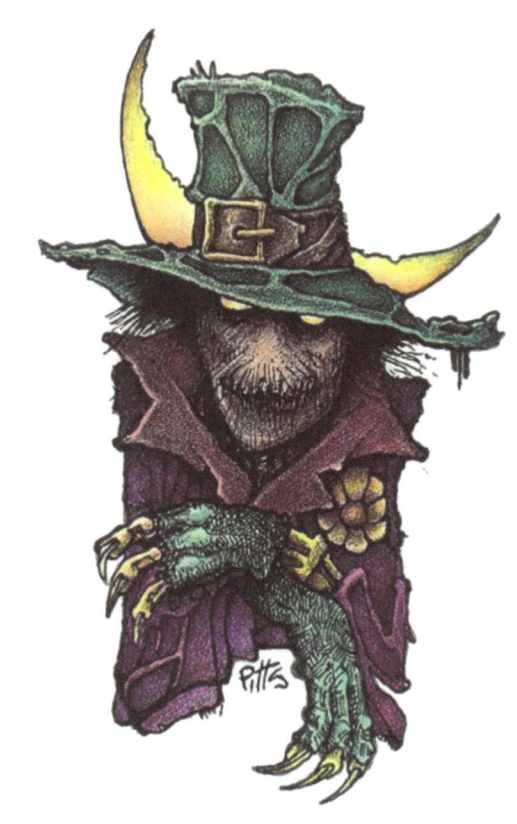

Rolling back the years...

PARALLEL UNIVERSE PUBLICATIONS

First Published in the UK in 2017
Volume One of the soft cover version First Published 2019
Jim Pitts artwork copyright © 2017 Jim Pitts
All other artists and photographers retain rights to their own work
All written contributions are copyright the individual authors
ISBN: 978-1-9161109-0-8

THIS BOOK IS DEDICATED TO THE MEMORIES OF

JOHN STEWART
DAVE MCFARREN
& KARL EDWARD WAGNER

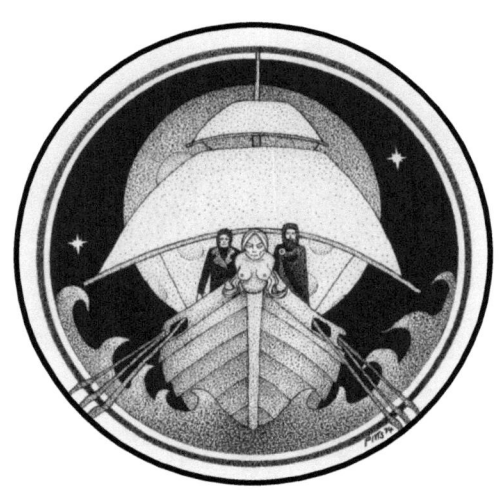

All rights reserved. No part of this publication may be reproduced, stored in a retrieval system, rebound or transmitted in any form or by any means, electronic, mechanical, photocopying, recording or otherwise, without the prior written permission of the author and publisher. This book is sold subject to the condition that it shall not by way of trade or otherwise be lent, resold, hired out or otherwise circulated without the publisher's prior consent in any form of binding or cover other than that in which it is published.

Parallel Universe Publications, 130 Union Road, Oswaldtwistle,
Lancashire, BB5 3DR, UK

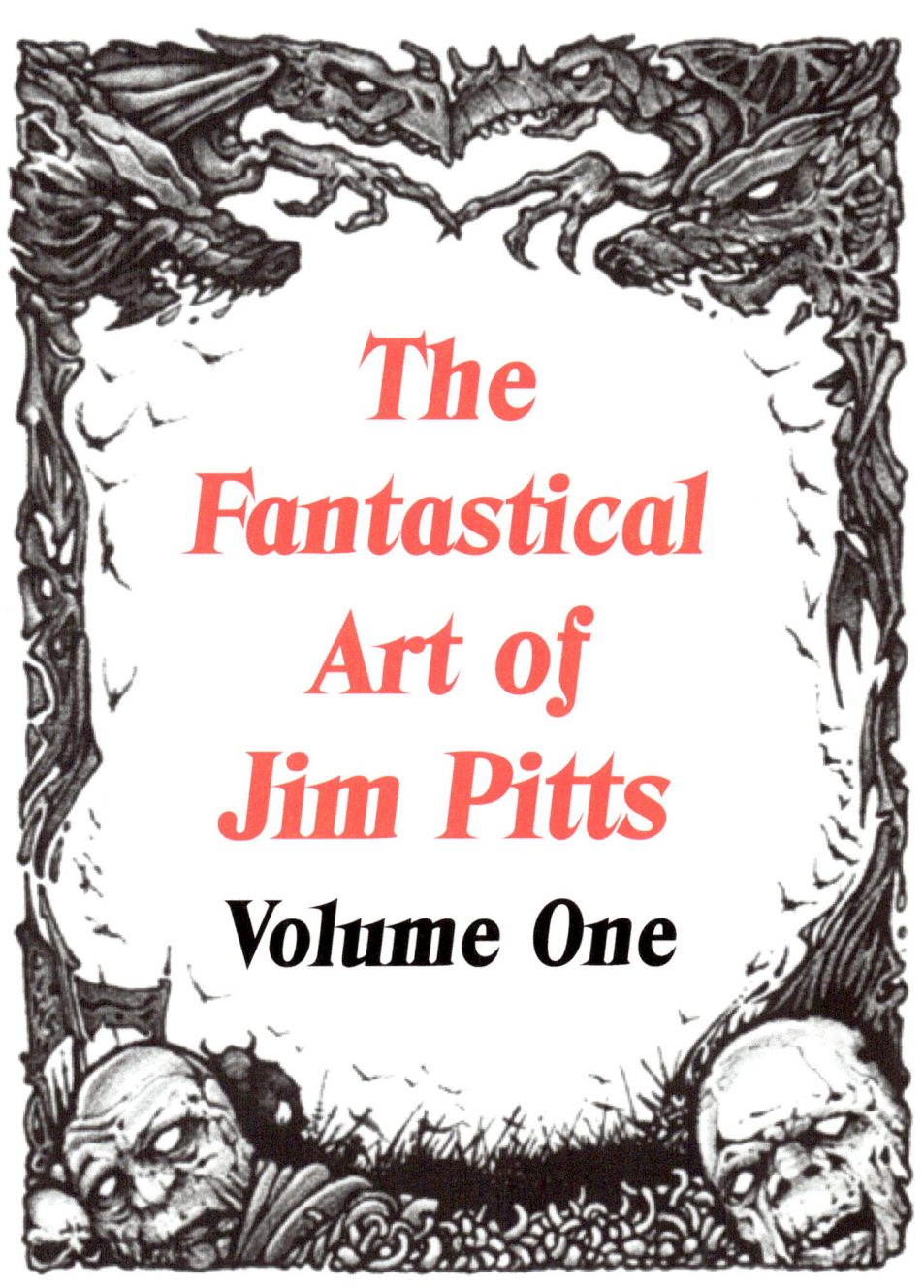

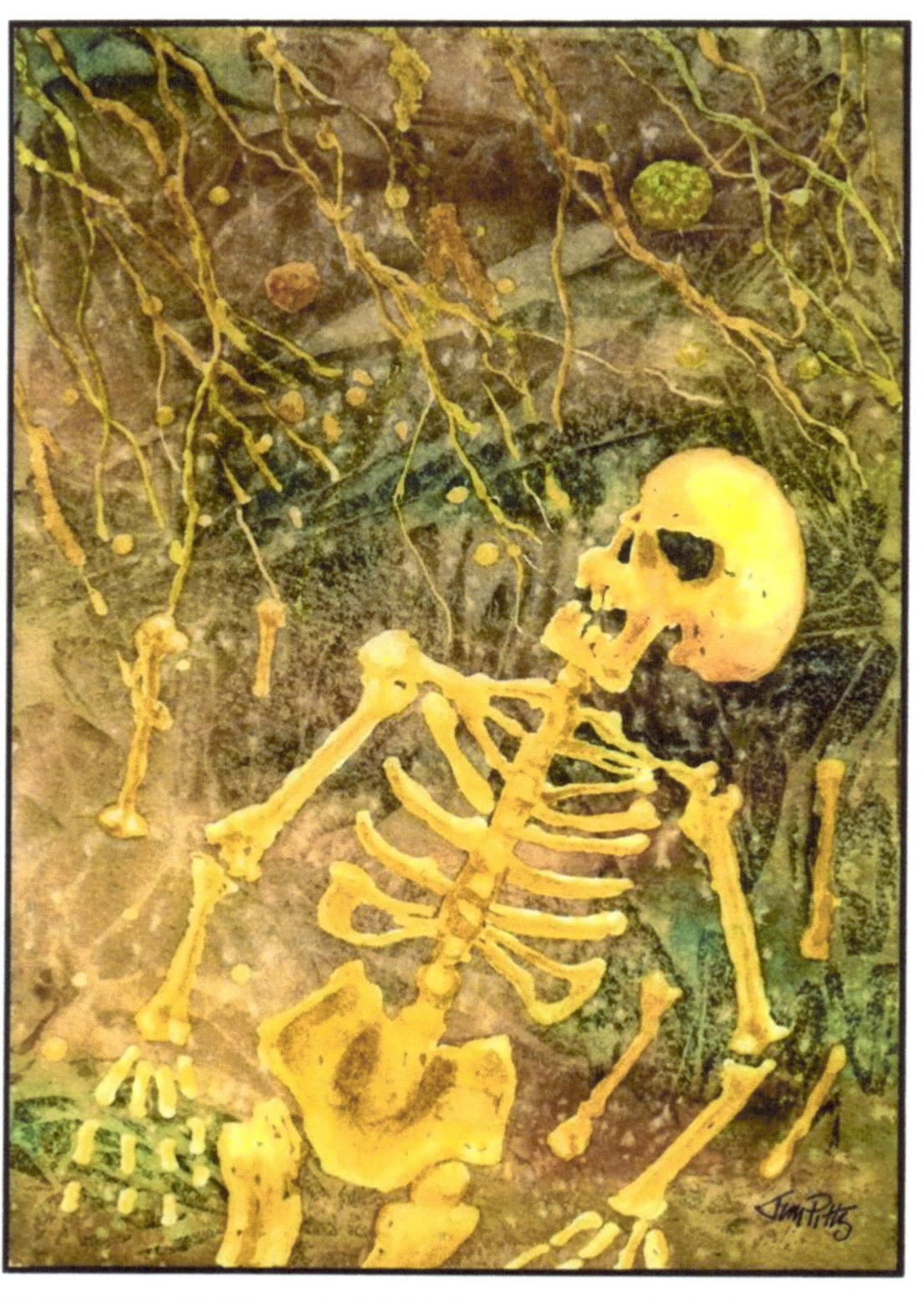

An experiment in water colour techniques using clingfilm and ink
Cover for *Worlds of the Unknown* # 1 (Spectre Press)

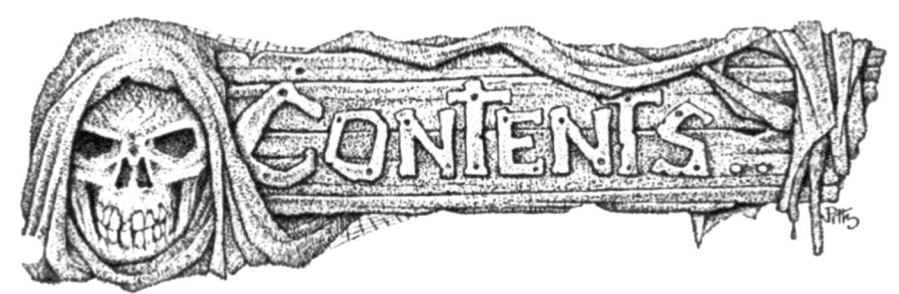

Introduction by David A. Riley	6
In Black and White: The Early Art of Jim Pitts by David A. Sutton	8
The British Fantasy Society: *Dark Horizons* and the *BFS Bulletin*	27
The Artist in Fandom: Jim Pitts interviewed by Nick Caffrey (1981)	31
"The Jim Pitts Folk Quartet"- Early years of a lifelong friendship by Nick Caffrey	40
World of Horror - 1975	44
Spaced Out & Savage Heroes - Michel Parry	50
Spectre Press - Jon M. Harvey	58
Jim Pitts and *Fantasy Tales* by Stephen Jones	80
Kadath magazine	97
Jim Pitts by Ramsey Campbell	102
Legend Horror Classics - 1975	105
Acknowledgements and Thanks	111

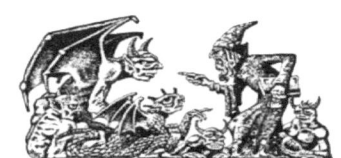

INTRODUCTION
by David A. Riley

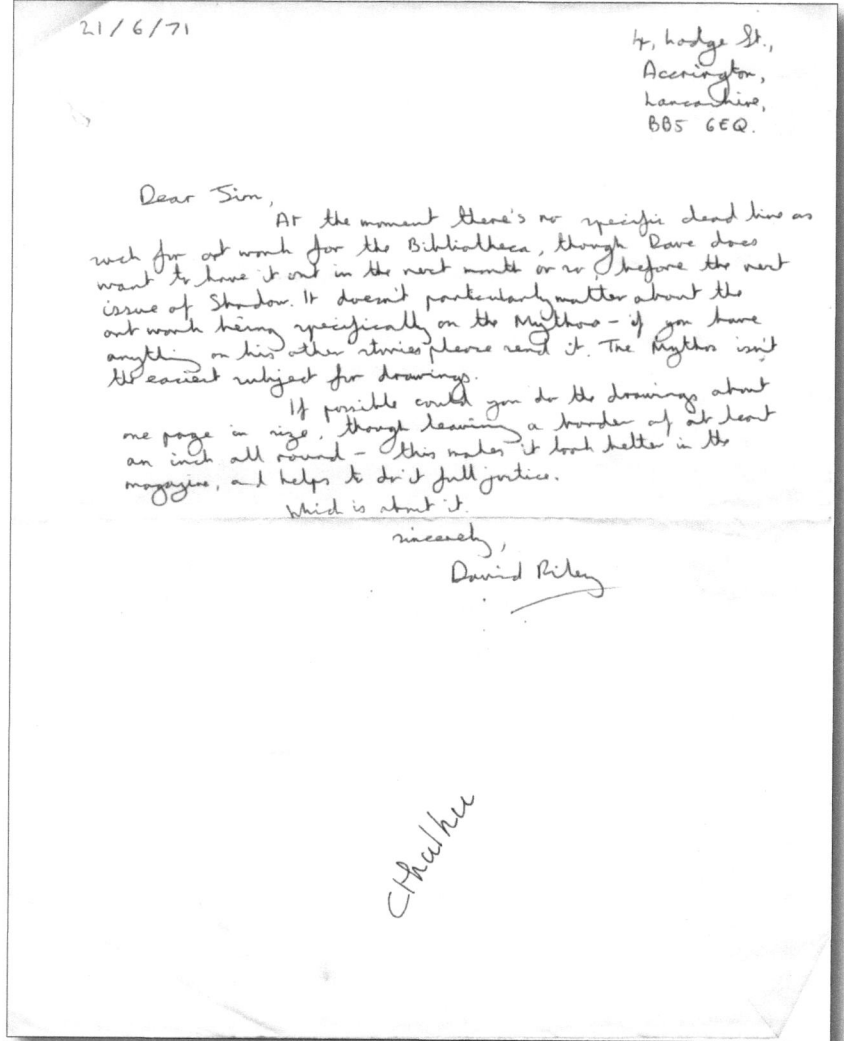

I can't claim to have "discovered" Jim Pitts as an artist. But I can claim to being the first person he submitted any artwork to, back in the days when I was art editor for Dave Sutton's fanzine, *Shadow*. Initially Jim posted some artwork to me. I don't, unfortunately, still have Jim's original letters, but he did keep my replies, which I have copied here. It was at this time that we met face to face for the first time. I think it may have been a Sunday afternoon when Jim and his friend, Nick Caffrey, turned up at my door, and handed me some of his first creations – destined to be published in *Bibliotheca H. P. Lovecraft*, which was a special issue of *Shadow*. Little was I to realise how long our relationship – now a firm friendship – was destined to last! Helped, of course, by the fact that we have never lived more than a few miles apart, me in Accrington and Jim in neighbouring Blackburn, where, unlike myself at the time, he was already a family man, with two young sons, Brian and Michael.

Nor was I to realise how rapidly Jim's talents as an artist would improve over the coming months, never mind years, with the amazing result that by 1972 he was awarded the prestigious Ken McIntyre Award at the Easter Science Fiction Convention in Chester for "The Gargoyle", which graced the front cover of Jon M. Harvey's fanzine *Balthus*. Interestingly, Jim's talents as an artist and his versatility in using different media, from his first stipplings in pen and ink, to coloured pencils, acrylics, water colours etc., has shown that he has never stopped improving his abilities, with better and better artwork flowing from him as time goes by. Which makes me certain we have not yet seen the best he is capable of creating yet!

By the mid-seventies we were members of the newly-formed British Fantasy Society. It was a time of great creativity, and the BFS was on the rise, with more and better publications and the organising of its own convention, Fantasycon, with which we were both, of course, involved. In 1974 we volunteered to publish the society's newssheet, *The BFS Bulletin*, which we upgraded from a few duplicated sheets to a full-blown lithographic publication. Before computers and word processors, it was an arduous process, me typing out columns on my manual typewriter, while Jim photocopied illustrations, etc., and letrasetted the headings, a time-consuming task with each letter having to be individually stuck to the original boards, which were twice the size of the final printed publication. No wonder we were glad to pass the editorship on to Gordon Larkin two years later!

That wasn't the end of our collaborations, though. In 1995, my wife and I published what was intended to be a fully professional SF/fantasy magazine called *Beyond*. Jim, of course, was the obvious choice for Art Editor. Alas, the magazine only lasted three issues before the money ran out due to poorer sales than we had planned for or could afford. But it was a project which gave me a taste for publishing – to which I returned some years later with Parallel Universe Publications. Which I suppose makes it all the more fitting that now, after more than forty years, I can help in the creation of this book, showcasing some of the best of the fantastical art of Jim Pitts.

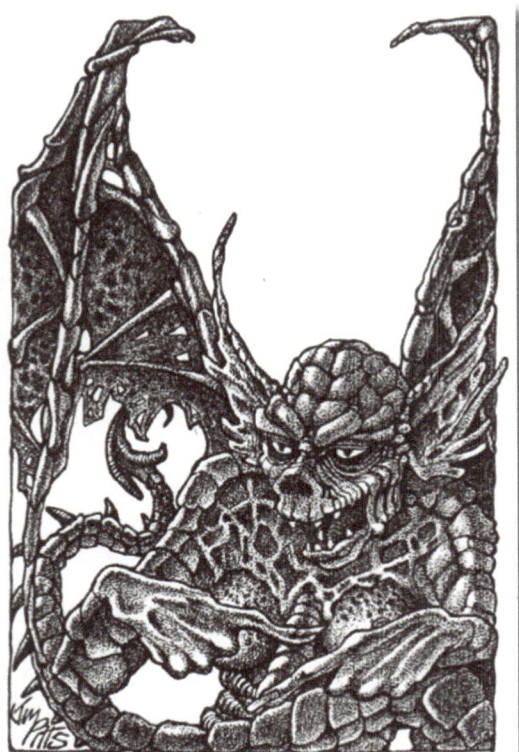

The early 90s at a Preston SF Group meeting organised by Stephen Gallagher and Bryan Talbot. In the photo are Ray Harryhausen, Martin McKenna, Jim Pitts, and David A. Riley

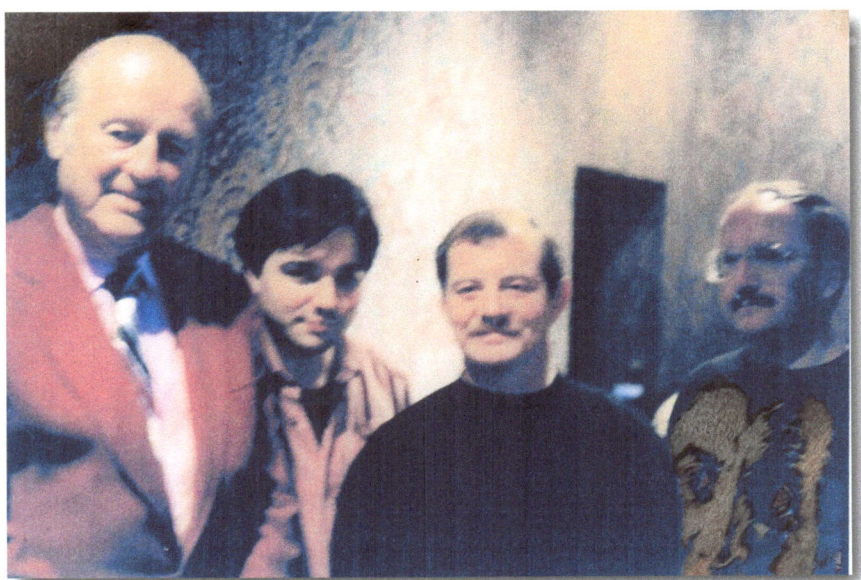

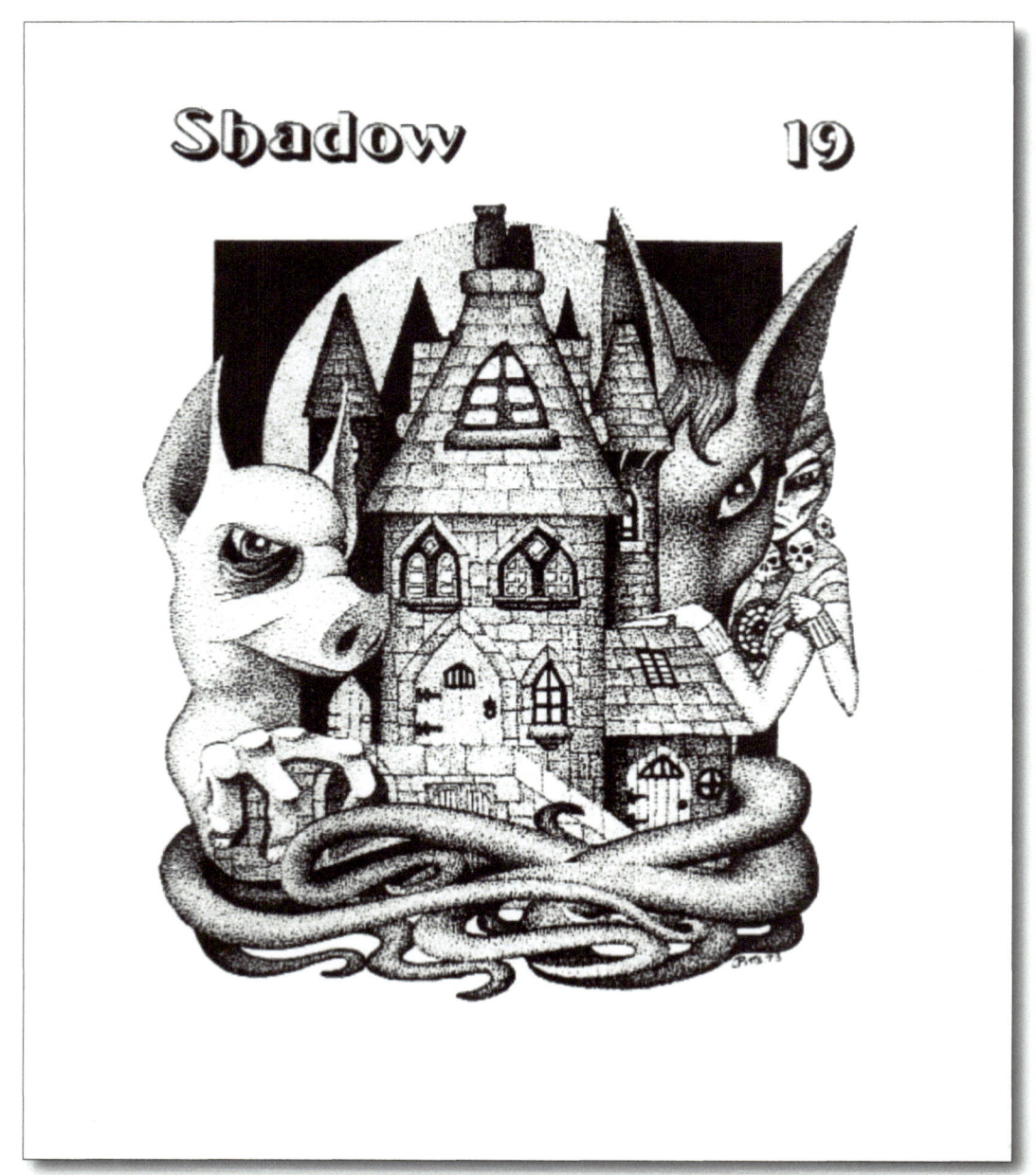

"But his cover artwork for *Shadow 19* (April 1973) was even better, a magnificent depiction of William Hope Hodgson's *The House on the Borderland*." David A. Sutton

THE 1970s *SHADOW* & OTHER FANZINES

In Black and White: The Early Art of Jim Pitts
by David A. Sutton

A stalwart of early British fantasy convention art shows and contributor to a number of key UK and American fanzines, Jim Pitts is one of the horror genre's unsung heroes. He's been an artist and illustrator for around forty years and I am pleased to say I have known him during that time and have had the opportunity to publish his work. He's a down-to-earth and self-effacing man. Jim just lets his artworks speak on his behalf.

In the early seventies I received two illustrations from Dave Riley, who had become art editor of my fanzine *Shadow: Fantasy Literature Review*. This new artist was Jim Pitts. At the time *Shadow* was a duplicated (mimeographed) fanzine, with litho printed covers. Jim had responded to an advertisement that I had put in the magazine, for artwork to illustrate a special publication I was doing called *Bibliotheca: H. P. Lovecraft*. This was published in July of 1971 and was a selection of bibliographical listings such as a chronological listing of the Cthulhu Mythos stories, a chronological listing of Lovecraft stories and novels and additions to the Jack L. Chalker bibliography published in Arkham House's *The Dark Brotherhood & Other Pieces* (1966).

These two early pen and ink pieces of artwork illustrated Lovecraft's 'The Outsider' and 'Pickman's Model'. The electro stencil reproduction did not do justice to Jim's technique, but this was in the days when litho printing was just starting to be used in genre fanzines in the UK and for *Shadow* at the time, only the cover artwork received the more professional litho finish.

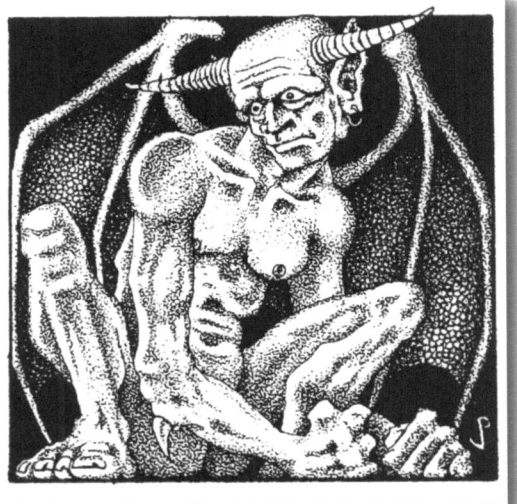

However, looking at the reproductions of these two examples, Jim's attention to detail can clearly be seen, and also the clever stippling work he used to create light, shade and movement.

Later that year, when I published *Shadow* issue 15 (December 1971), I used two more pieces from Jim's pen. This time the two interiors were full page pieces printed using litho. One graced James Wade's story 'A Weirder Shadow Over Innsmouth' and an even more elaborate and startling piece called 'Skullface'. The skull was slightly cartoonish, against a background of moon and stars. It was very delicately stippled work and showed a less busy and more dramatic evocation of its subject than 'Pickman's Model' in the *Bibliotheca*. One felt that Jim was practicing his techniques, honing them and developing his own style.

For *Shadow* 17 (June 1972) I again published two pieces, but this time one featured on the cover: A striking image of a ghoulish figure reading a book with a dripping candle at his side, against a background of an arched window with crescent moon and stars. His interior piece illustrated C. L. Moore's 'The Black God's Kiss'. Both were very striking ink illustrations, with very understated stippling. Jim's artwork was now evoking Hannes Bok (a favourite artist of Jim's) and perhaps Virgil Finlay. Jim had also developed a compact style: his imagery did not extend to fill the page, it was contained, constrained, its frame was the outline of the image features themselves; a technique that displays through much of his early work.

By *Shadow 18* (November 1972) I had moved to full lithographic printing and the magazine's appearance was a lot more professional. Jim's 'Demons' was lit with flames and the shading and light were amazing. His other piece in the issue was a departure from the stippling technique, a carbon pencil rendering of a chained man facing a cowled figure writing in a huge tome, with demons lurking in the background: 'The Reckoning' was very different from Jim's earlier work. In the letter column of that issue, there was universal praise for Jim's illustrations in the previous number.

Lovecraft's 'The Strange High House in the Mist' received Jim's evocative treatment, with mist-swirled demons circling a strangely askew house at moonrise. But his cover artwork for *Shadow 19* (April 1973) was even better, a magnificent depiction of William Hope Hodgson's *The House on the Borderland*. The detail and the imagery he packs into this piece of artwork is surprising and shows an artist in full control in depicting his subject. In the letter column of the following issue, Ramsey Campbell commented on the Borderland illustration: "Cover – well Bok lives again, that's the obvious comment; but I'm prepared to go further and say I prefer it to the Bok cover on the Arkham Hodgson [Arkham House, 1946], largely because Pitts' grotesquerie has more conviction". Jim has cited the influence of Hannes Bok on his own artistic creations. He came to understand that Bok used a combination of techniques, stippling and embossed paper with ink and pencil to achieve shading. Jim achieved his with pure stippling in his early work.

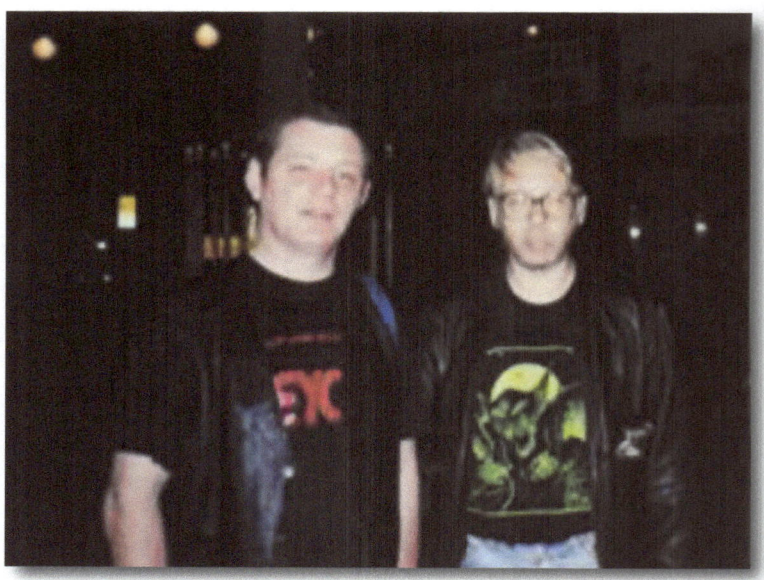

Jim with Dave Sutton in the mid 1990s

There were to be only two more issues of *Shadow*. In number 20 (October 1973) Jim's vampire and bat glared from the front cover, illustrating an article on vampires in fiction and inside he depicted William Hope Hodgson's short story 'The Phantom Ship'. Gordon Larkin's story 'The Rack' received a fantastic rendering in issue 21 (August 1974), possibly the finest piece he did for the magazine: A dungeon torture chamber lit by a wall sconce and plagued by beady-eyed rats, the central section depicts the cowled, menacing torturer and his agonized victim on the rack.

Shadow had one final fling, though. In 1994 I published *Voices From Shadow*, a 20th anniversary celebration updating and reprinting some of the best articles from the magazine. Naturally I asked Jim for artwork and his cover was a stunning vampirish bat-winged creature limned by a full moon. (I am pleased to say that I own the original). The textures and detail are evoked not by stippling, but a combination of very skilled hatching and cross-hatching work. Very different from his method of twenty years earlier.

The output of comic artists interested Jim early on, Frank Frazetta and Steve Ditko. Then later Bok, Maxfield Parrish, Sidney Sime, Harry Clarke and Ed Cartier. And his extensive reading of sword and sorcery and horror fiction meant he found the inspiration to try his hand at illustration. We should all be grateful that he did! The results, as they say, speak for themselves.

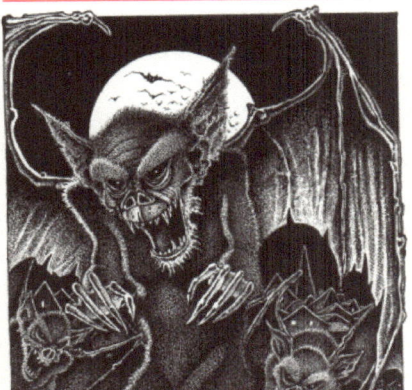
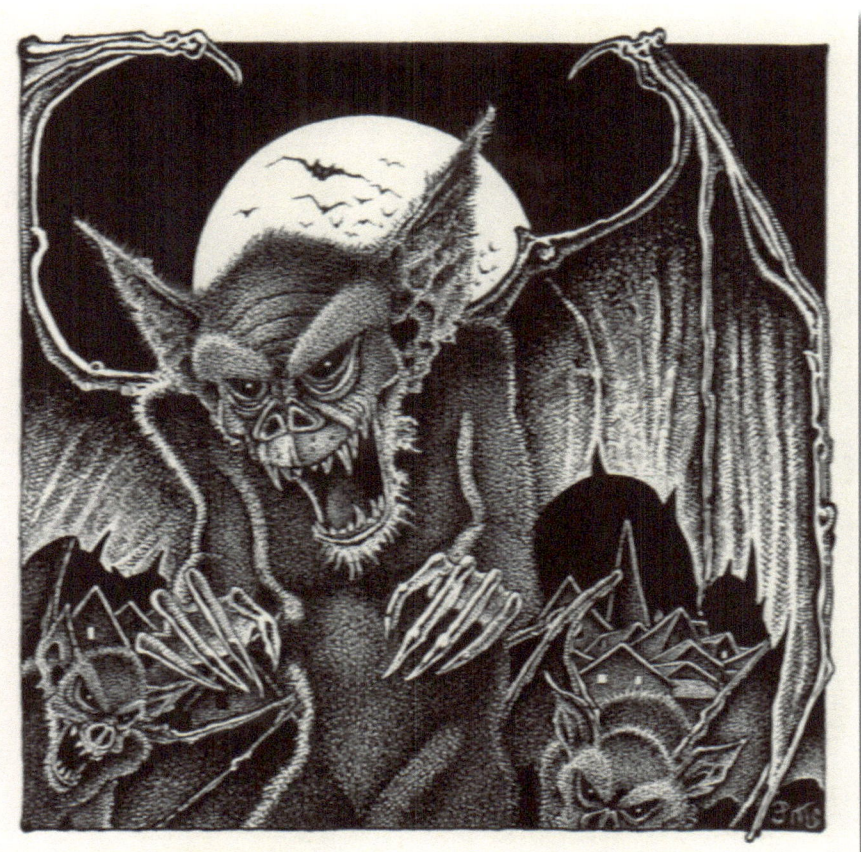
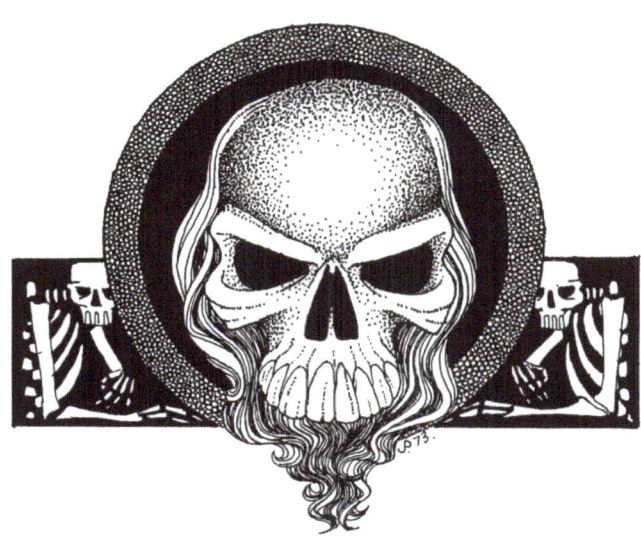

Illustrations used in *Voices from Shadow*

To the right is an illustration for William Hope Hodgson's Carnacki story *The Hog*.

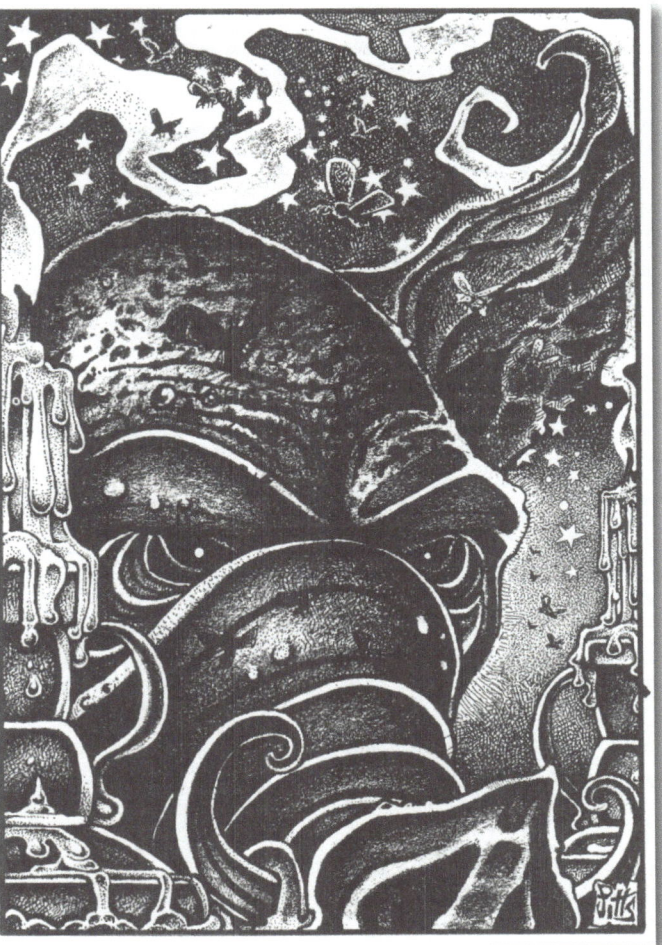

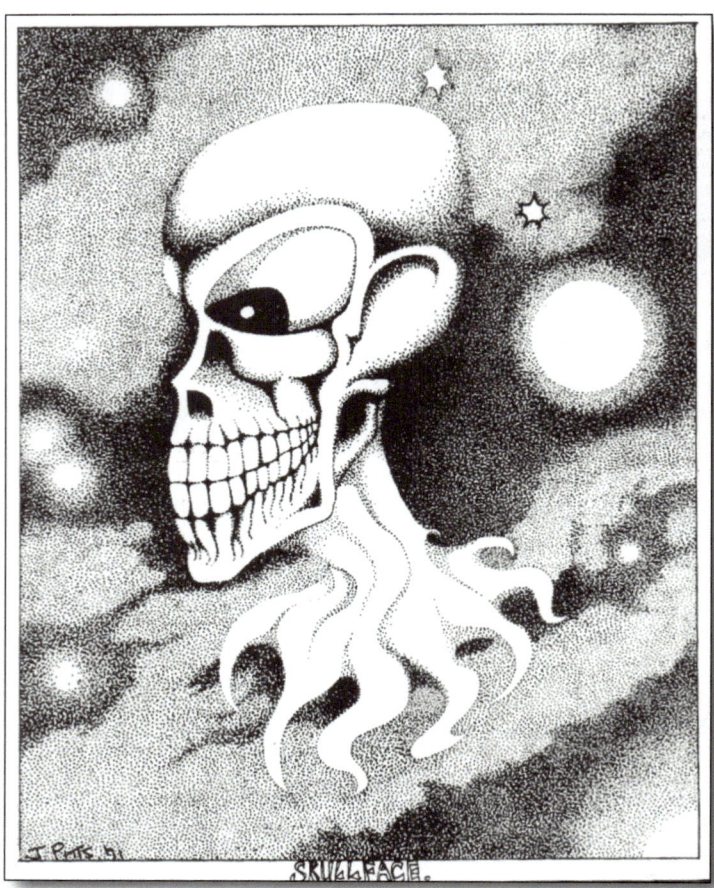

"...an even more elaborate and startling piece called 'Skullface'. The skull was slightly cartoon-ish, against a background of moon and stars. It was very delicately stippled work and showed a less busy and more dramatic evocation of its subject than 'Pickman's Model' in the *Bibliotheca*. One felt that Jim was practicing his techniques, honing them and developing his own style."
    David A. Sutton

The Black God's Kiss - a Jirel of Joiry story by C. L. Moore

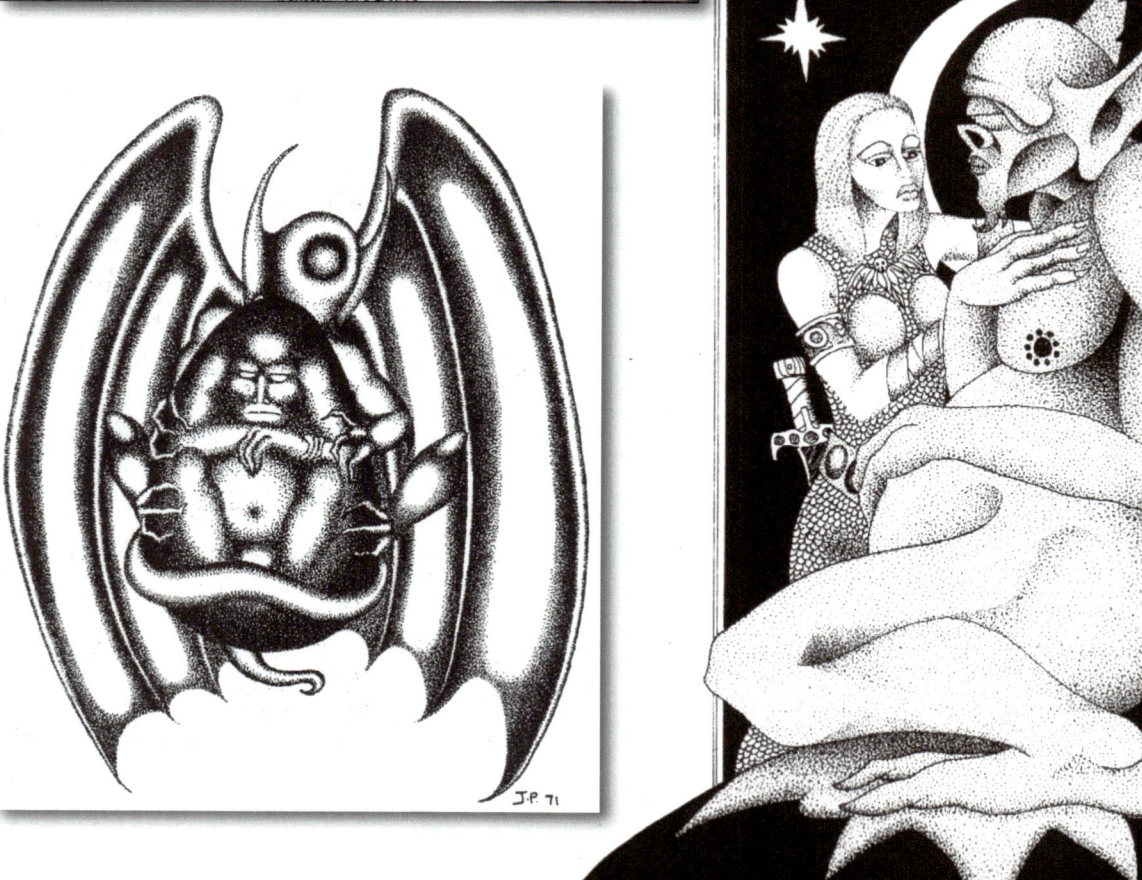

Fantasycon 1975 interior art in the convention program, illustrating H. P. Lovecraft's *The Strange High House in the Mist*

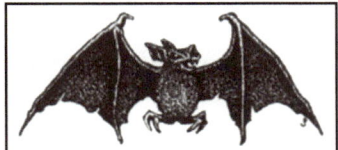

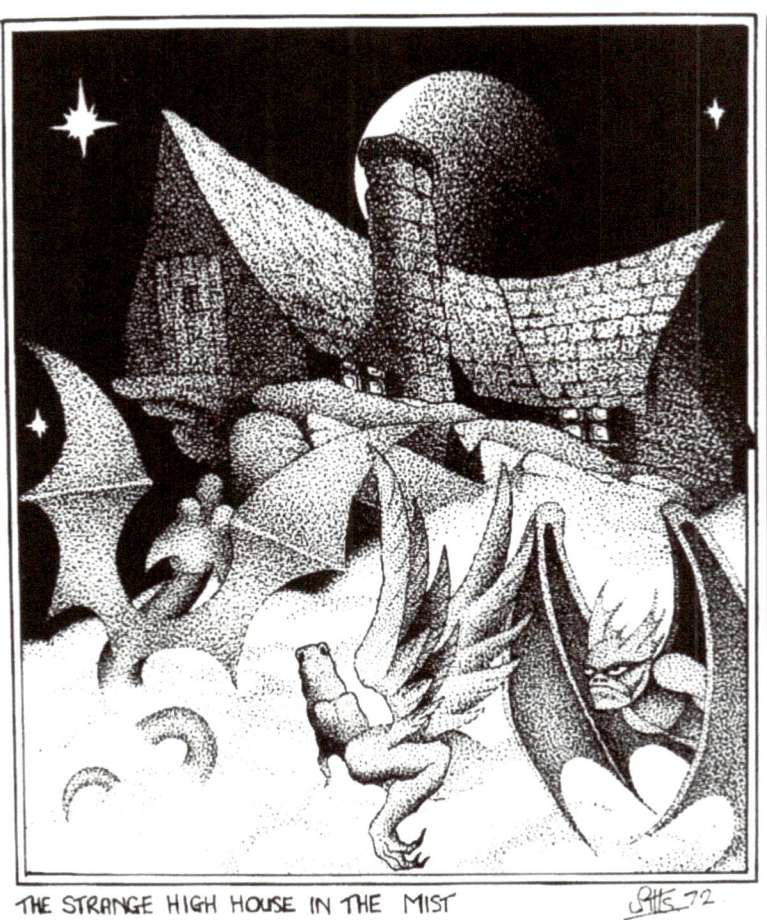

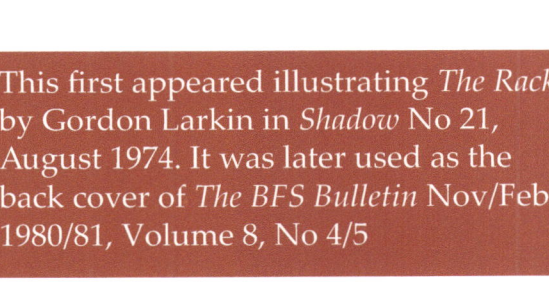

This first appeared illustrating *The Rack* by Gordon Larkin in *Shadow* No 21, August 1974. It was later used as the back cover of *The BFS Bulletin* Nov/Feb 1980/81, Volume 8, No 4/5

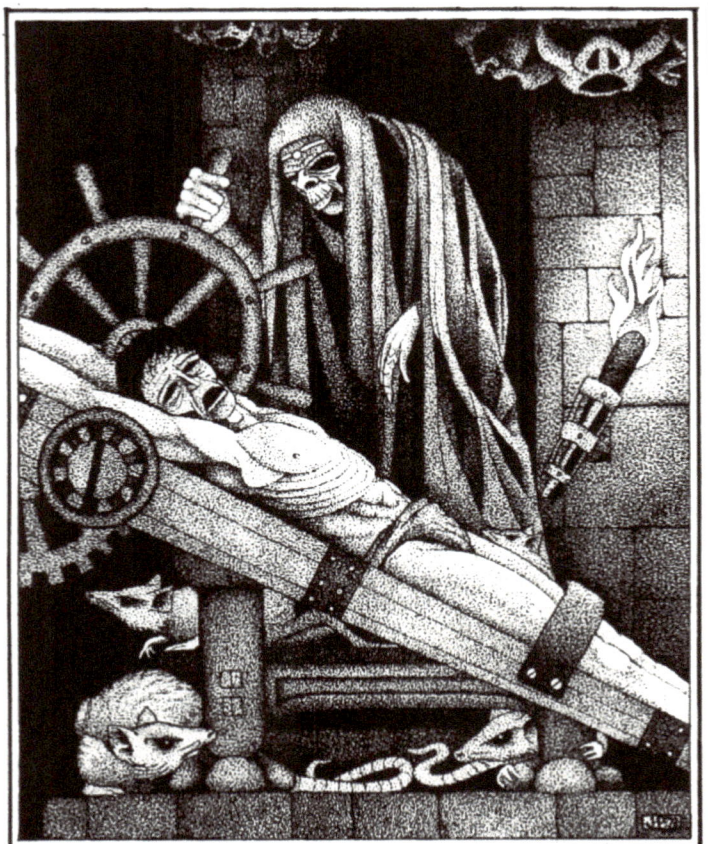

Shadow 17

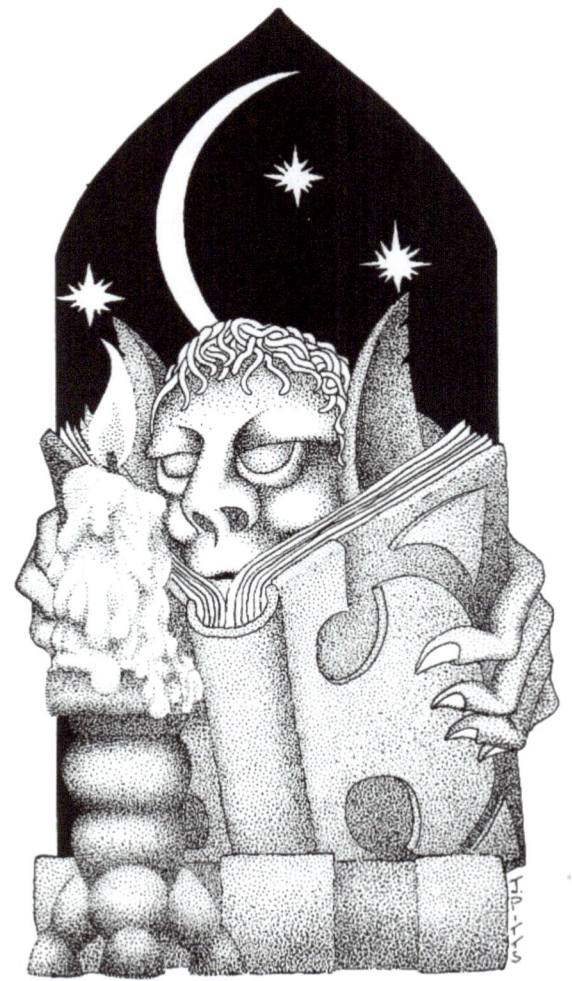

"For *Shadow 17* (June 1972) I again published two pieces, but this time one featured on the cover: A striking image of a ghoulish figure reading a book with a dripping candle at his side, against a background of an arched window with crescent moon and stars."
David A. Sutton

Shadow 20

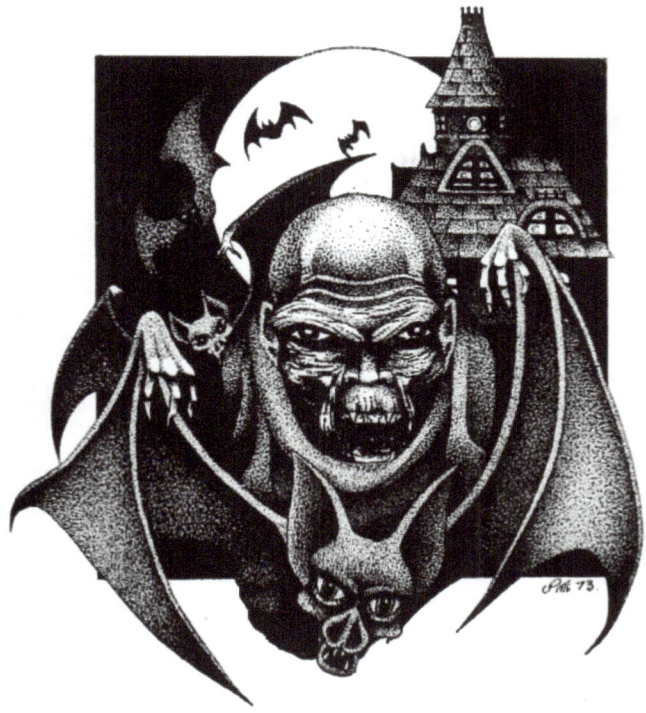

HOPE HODGSON * VAMPIRES * FICTION

"In number 20 (October 1973) Jim's vampire and bat glared from the front cover, illustrating an article on vampires in fiction."
David A. Sutton

Bibliotheca: H. P. Lovecraft (cover by Kevin O'Neill) contained the first published drawings by Jim Pitts.

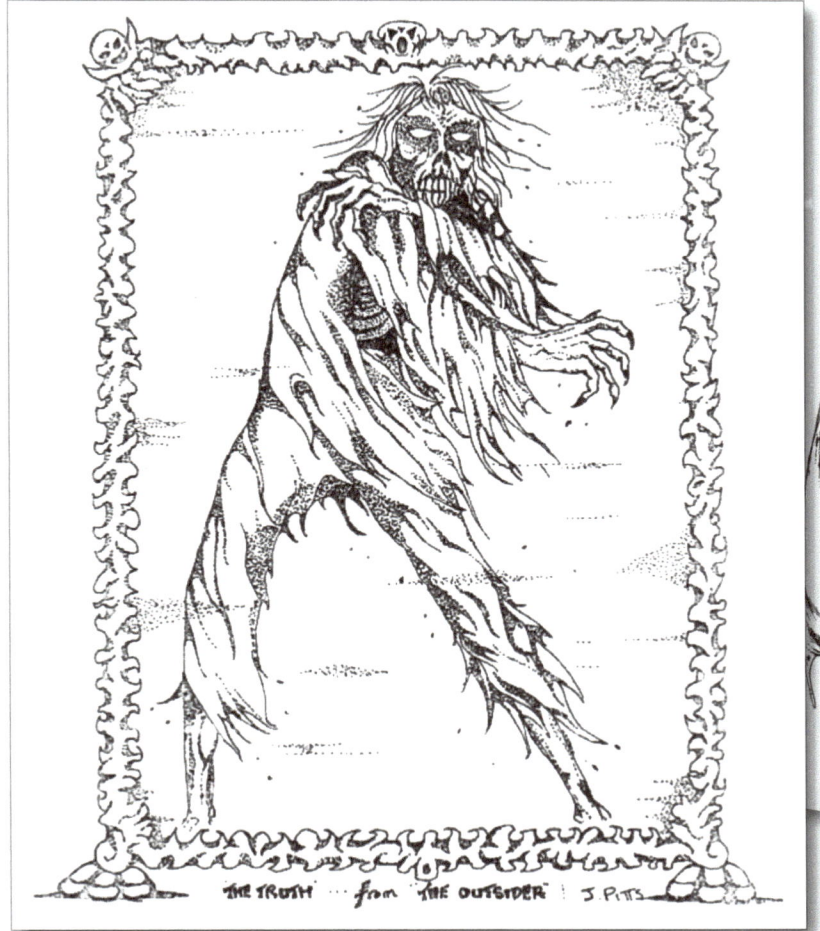
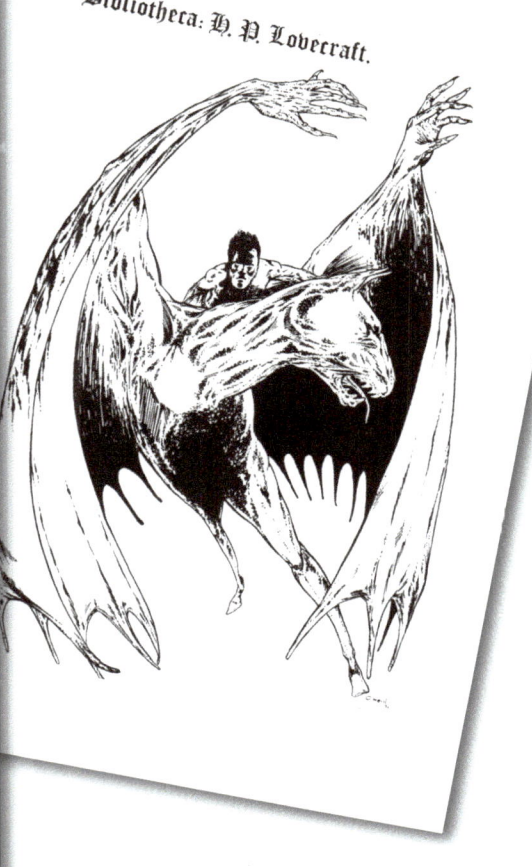
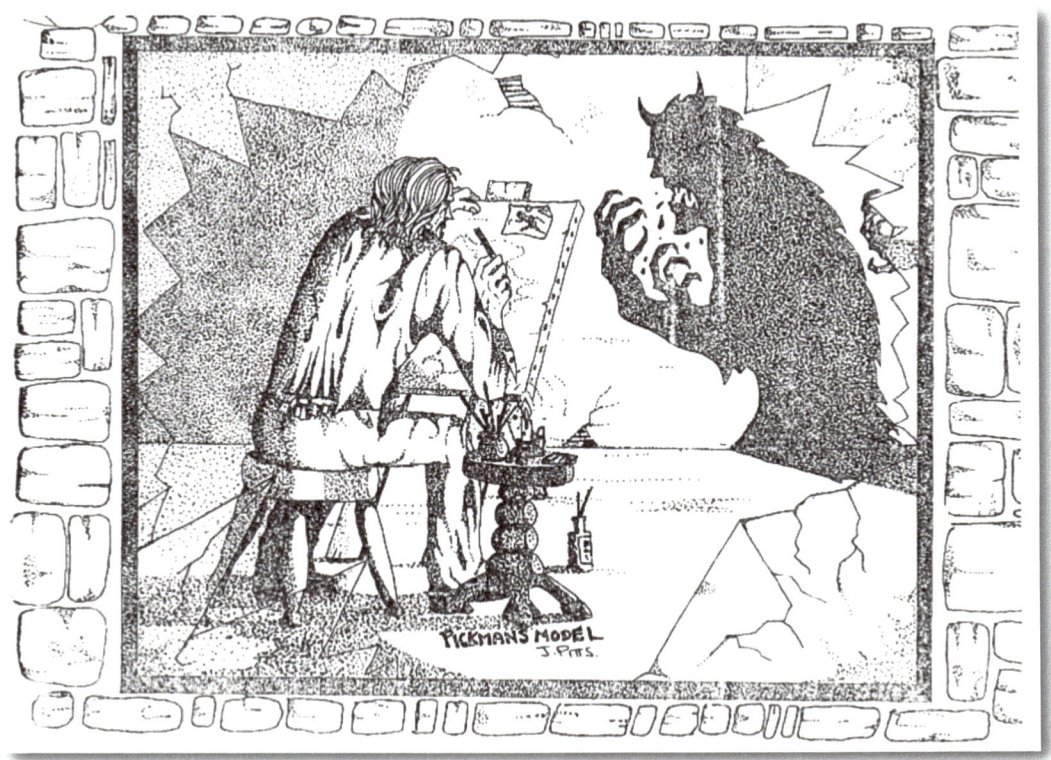

Balthus was edited by Jon M. Harvey in 1971. This issue contained an article about Abraham Merritt by Brian J. Frost, *The Eternal Huntsmen* by Jon M. Harvey, *The Smugglers of Penrose* by S. L. Eneys, and a short story, *Ash Shadow*, by Mark Adlard.

Jim's cover illustration, *The Gargoyle*, won him the coveted Ken McIntyre Award at the next British Science Fiction Convention.

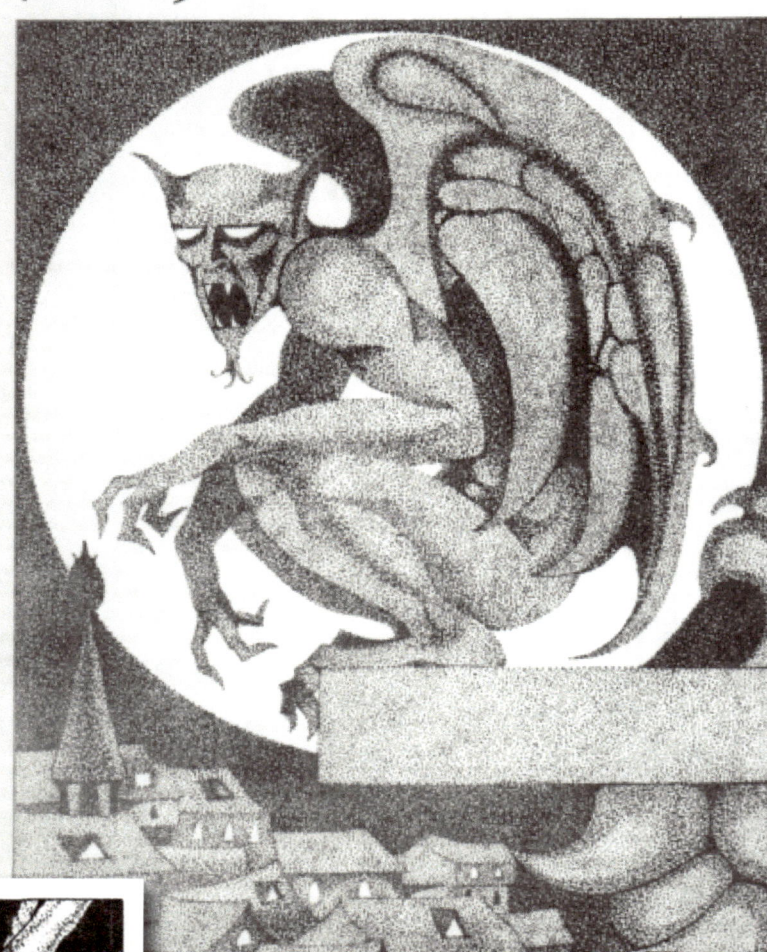

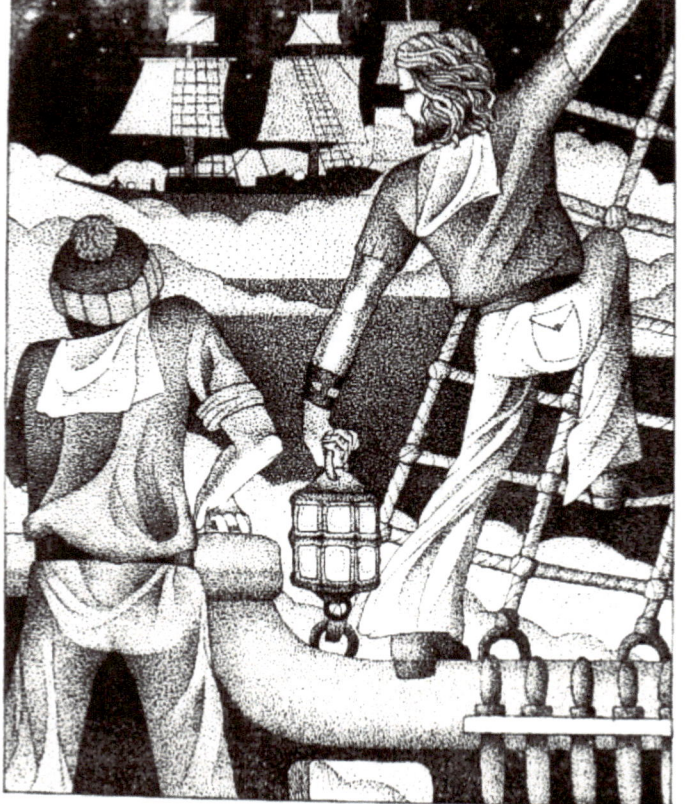

An illustration of William Hope Hodgson's *The Ghost Pirates*, published in *Balthus*.

Anduril #6 was edited and published by John Martin in 1976, eight and a half by eleven inches in size, with card covers.

The cover was the work of talented artist Russ Nicholson.

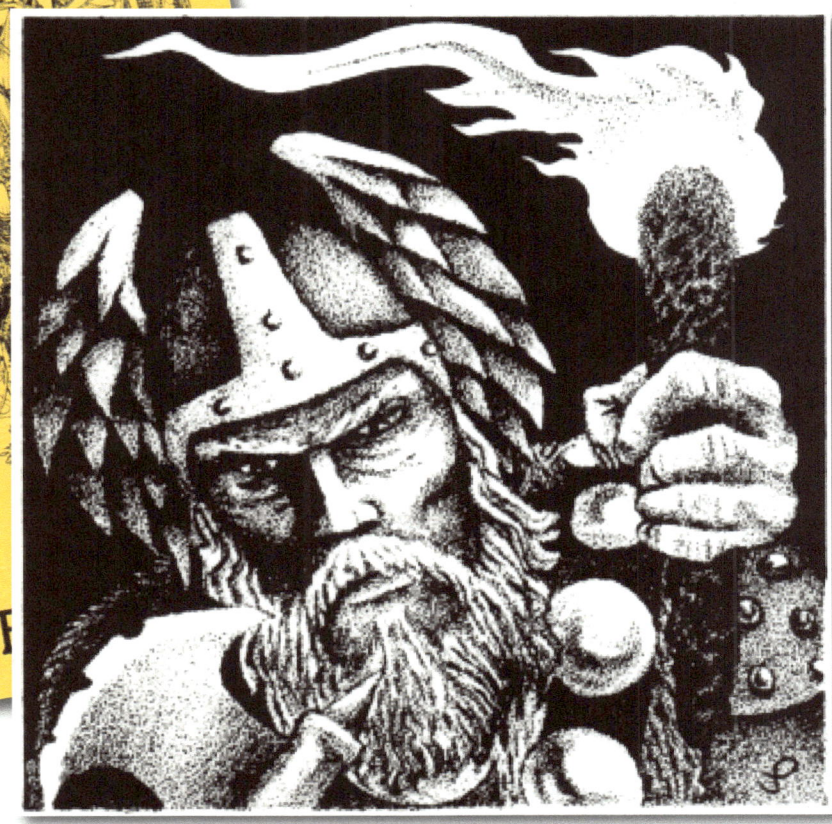

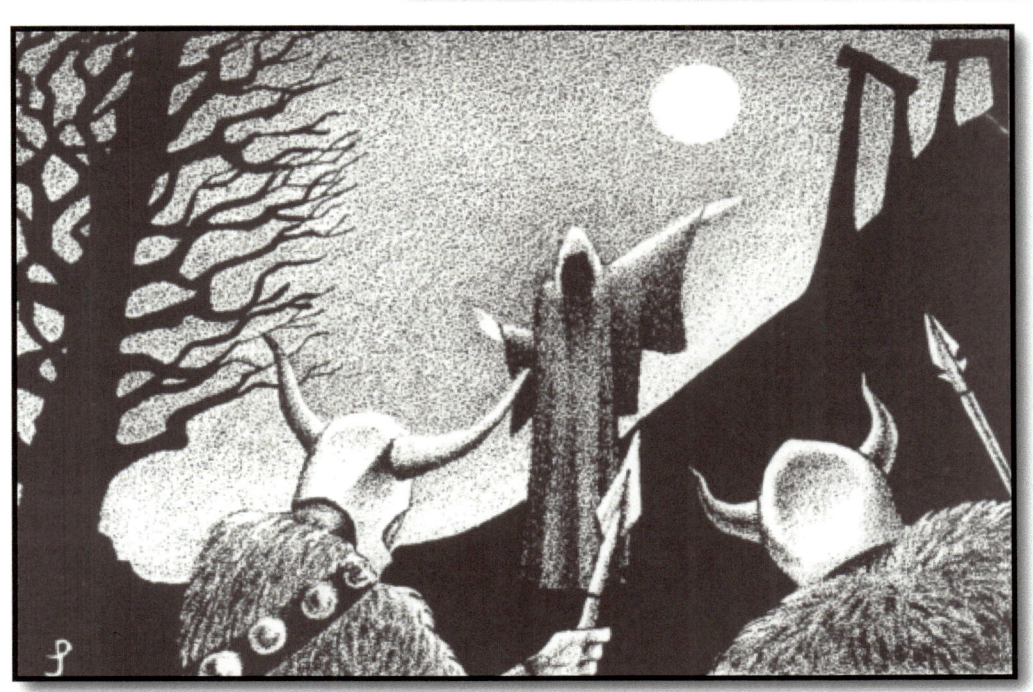

Title page and two smaller illustrations for Adrian Cole's story *The Sleeping God* in *Anduril* #6.

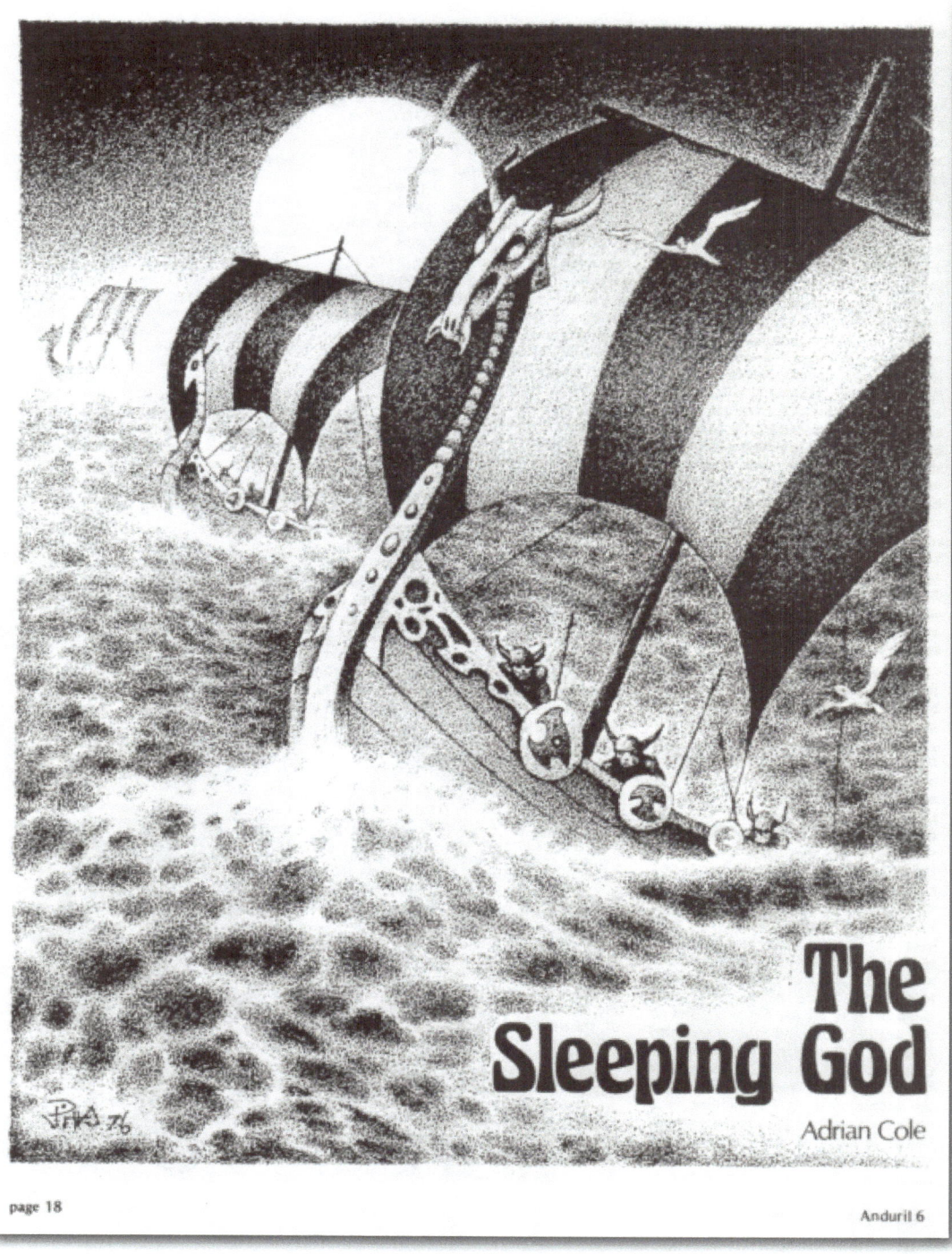

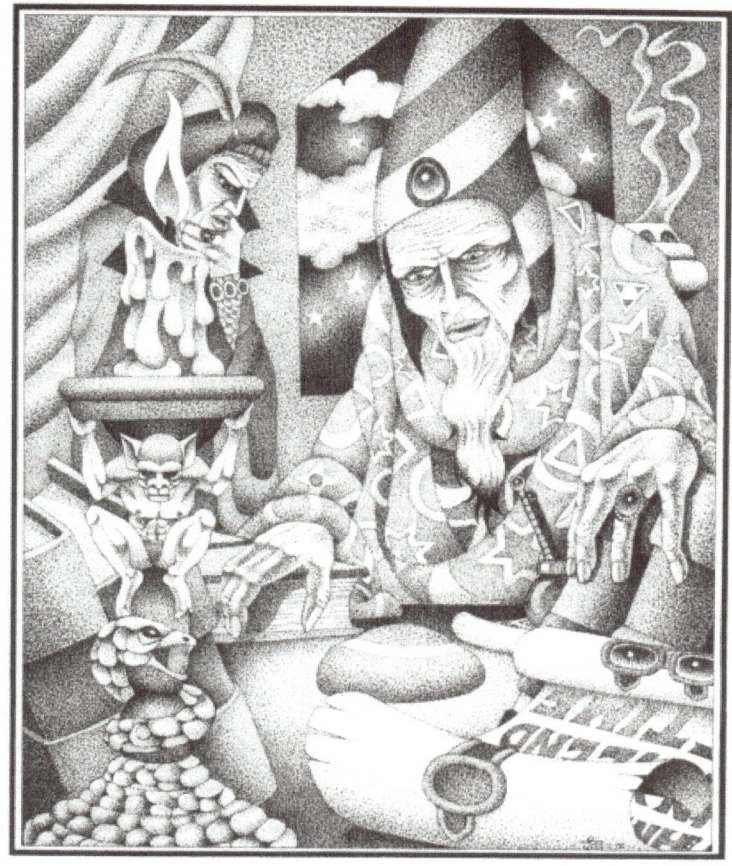

Two full-page illustrations from *Balthus* #4

These early illustrations were completed "stippled" as Jim had not yet discovered the embossed/coquile paper yet.

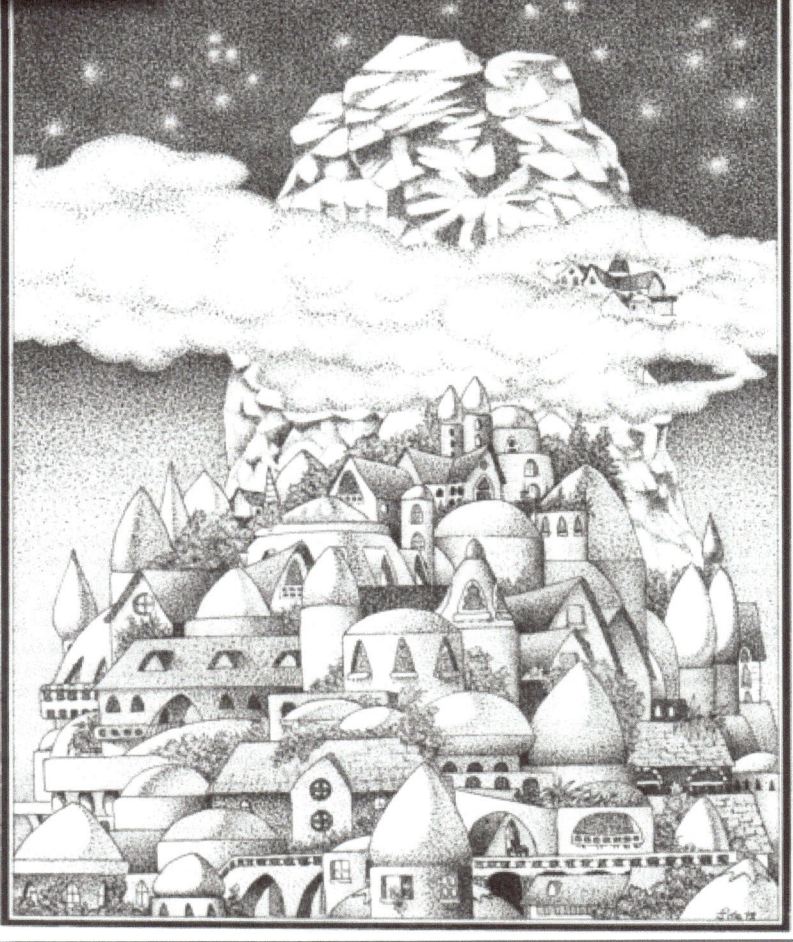

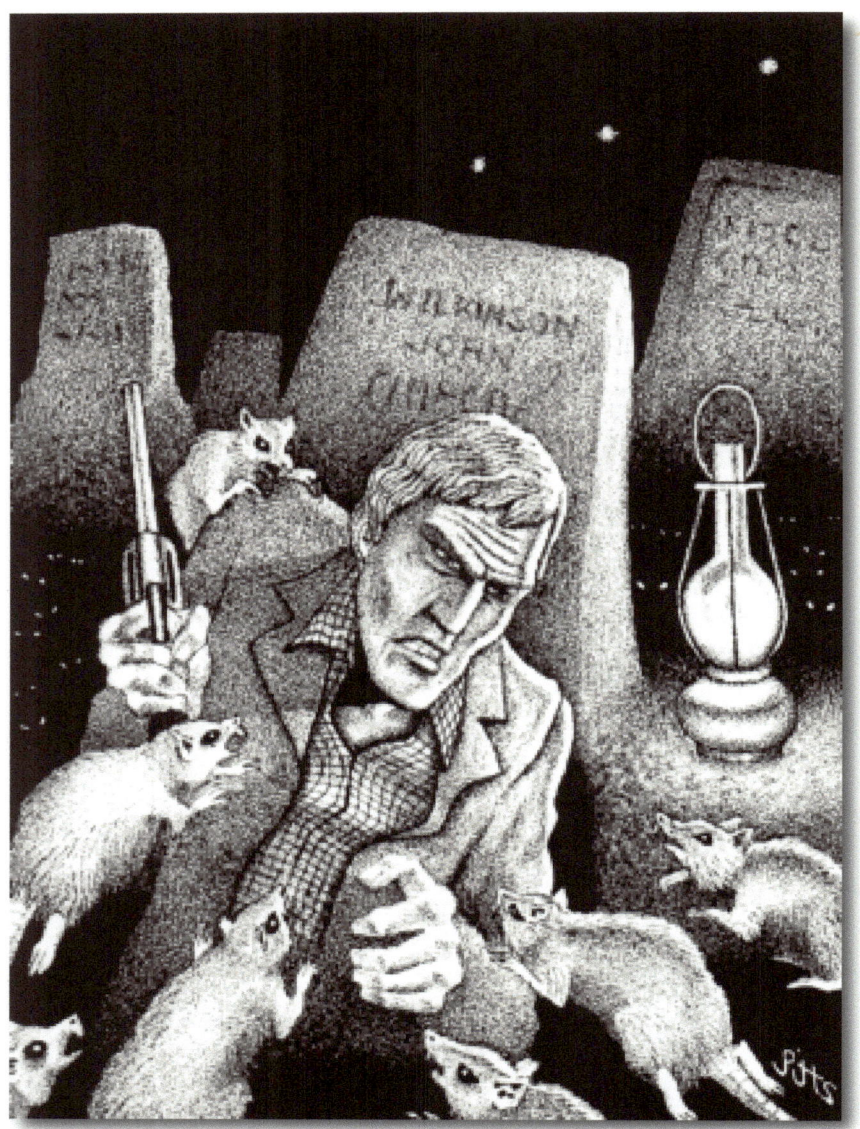

Phantasy Digest No 1, 1976, edited by Wayne Warfield, published by William P. Hall.

Illustration for Robert E. Howard's *Graveyard Rats*.

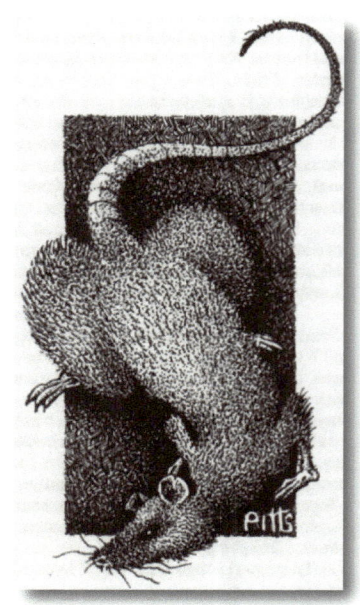

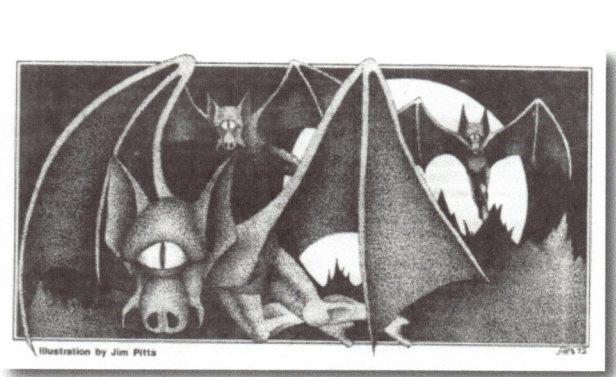

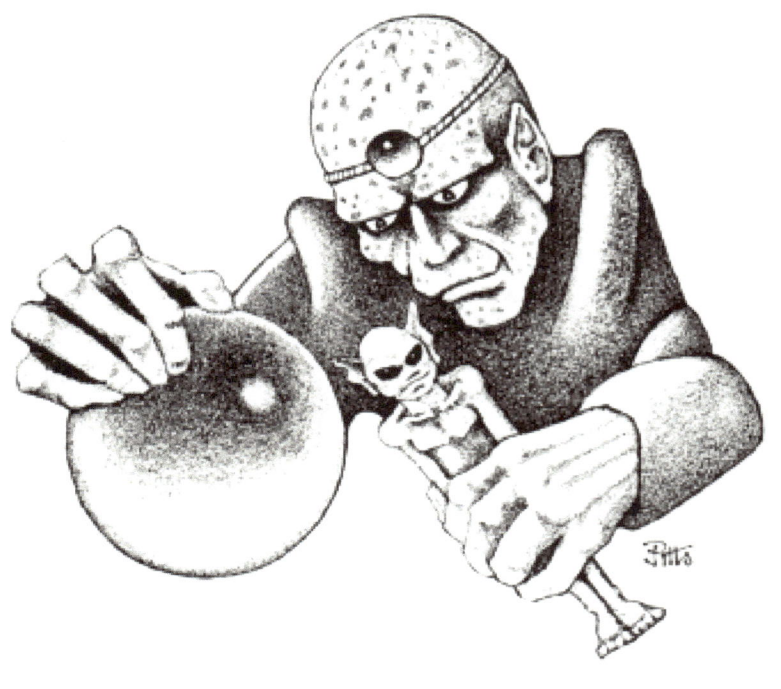

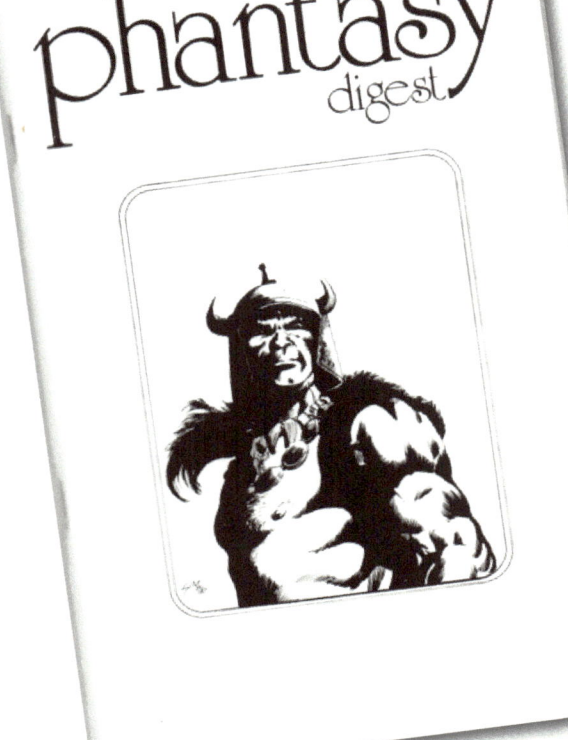
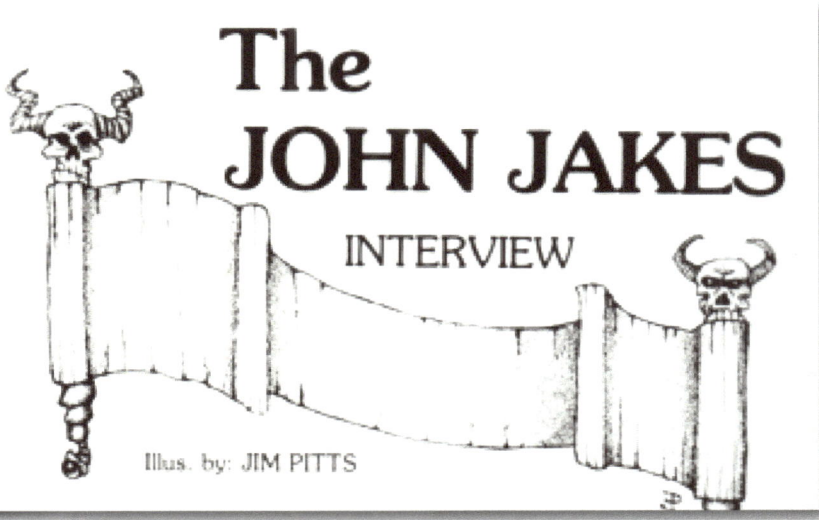

Phantasy Digest # 2, 1977, edited by Wayne Warfield, published by William P. Hall. Cover by Dave Sim.

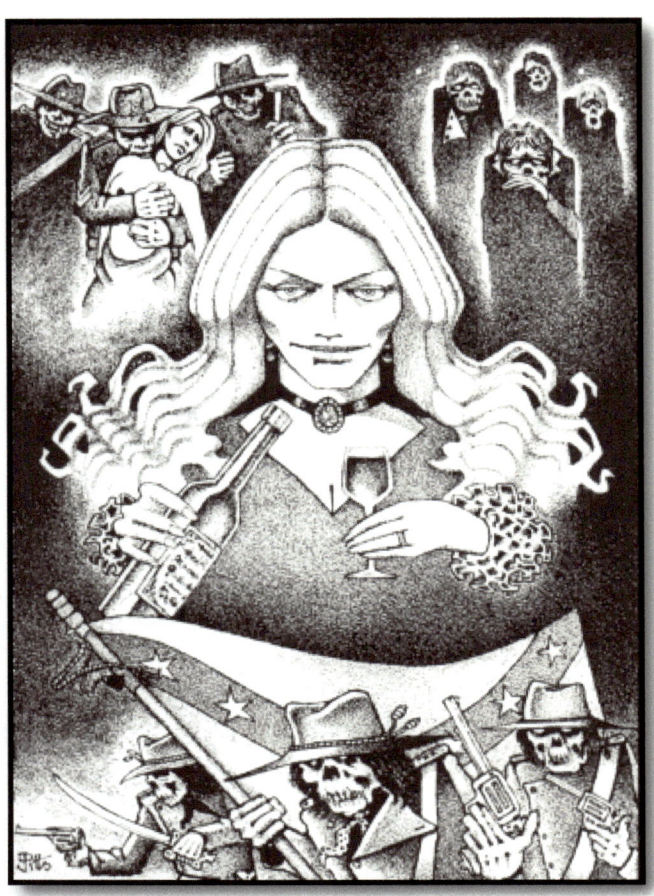
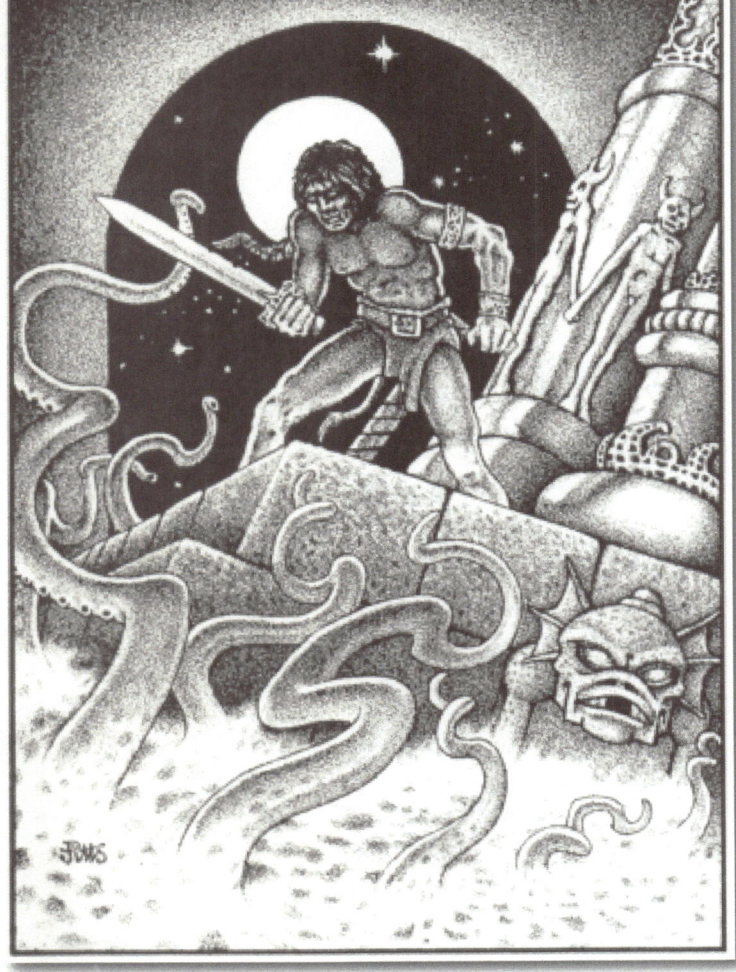

Mallorn 6

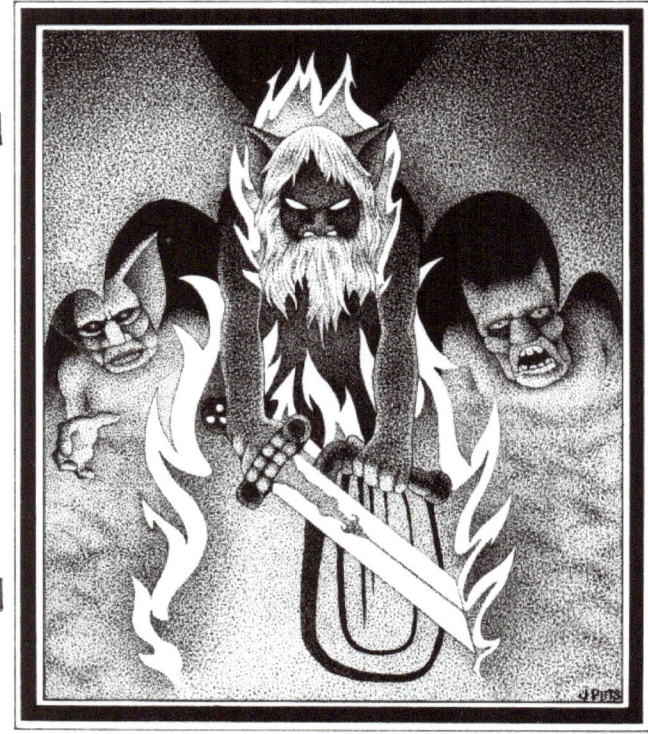

Front cover for *Mallorn 6, The Journal of the Tolkien Society*, edited by Jon M. Harvey, 1972

The illustration is titled "The Balrog"

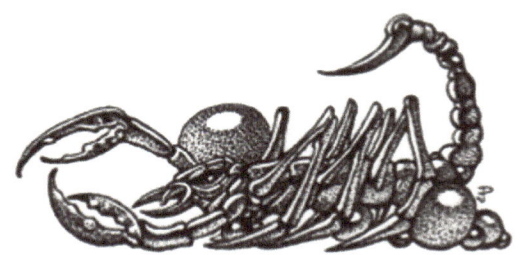

Below: *Fantasy Tales*, USA, Carrol & Graf Vol 1 No 1, 1990. Illustrating *Into the Dark Land* by Darrel Schweitzer and another.

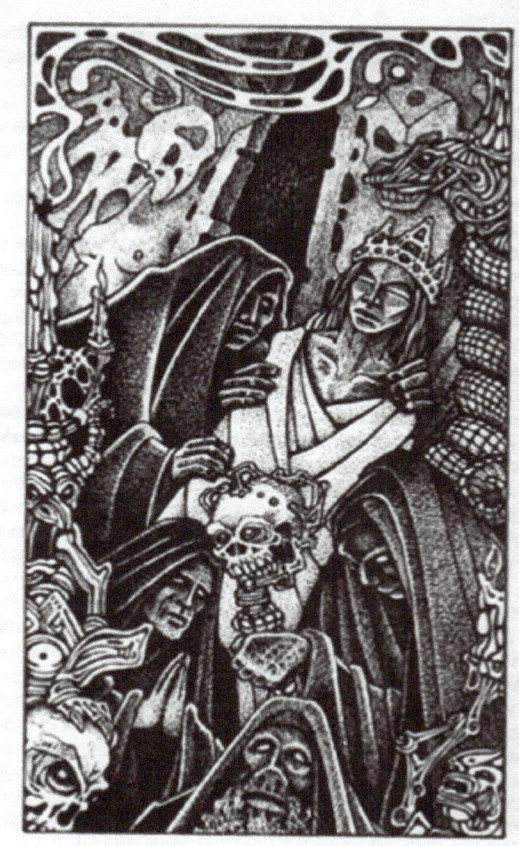

Besides the cape, he wore silver helmet with a visor. (Art: Jim Pitts)

"My daughter has arrived" said the King aloud, "Let all lights be lit." (Art: Jim Pitts)

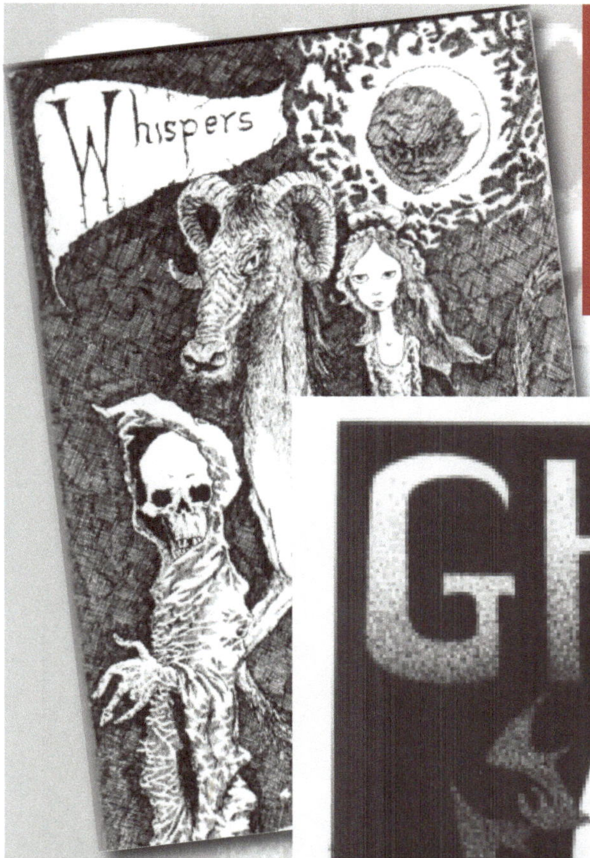

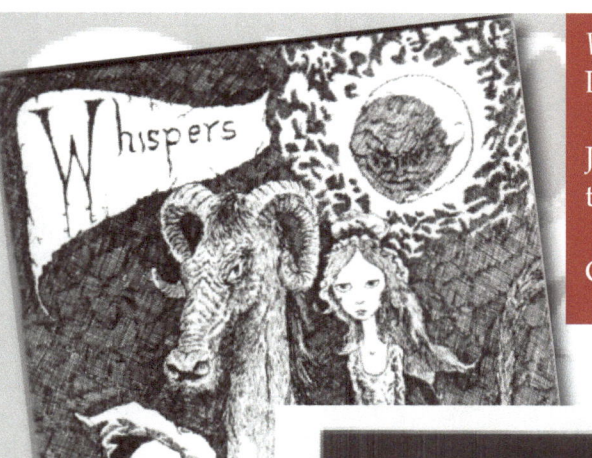

Whispers No 8, December 1975, published and edited by David Stuart Schiff.

Jim drew a special series of illustrations commemorating the ghost stories of M. R. James

Cover by John Linton

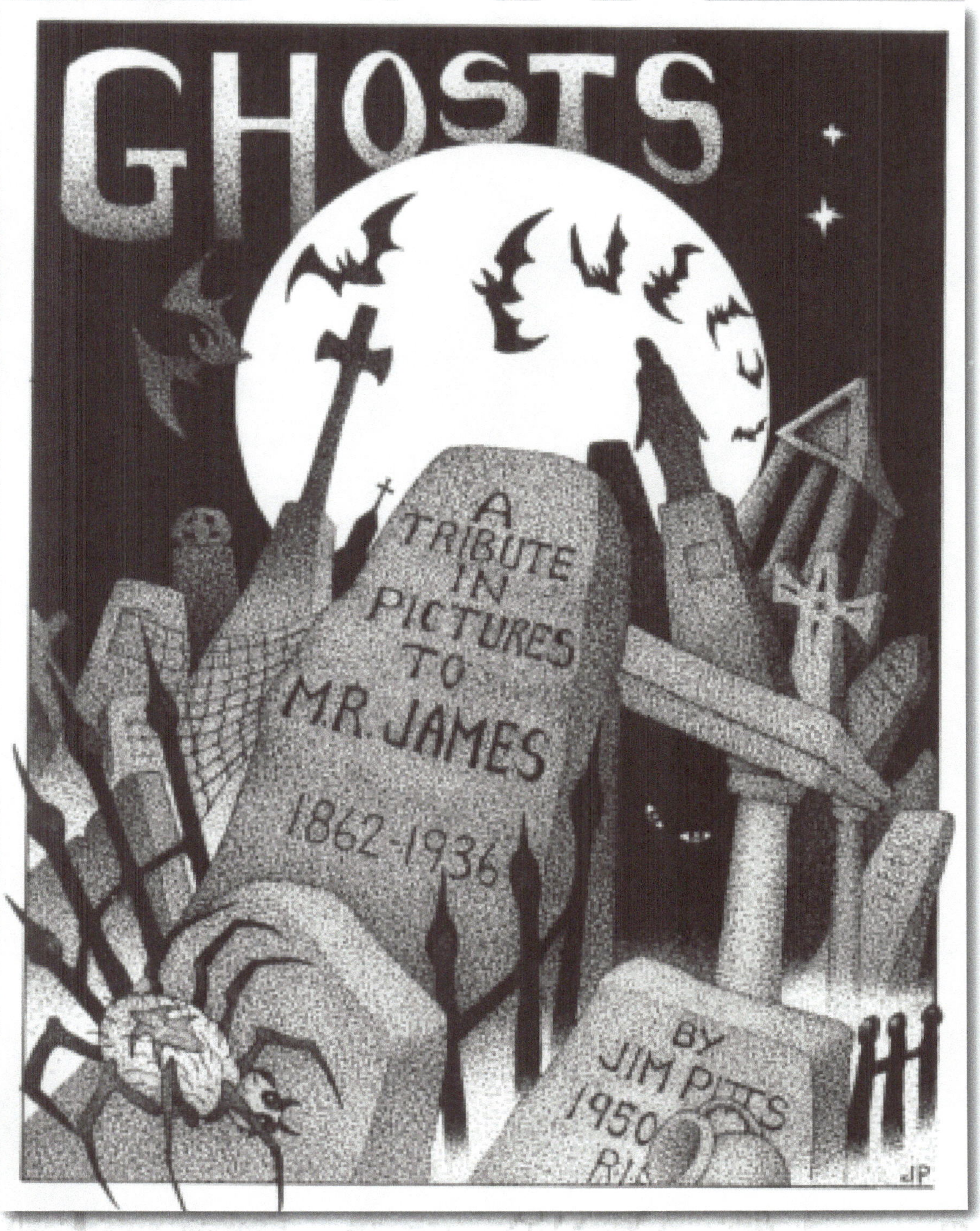

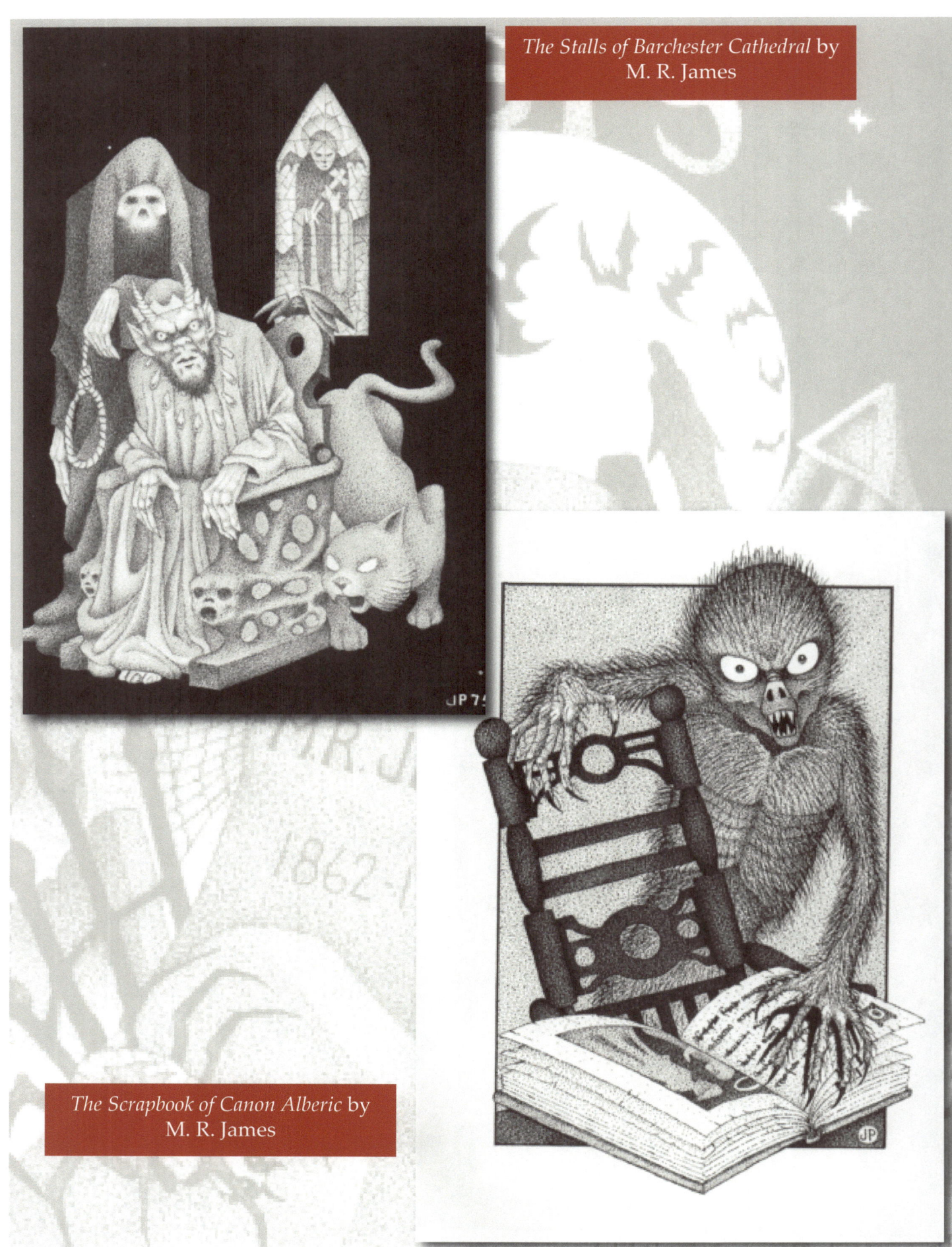

The Stalls of Barchester Cathedral by M. R. James

The Scrapbook of Canon Alberic by M. R. James

Lost Hearts by M. R. James

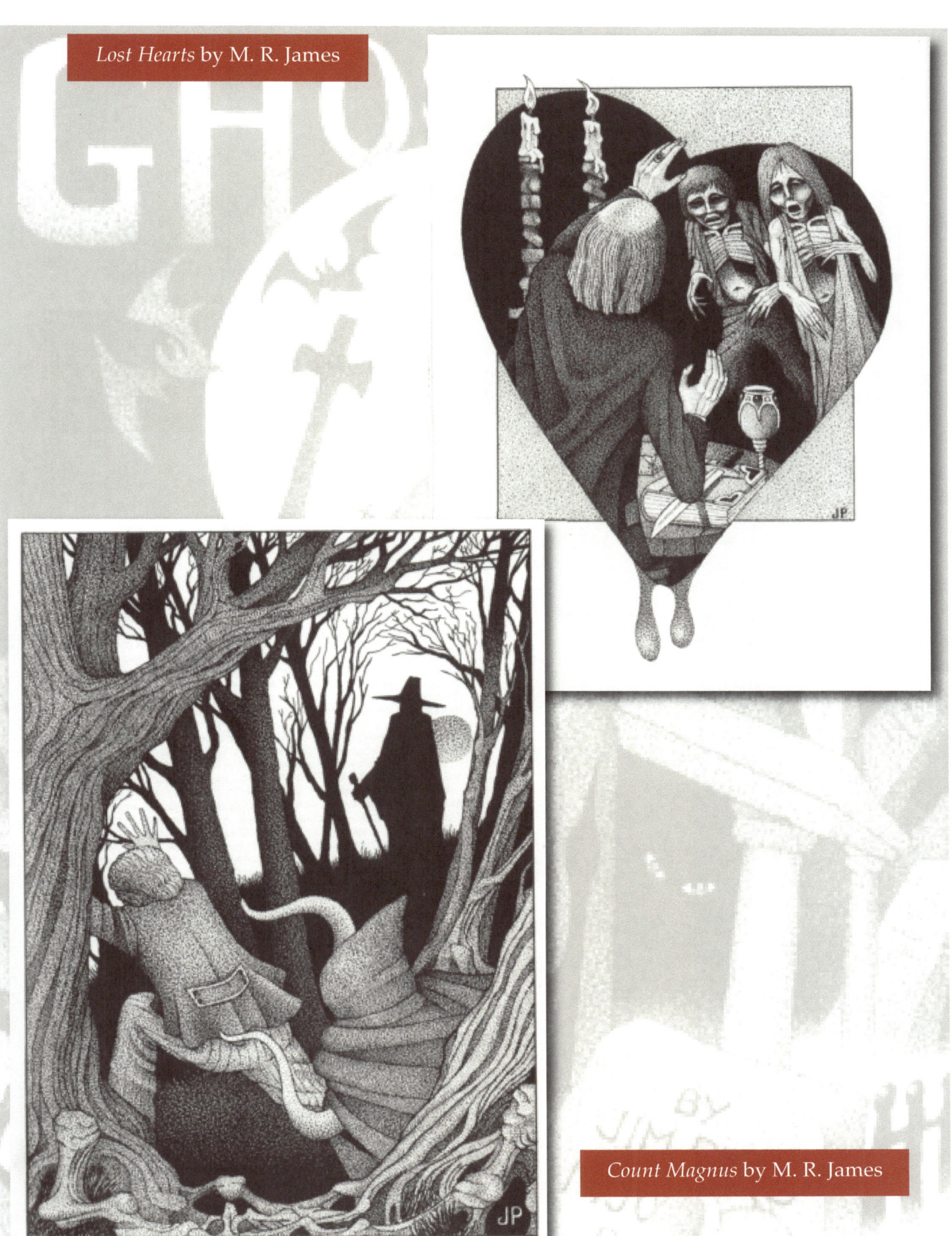

Count Magnus by M. R. James

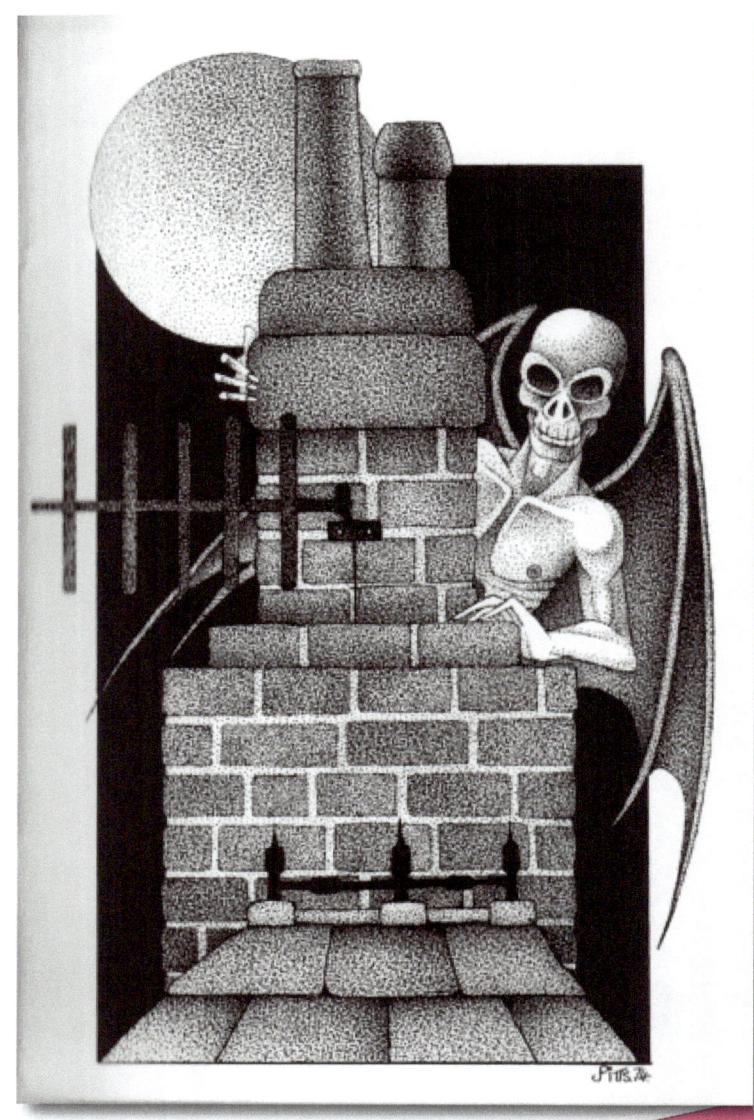

Whispers Volume 2, No 1, November 1974, published and edited by David Stuart Schiff.
Inside back cover

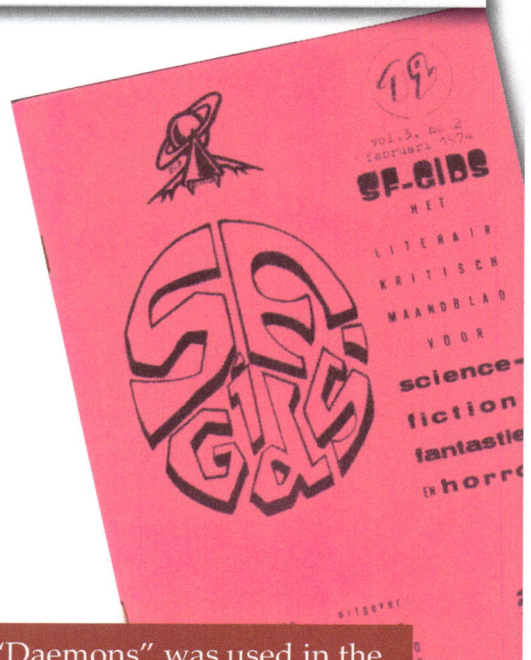

The illustration "Daemons" was used in the Belgian fanzine *SF-Gibs*, Volume 3, No 2, February 1974'

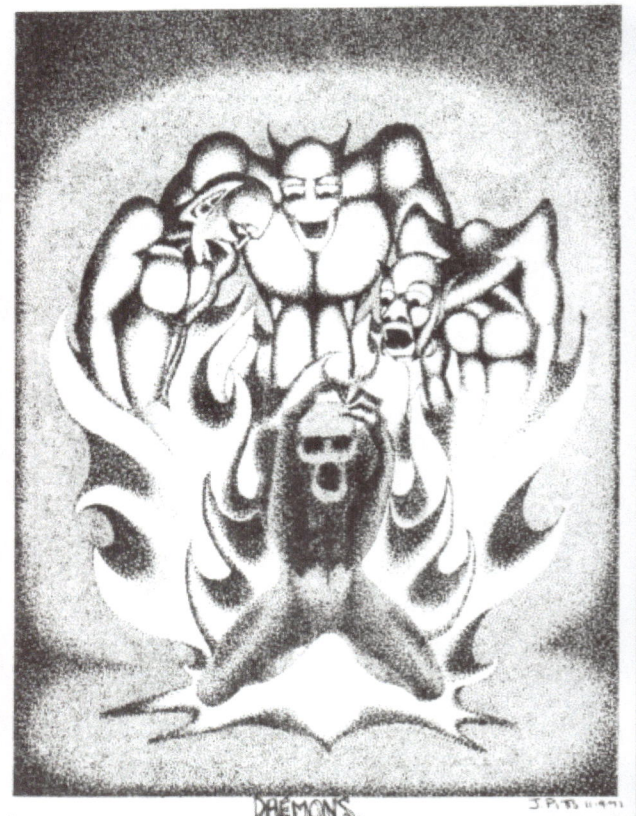

The British Fantasy Society
Dark Horizons and the *BFS Bulletin*

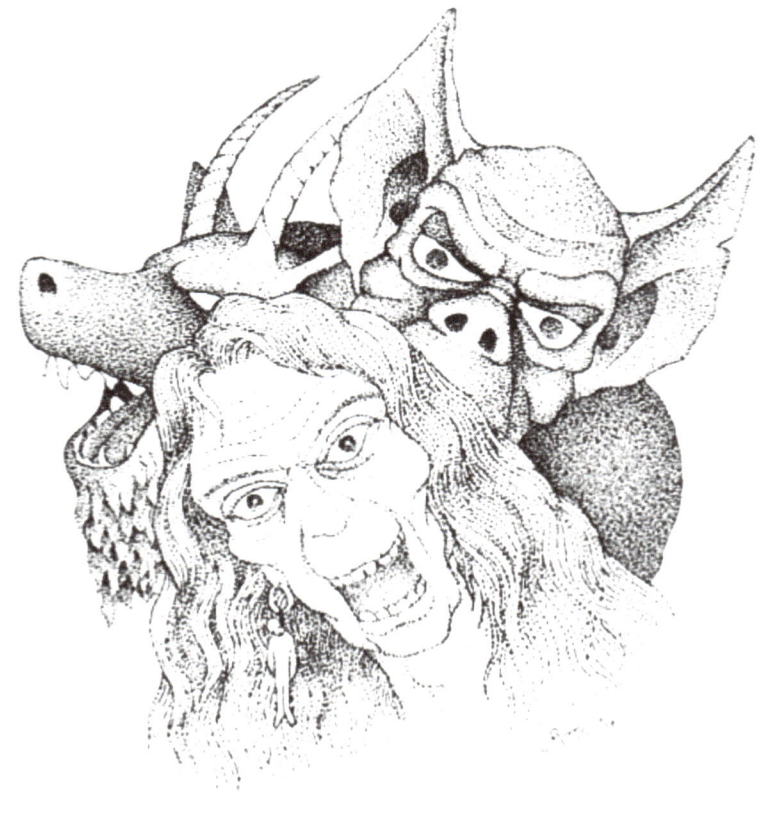

Early self portrait

From the very outset Jim's art became a familar sight in all of the British Fantasy Society's periodicals, whether it was the *BFS Bulletin*, *Dark Horizons* or the various other publishing projects the BFS undertook.

When the BFS decided to make its first British Fantasy Award - the August Derleth Award - the statuette was originally designed by Jim, and would not be replaced for several years.

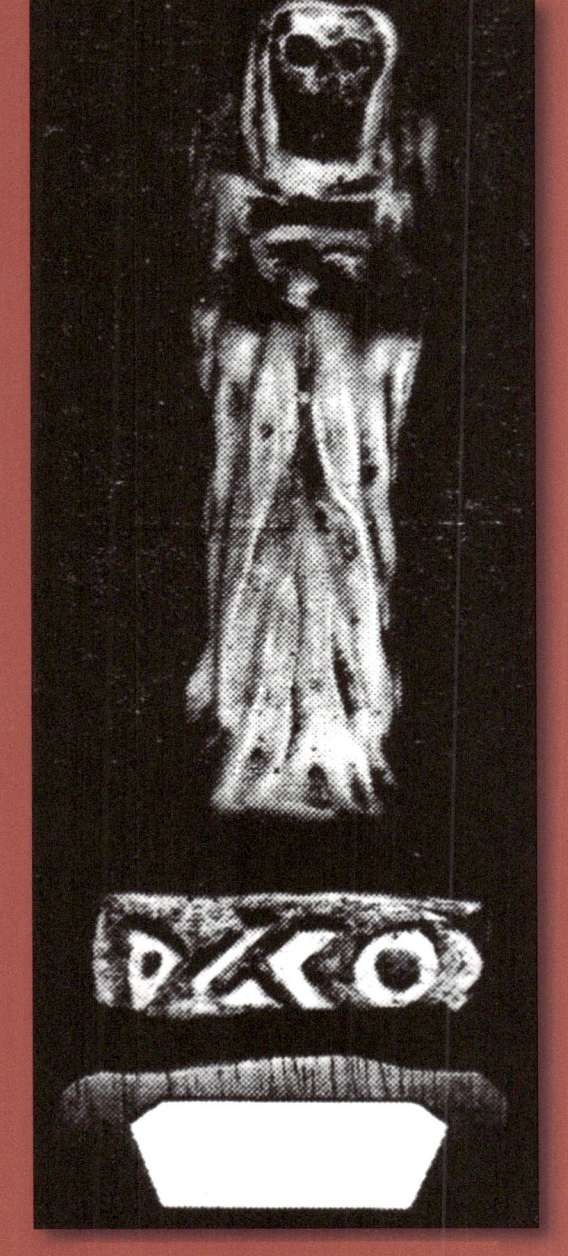

Jim's design for the August Derleth Award

Dark Horizons
issue 9 • summer 1974

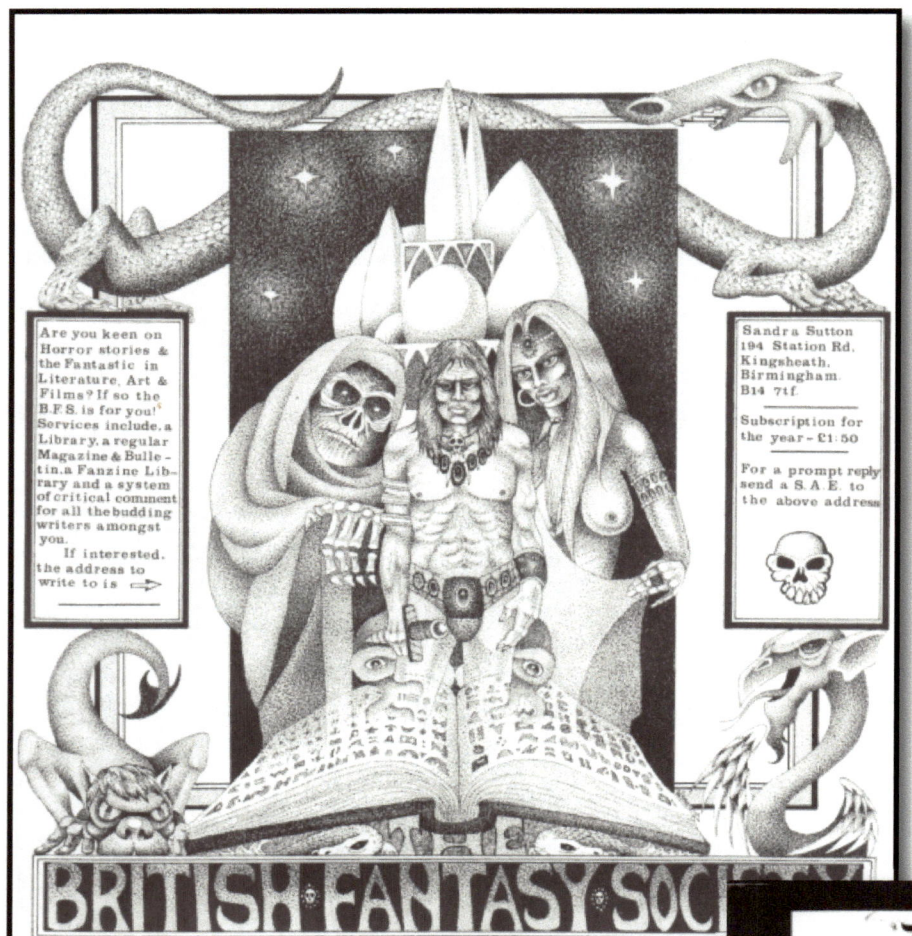

Flyer designed by Jim for the British Fantasy Society in the 1970s

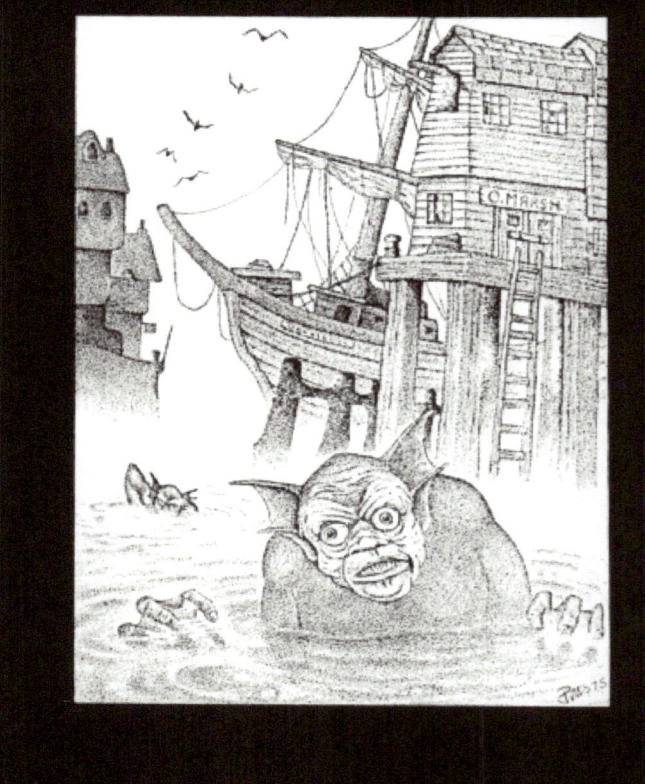

To the right: *Dark Horizons* issue 13, Spring, 1976 - An inhabitant of H. P. Lovecraft's Innsmouth.

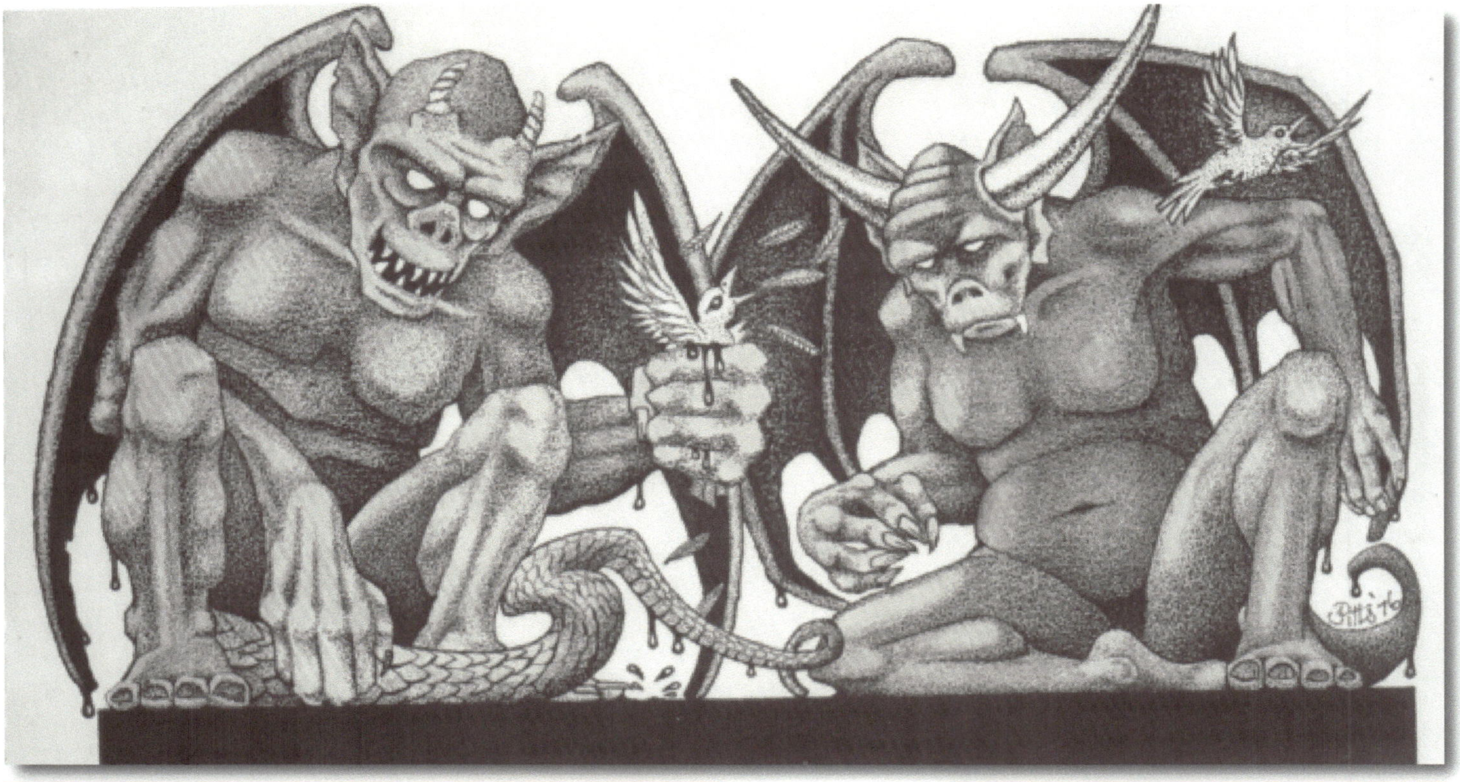

Below: Advert for the British Fantasy Society published in the programme booklet of the 5th Annual Comicon, London 1972

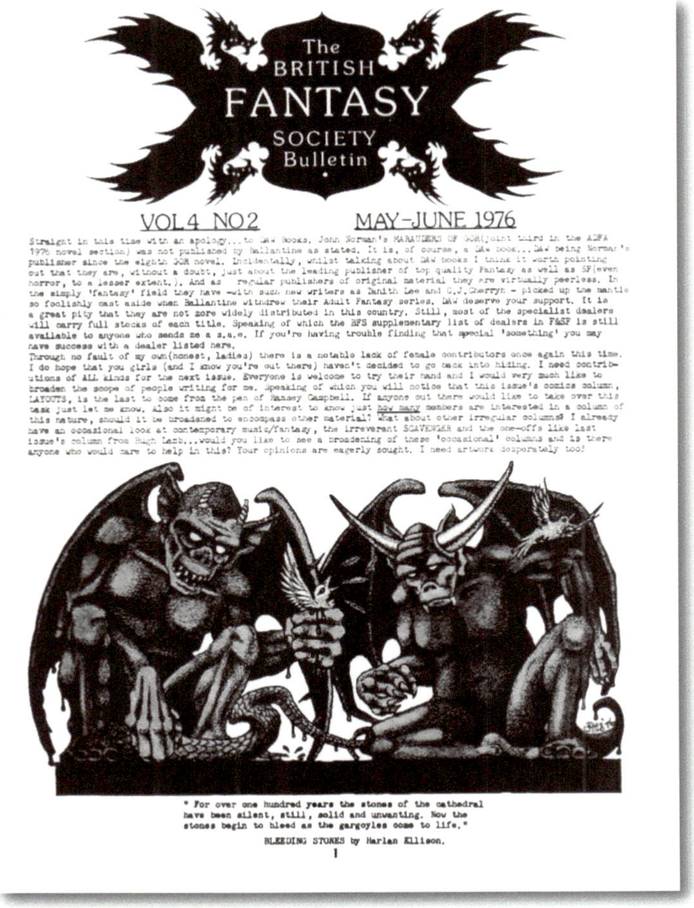

The above illustration was inspired by Harlan Ellison's story *Bleeding Stones*.

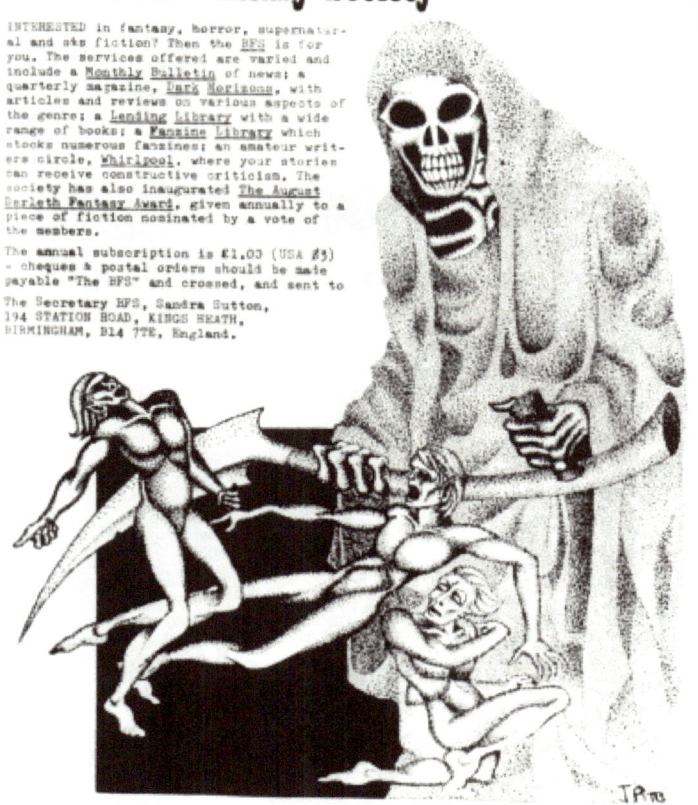

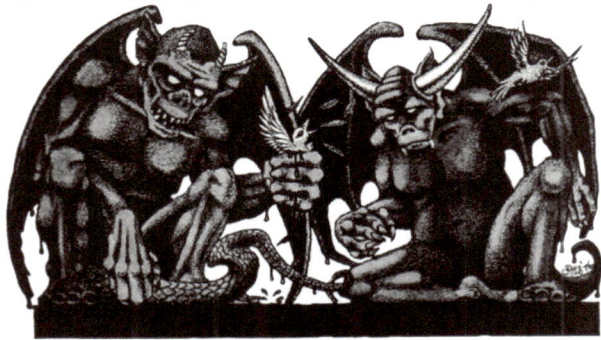

Winter Chills 1 was published by the British Fantasy Society in 1987. Edited by Peter Coleborn, it included six stories by R. Chetwynd-Hayes, Ramsey Campbell, Sydney J. Bounds, Peter Tremayne, David Sutton, and Brian Lumley. Jim illustrated *The Hanging Tree* by R. Chetwynd-Hayes.

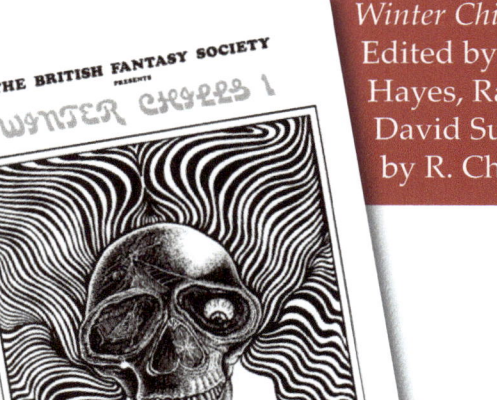

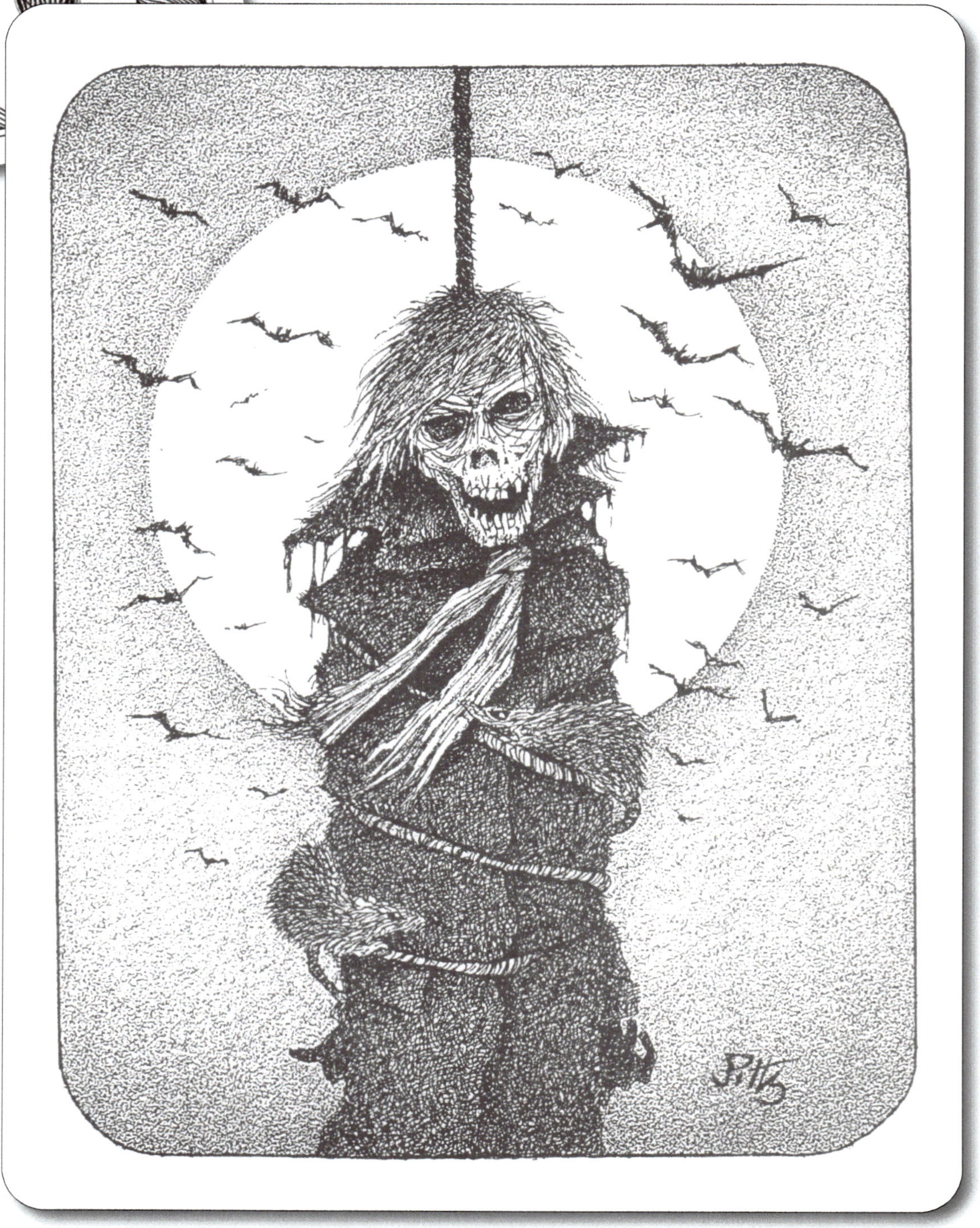

The British Fantasy Society ran two interviews with Jim Pitts over the years. The second, *The Artist in Fandom: Jim Pitts*, appeared in the May-June 1981 issue of the *BFS Bulletin* and was conducted by long-time friend, folk singer Nick Caffrey. You can read the full interview on the next two pages.

THE ARTIST IN FANDOM JIM PITTS

Interviewed by Nick Caffrey

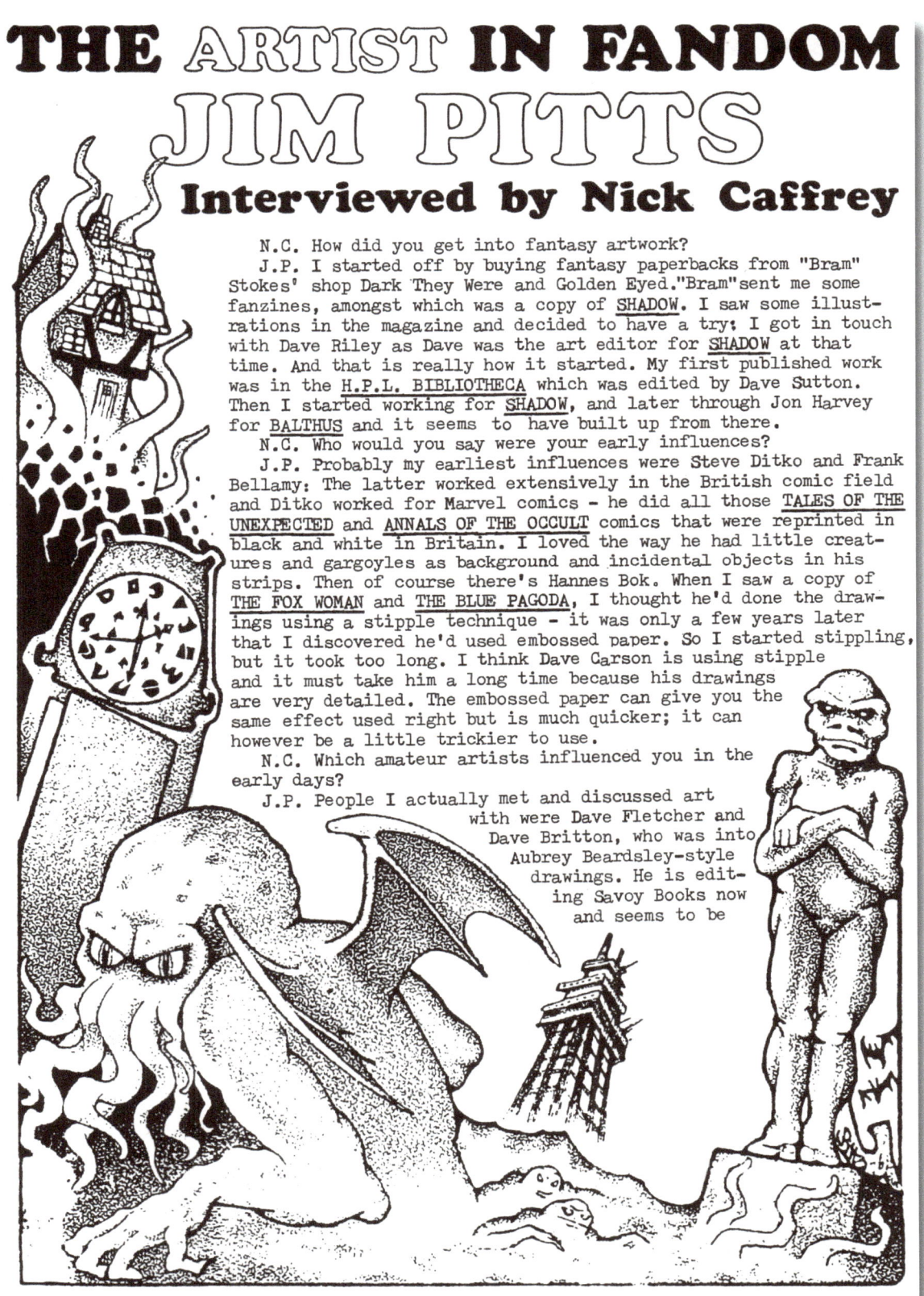

N.C. How did you get into fantasy artwork?

J.P. I started off by buying fantasy paperbacks from "Bram" Stokes' shop Dark They Were and Golden Eyed."Bram" sent me some fanzines, amongst which was a copy of SHADOW. I saw some illustrations in the magazine and decided to have a try: I got in touch with Dave Riley as Dave was the art editor for SHADOW at that time. And that is really how it started. My first published work was in the H.P.L. BIBLIOTHECA which was edited by Dave Sutton. Then I started working for SHADOW, and later through Jon Harvey for BALTHUS and it seems to have built up from there.

N.C. Who would you say were your early influences?

J.P. Probably my earliest influences were Steve Ditko and Frank Bellamy: The latter worked extensively in the British comic field and Ditko worked for Marvel comics - he did all those TALES OF THE UNEXPECTED and ANNALS OF THE OCCULT comics that were reprinted in black and white in Britain. I loved the way he had little creatures and gargoyles as background and incidental objects in his strips. Then of course there's Hannes Bok. When I saw a copy of THE FOX WOMAN and THE BLUE PAGODA, I thought he'd done the drawings using a stipple technique - it was only a few years later that I discovered he'd used embossed paper. So I started stippling, but it took too long. I think Dave Carson is using stipple and it must take him a long time because his drawings are very detailed. The embossed paper can give you the same effect used right but is much quicker; it can however be a little trickier to use.

N.C. Which amateur artists influenced you in the early days?

J.P. People I actually met and discussed art with were Dave Fletcher and Dave Britton, who was into Aubrey Beardsley-style drawings. He is editing Savoy Books now and seems to be

THE ARTIST IN FANDOM

Jim Pitts interviewed by Nick Caffrey
The BFS Bulletin May-June, 1981

NC: How did you get into fantasy artwork?

JP: I started off by buying fantasy paperbacks from Bram Stokes' shop Dark They Were and Golden Eyed. Bram sent me some fanzines, amongst which was a copy of *Shadow*. I saw some illustrations in the magazine and decided to have a try; I got in touch with Dave Riley as Dave was the art editor for *Shadow* at that time. And that is really how it started. My first published work was in the *H.P.L. Bibliotheca*, which was edited by Dave Sutton. Then I started working for *Shadow*, and later through Jon Harvey for *Balthus*, and it seems to have built up from there.

NC: Who would you say were your early influences?

JP: Probably my earliest influences were Steve Ditko and Frank Bellamy. The latter worked extensively in the British comic field and Ditko worked for Marvel comics – he did all those *Tales of the Unexpected* and *Annals of the Occult* comics that were reprinted in black and white in Britain. I loved the way he had little creatures and gargoyles as background and incidental objects in his strips. Then of course there's Hannes Bok. When I saw a copy of *The Fox Woman* and *The Blue Pagoda*, I thought he'd done the drawings using a stipple technique – it was only a few years later that I discovered he'd used embossed paper. So I started stippling, but it took too long. I think Dave Carson is using stipple and it must take him a long time because his drawings are very detailed. The embossed paper can give you the same effect used right but is much quicker; it can however be a little trickier to use.

NC: Which amateur artists influenced you in the early days?

JP: People I actually met and discussed art with were Dave Fletcher and Dave Britton, who was into Aubrey Beardsley-style drawings. He is editing Savoy Books now and seems to be doing quite well. There was Brian Frost, and Dave Riley was doing some drawing as well. It was Dave Fletcher who was the greatest help in those days.

NC: Was it Dave who introduced you to the works of Maxfield Parrish and Harry Clarke?

JP: Yes. I had heard of them through reading about Hannes Bok, but Dave actually had examples of their work in his book collection. I used to go over to his home and stay for the weekend and we experimented in colour techniques, as Dave was doing a lot of colour then. I don't think he was very happy with his colour work and I was just trying to get into it.

NC: In the early 1970s you became fairly well known in the amateur fantasy publications and you took over the *BFS*

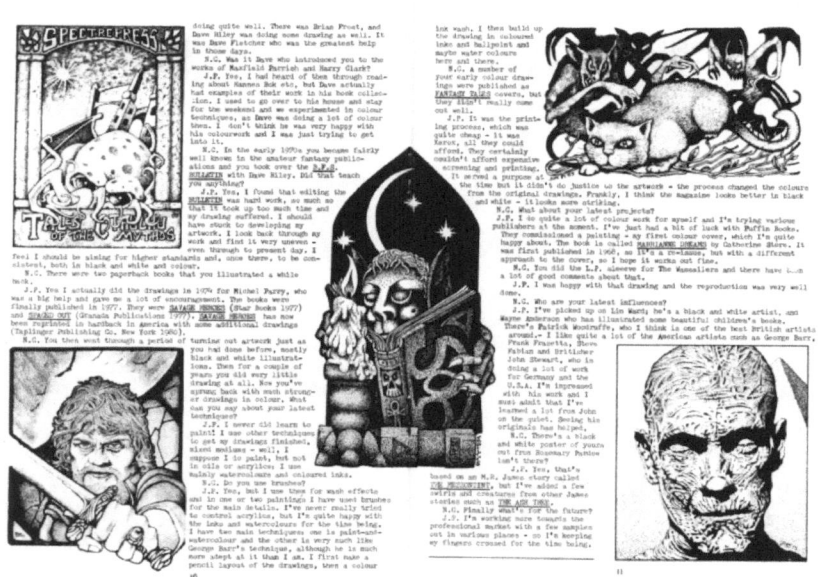

Bulletin with Dave Riley. Did that teach you anything?

JP: Yes, I found that editing the *Bulletin* was hard work, so much so that it took up too much time and my drawing suffered. I should have stuck to developing my artwork. I look back through my work and find it very uneven – even through to the present day. I feel I should be aiming for higher standards and, once there, to be consistent, both in black and white and colour.

NC: There were two paperback books that you illustrated a while back.

JP: Yes, I actually did the drawings in 1974 for Michel Parry, who was a big help and gave me a lot of encouragement. The books were finally published in 1977. They were *Savage Heroes* (Star Books, 1977) and *Spaced Out* (Granada Publications, 1977). *Savage Heroes* has now been reprinted in hardback in America with some additional drawings (Taplinger Publishing Co. New York. 1980).

NC: You then went through a period of turning out artwork just as you had done before, mostly black and white illustrations. Then for a couple of years you did very little drawing at all. Now you've sprung back with much stronger drawings in colour. What can you say about your latest techniques?

JP: I never did learn to paint! I use other techniques to get my drawings finished. Mixed mediums – well, I suppose I do paint, but not in oils or acrylics. I use mainly watercolours and coloured inks.

NC: Do you use brushes?

JP: Yes, but I use them for wash effects and in one or two paintings I have used brushes for the main details. I've never really tried to control acrylics. But I'm quite happy with the inks and watercolours for the time being. I have two main techniques: one is paint-and-watercolour, and the other is very much like George Barr's technique, although he is much more adept at it than I am. I first make a pencil layout of the drawings, then a colour ink wash. I then build up the drawing in coloured inks and ballpoint and maybe water colours here and there.

NC: A number of your early colour drawings were published as *Fantasy Tales* covers, but they didn't really come out well.

JP: It was the printing process, which was quite cheap – it was Xerox, all they could afford. They certainly couldn't afford expensive screening and printing. It served a purpose at the time but it didn't do justice to the artwork – the process changed the colours from the original drawings. Frankly, I think the magazine looks better in black and white – it looks more striking.

NC: What about your latest projects?

JP: I do quite a lot of colour work for myself and I'm trying various publishers at the moment. I've just had a bit of luck with Puffin Books. They commissioned a painting – my first colour cover, which I'm quite happy about. The book is called *Marianne Dreams* by Catherine Store. It was first published in 1968, so it's a re-issue, but with a different approach to the cover, so I hope it works out fine.

NC: You did the L.P. sleeve for The Wassailers and there have been a lot of good comments about that.

JP: I was happy with that drawing and the reproduction was very well done.

NC: Who are your latest influences?

JP: I've picked up on Lin Ward; he's a black and white artist, and Wayne Anderson who has illustrated some beautiful children's books. There's Patrick Woodruffe, who I think is one of the best British artists around. I quite like a lot of the American artists such as George Barr, Frank Frazetta, Steve Fabian and Britisher John Stewart, who us doing a lot of work for Germany and the USA. I'm impressed with his work and I must admit that I've learned a lot from John on the quiet. Seeing his originals has helped.

NC: There's a black and white poster of yours out from Rosemary Pardoe, isn't there?

JP: Yes, that's based on an M. R. James story called *The Mezzotint*, but I've added a few swirls and creatures from other James stories, such as *The Ash Tree*.

NC: Finally, what's for the future?

JP: I'm working more towards the professional market with a few samples out in various places – so I'm keeping my fingers crossed for the time being.

Cover artwork for *Dark Horizons* # 15 used by then *DH* editor Stephen Jones in 1976

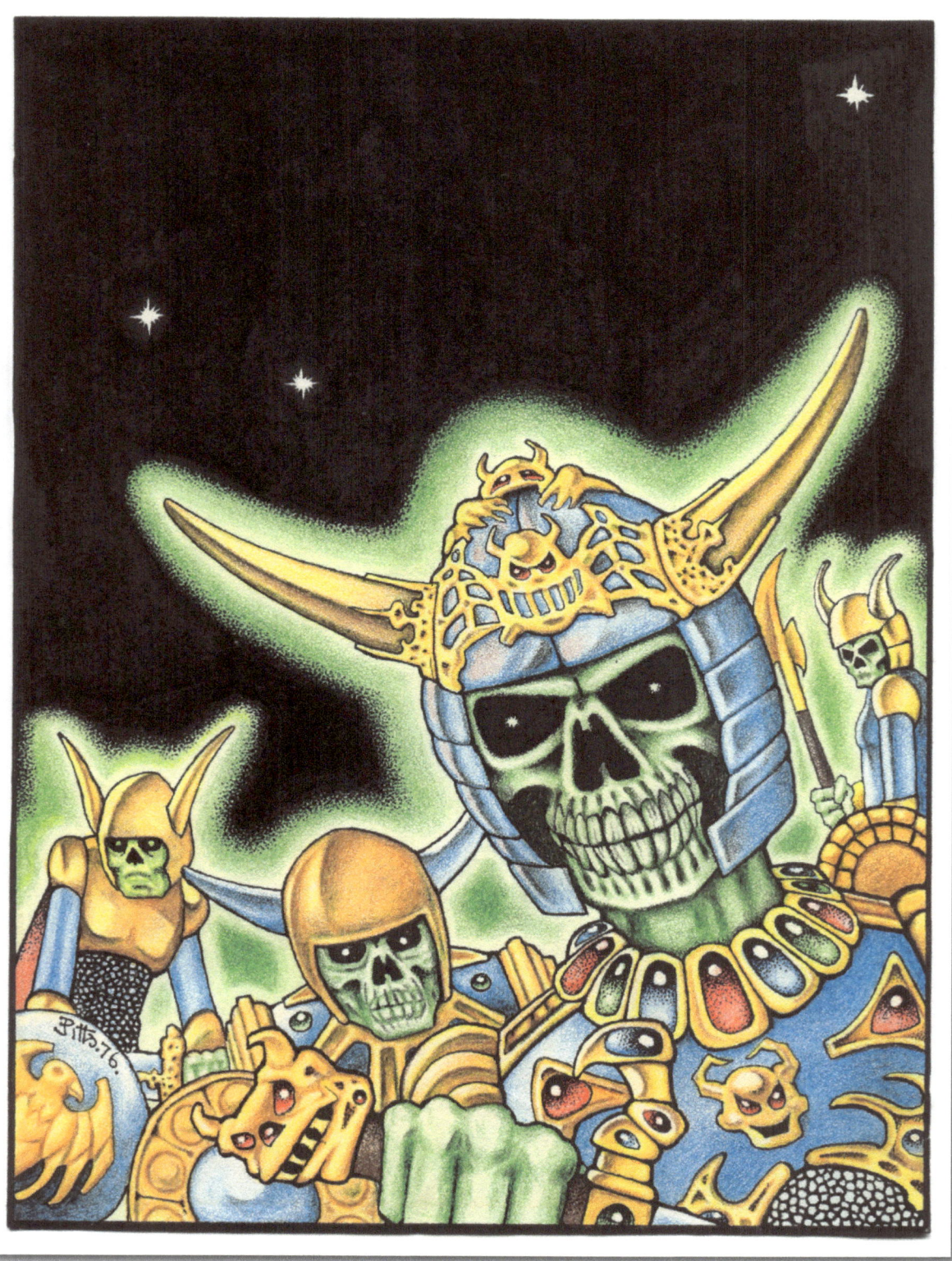

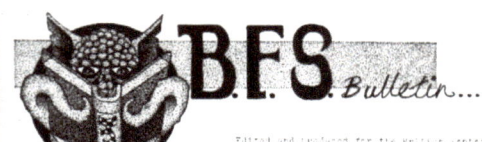

In 1974 Jim Pitts and David A. Riley collaborated on editing and producing the *BFS Bulletin*, which up until then had been printed as a gestetner duplicated newsheet. From now on the *Bulletin* would be published by all successive editors using lithographic printing. It was a big step forward for the British Fantasy Society and not initially welcomed by all. Some criticised the new printing process as too costly. It did, however, start the BFS on the road to producing increasingly more professional-looking publications, a process that has continued to this day.

To the left is a copy of the first of the new-style-*Bulletins*, published in May/June 1974.

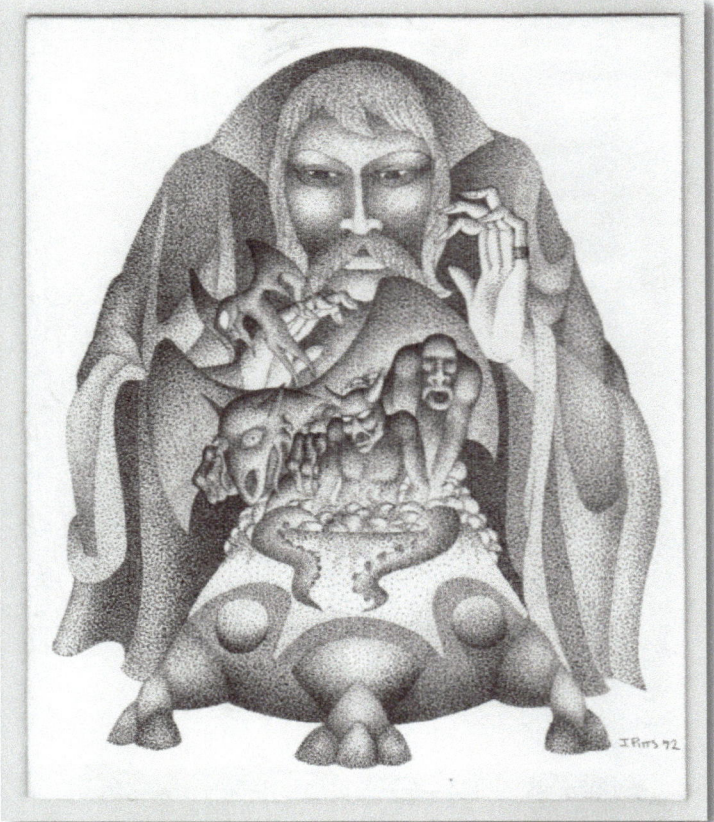

Dark Horizons summer 1974 with the first ever interview of Jim Pitts: *The Artist in Fandom*, conducted by David A. Riley and Nick Caffrey.

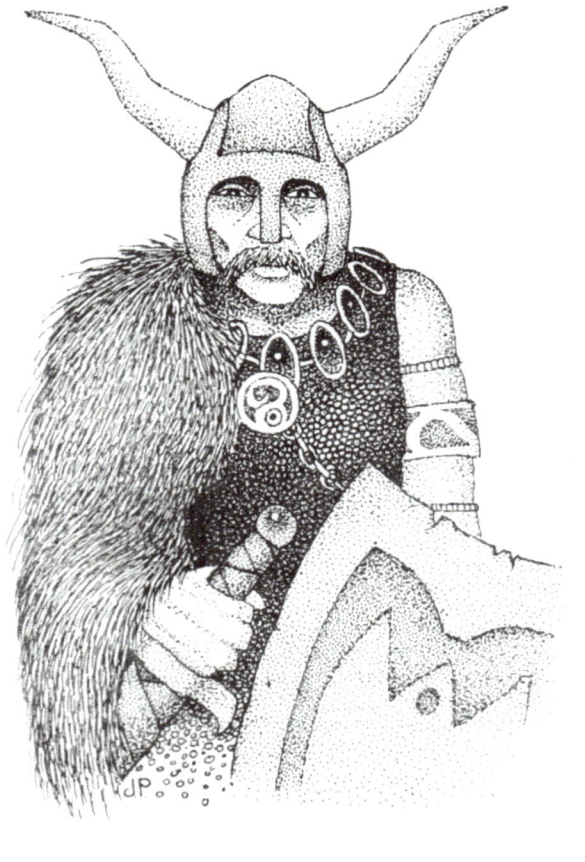

Used in the first *Fantasycon Programme Booklet* in February 1975

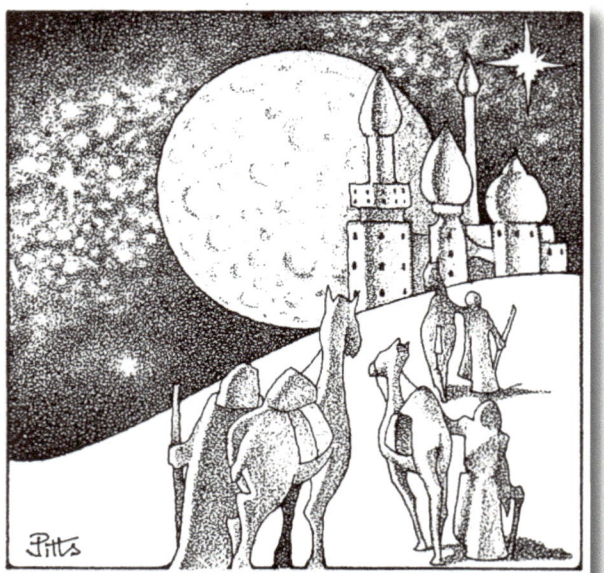

Above is an illustration from the 1976 Yuletide issue of *The BFS Bulletin*.

Below is the cover to *Dark Horizons* No 33, 1992.

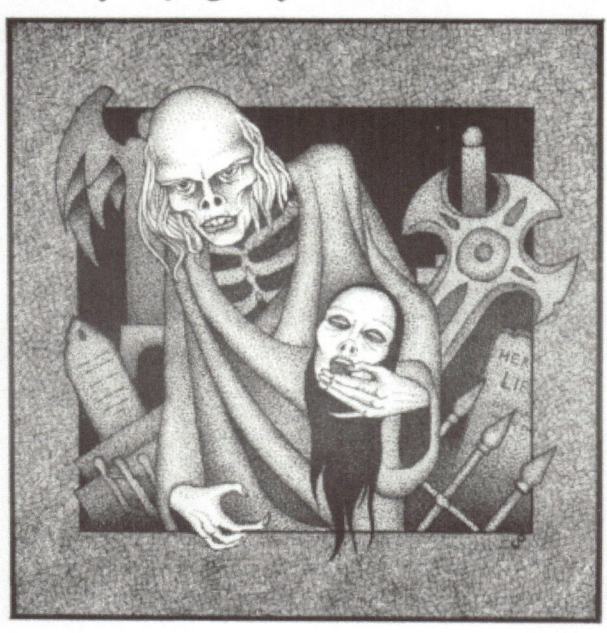

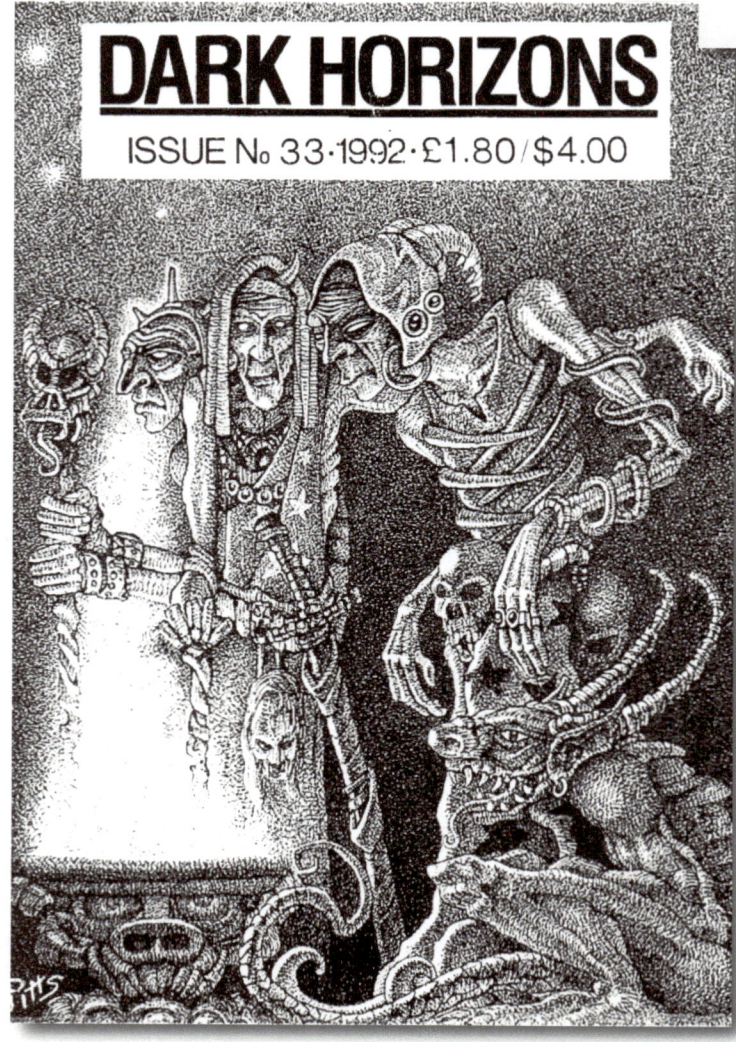

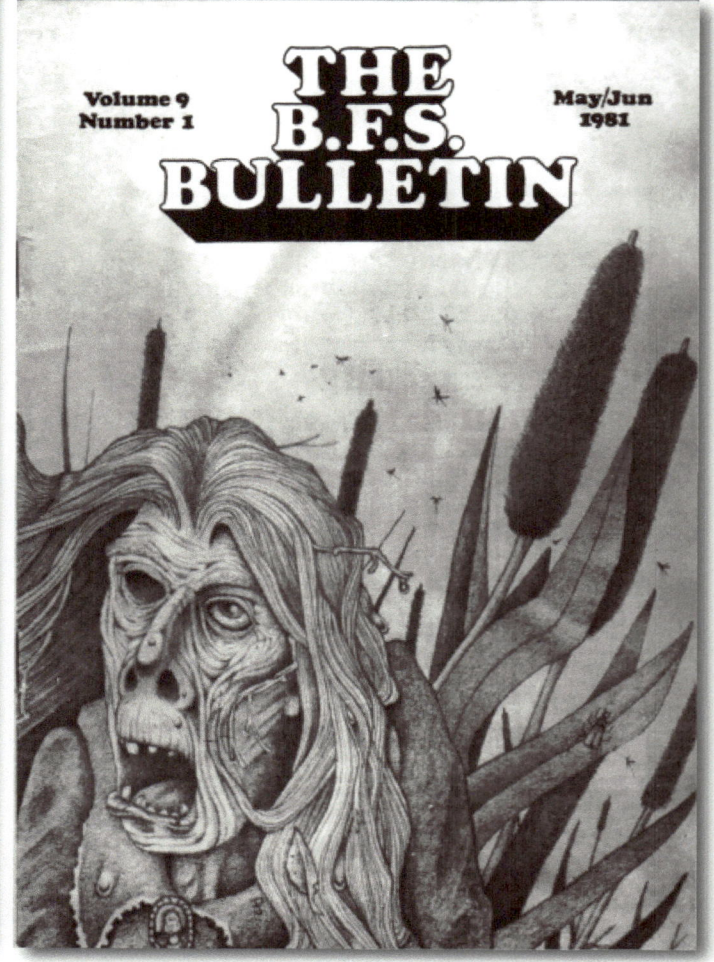

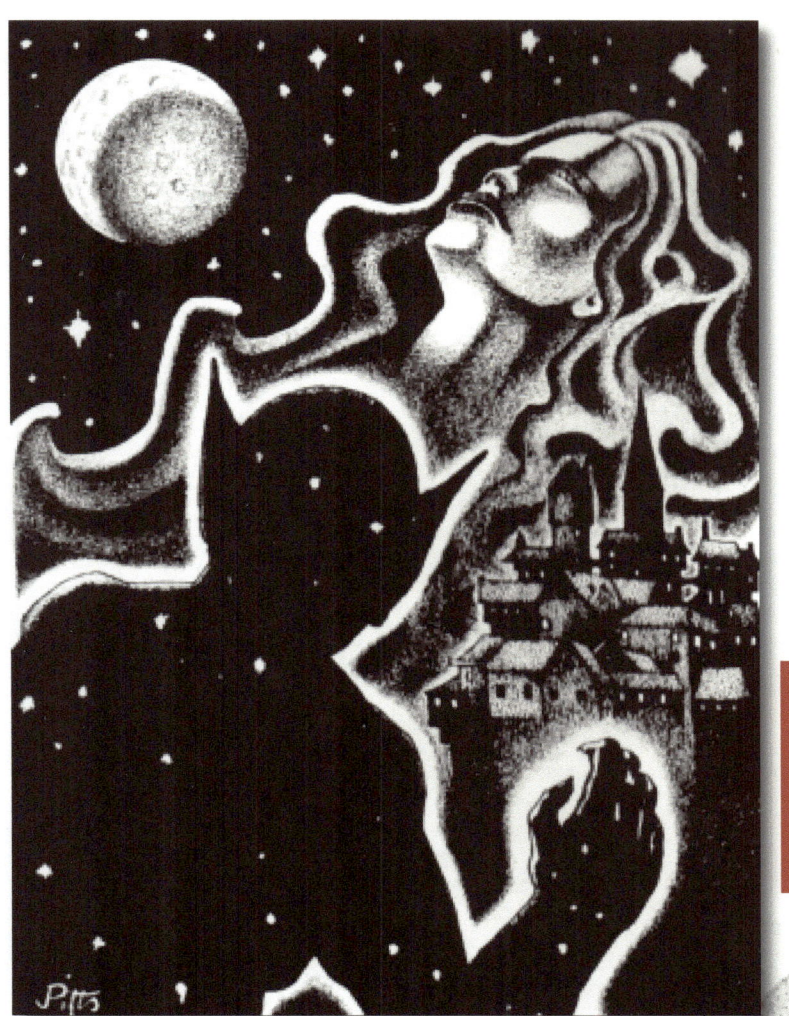

Dark Horizons issue 14, Summer 1976 inside front cover: "The Lay of the Last Zydrin"

Below: Dark Horizons issue 10, Autumn/Winter 1974

Interior illustration for *The Second Dragons* by Mike Chinn

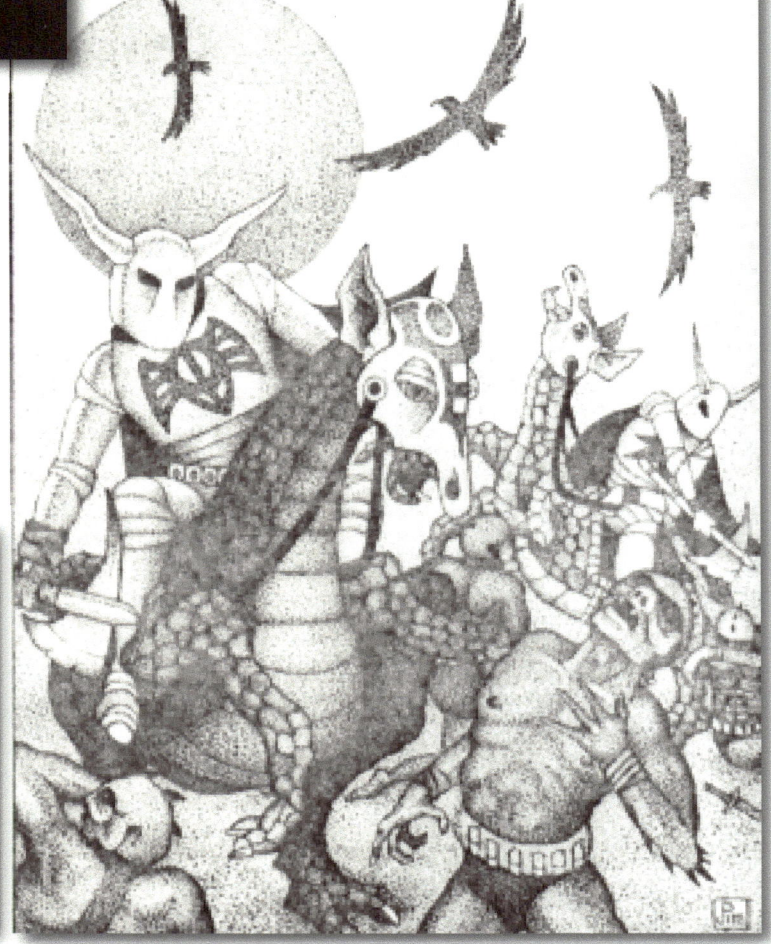

Below, title heading for *Parasites* by Alan Eames

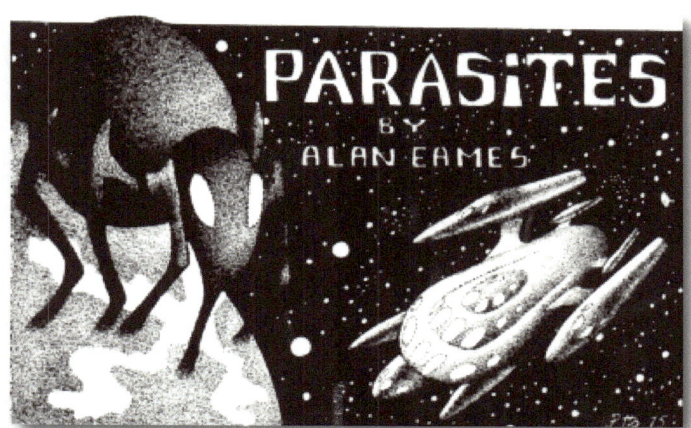

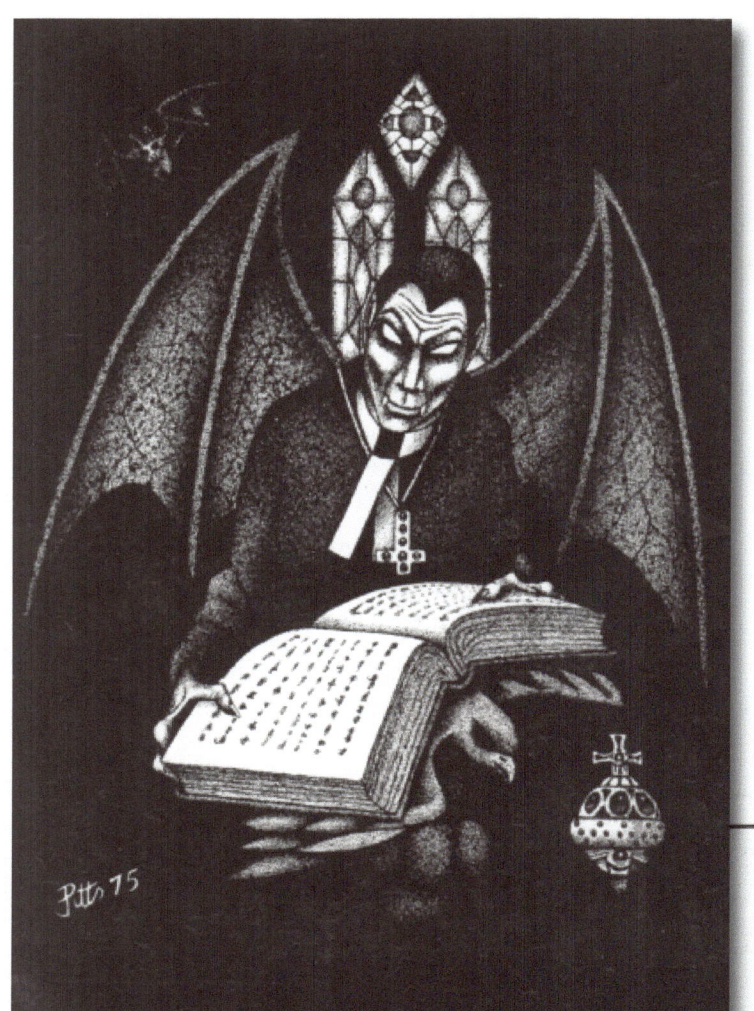

To the left: back cover illustration for *Dark Horizons* issue 14, Summer 1976 "A Question of Faith"

Dark Horizons issue 14, Summer 1976

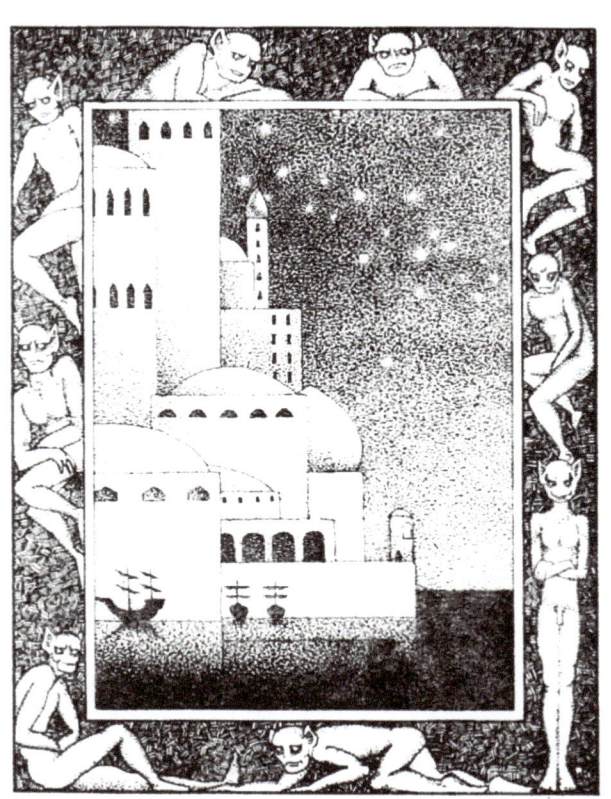

SARNATH - H.P. Lovecraft

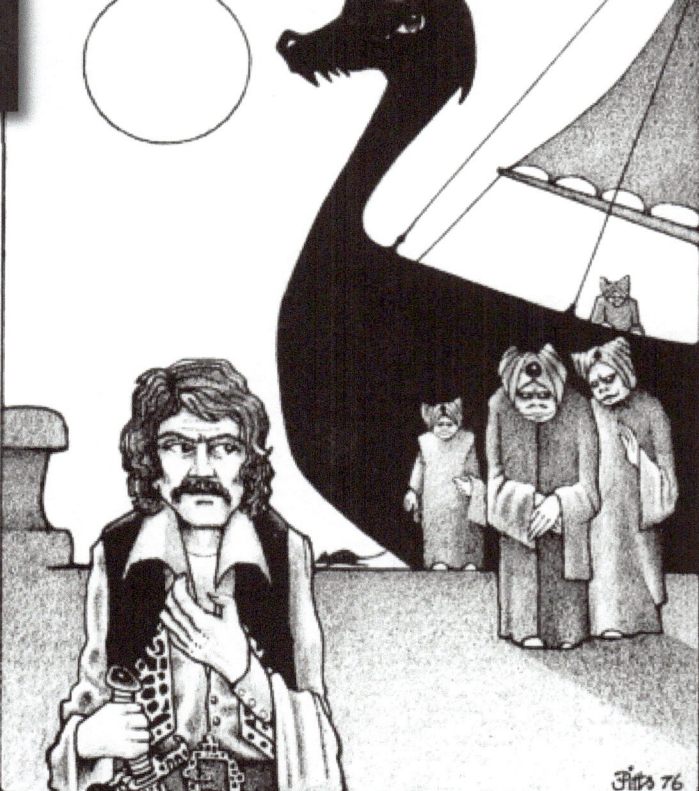

DYLATH-LEEN

"Why should those black galleys come in to harbour, disharge their four or five traders, and then simply lie there at anchor, emitting their foul odours, showing never a sign of their silent crews?"

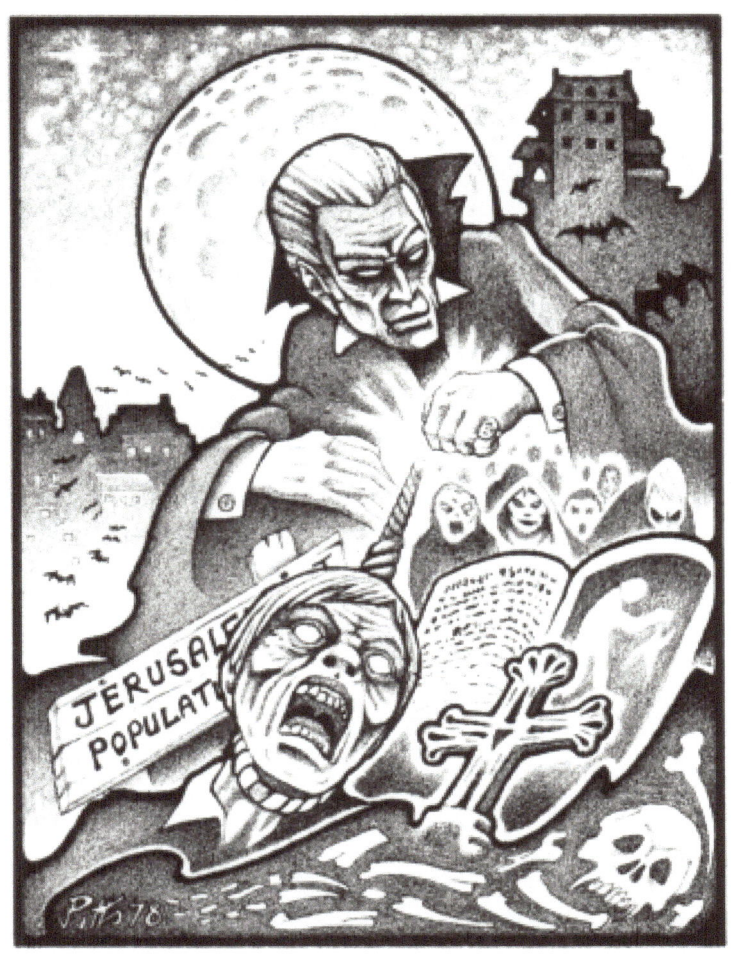

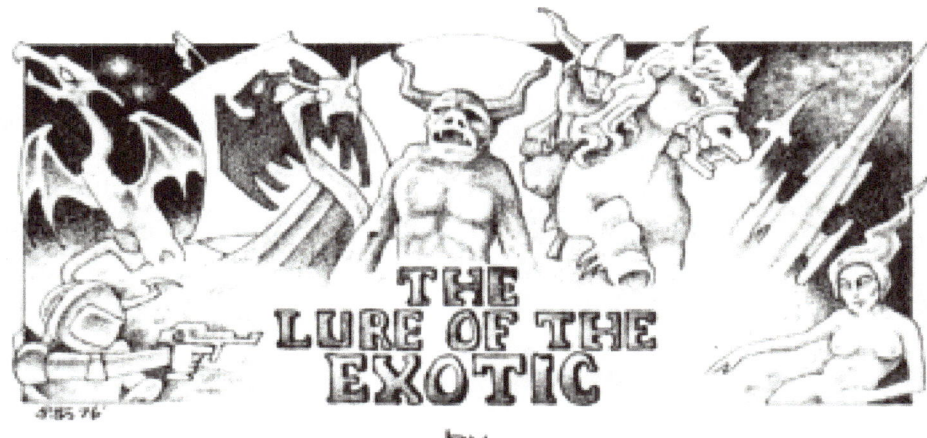

Fantasycon IV programme booklet in 1977. The illustration was inspired by Stephen King's *Salem's Lot* as he was due to attend that year's convention. Unfortunately his appearance was cancelled for medical reasons.

Interior heading for H. Ken Bulmer's *The Lure of the Exotic*

"THE JIM PITTS FOLK QUARTET"
EARLY YEARS OF LIFELONG FRIENDSHIP
by Nick Caffrey

I am not sure just when I first met Jim Pitts, he was one of a dozen other kids on the housing estate with whom I swapped comics. Initially they were the British comics: *Dandy, Beano, Eagle, Topper, Film Fun, Knockout, Hotspur*. Jim lived nearby, just up the road, across the Main Road, through the ginnel and fifth house on the left.

In the early nineteen sixties we both attended the local secondary school. At this time Jim and I were casual friends, swapping comics, chatting about the comic strips and artwork, the new rock bands, Jim and I were definitely Stones fans, all the stuff that kids talk about. Neither of us was sporty, so football and cricket didn't enter the conversation.

The UK started to receive some of the American comics, mainly *Superman, Batman, Archie, Aquaman* and other DC comics, we were both fans of *MAD* magazine and loved Jack Davis and Don Martin's illustrative styles and humour. There was also a new style of British comic that reprinted some of the American comics in black and white, these had titles such as *Secrets of the Unknown, Out of This World, Uncanny Tales, Sinister Tales*. One of our favourite artists in these was Steve Ditko, we loved his strange gaunt characters, the little background details of an imp, or half-seen demon peeping out from a corner of the weird occult shops that his characters seemed to visit.

The popularity of The Beatles, Rolling Stones and Bob Dylan brought a growth in local kids getting together to form bands, pseudo Stones, Shadows, Animals could be heard from many garages and front rooms as one travelled round the estate. Around 1963/4 I became part of a folk band, made up of other school kids from my class, we started singing copies of Bob Dylan, Dubliners and Spinners records. We played local youth clubs, church concerts and Working Men's Clubs.

After a couple of years one of the lads in the band dropped out, so we looked around for a replacement. How we came to ask Jim to join I cannot remember, but he soon took to playing the string bass and harmonica; Jim played a mean harmonica in the style of Cyril Davis who played with Alexis Korner's Blues Band. We called the band the James Pitts Folk Quartet, the name was probably a cop out from trying to think up a group name. It was from this time that Jim and I became much closer friends. Jim used to doodle little comic drawings, usually when he became bored of the discussions about what songs we going to put in that night's programme, or working out new songs when he was not directly involved. The doodles were often of the Stones, especially Mick and Brian, he also did funny little creatures reminiscent of the Ditko characters we loved from the comics.

As well as comics we both enjoyed fantasy, horror and science fiction books. I collected the Doc Savage books that had begun to be published by Bantam books with excellent covers by James Bama; we enjoyed the classic ghost stories and novels such as *Dracula* and *Frankenstein* along with American writers such as Ray Bradbury. We also became followers of Michael Moorcock's Elric stories that were printed in the *Science Fantasy* magazine. It was that magazine that brought Mervyn Peake to our attention when Moorcock wrote an an essay about Peake and the magazine printed two of his short stories. We soon discovered that

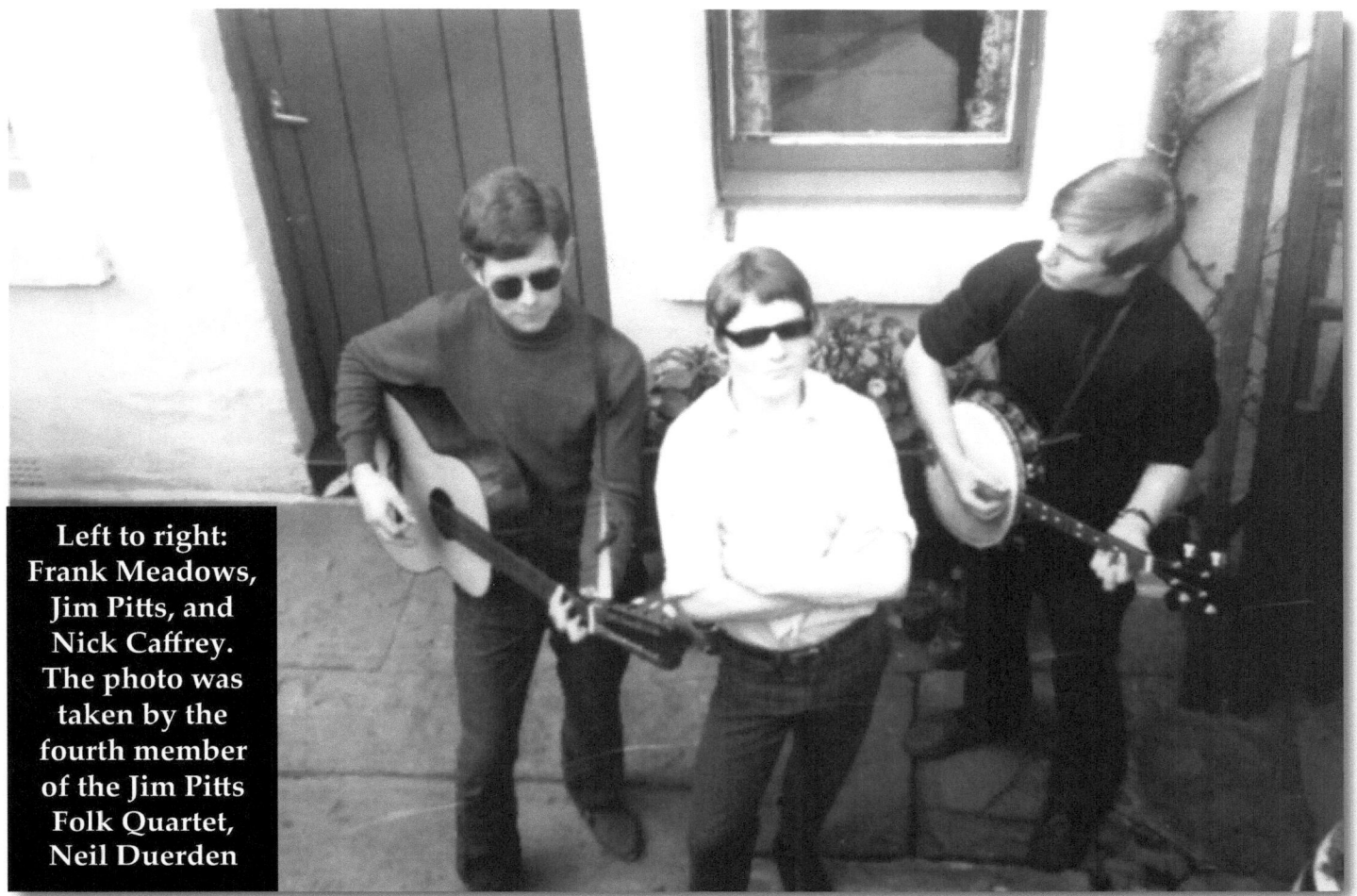

Left to right: Frank Meadows, Jim Pitts, and Nick Caffrey. The photo was taken by the fourth member of the Jim Pitts Folk Quartet, Neil Duerden

Mervyn Peake was an artist, producing drawings that really appealed.

It was Jim who discovered Dark They Were And Golden Eyed, a shop in London that specialised in fantasy books, he wrote off for the booklist and we soon began to order imported fantasy books. We became fans of Robert E Howard with Frazetta covers, H P Lovecraft and Edgar Rice Burroughs (whom we had only associated with the Tarzan series of books). We became aware of Hannes Bok, Virgil Finley, and other artists that had been published in *Weird Tales*.

We began to ring the shop for more information and recommendations, its owner Bram Stokes was very pleasant and helpful. It was Bram Stokes who told us about fanzines (amateur magazines with reviews and articles about fantasy books, films and artists). The fanzines came in a wide variety of quality and content, the drawings ranged from dreadful to very professional. Jim felt he could draw better, more competent illustrations than many of the ones published in the fanzines, and proceeded to prove this.

In 1969 I married Anna and we moved to a council house that was near to where Jim lived. Jim had dropped out of the band by this time, it had been reformed in a variety of different formats, until I too dropped out and didn't sing in a band for a few years.

During the early 1970s we saw a lot of each other, swapping books and getting nvolved with the British Fantasy Society (it was named The British Weird Fantasy Society when we first joined). Jim had had a few drawings published and won the Ken Macintyre award for The Gargoyle. His drawing techniques had improved greatly and were of a high standard.

Around 1972 I started a new duo with Ed McGurk who lived nearby at that time, we named the band Litany and later, when it came to producing some publicity leaflets and business cards, I asked Jim if he would put something together. The poster was of a jester holding a placard with Ed's address and contact number, it was beautiful, eye-catching and just perfect for the job; the business card followed this theme and was also a delight.

Jim and I ventured into Manchester and got to know Dave Britton, whose artwork was quite surreal and witty. Dave ran a bookshop near to the Free Trade Hall and sold fantasy, horror and science fiction books. He had also started publishing books and had reprinted some of the Ken Reid's *Fudge the Elf* comic strips in book form. Sometime in the early 1970s we met up with David Riley, Jim contacted him and we went round to his house in Accrington. David and Jim later produced the *BFS Bulletin* using Dave Britton's publishing facilities to print them. The newsletter was lively, with good reviews and plenty of good illustrations.

We attended Fantasy Conventions in Birmingham and met like-minded eccentrics who loved fantasy books, films and art. Jim's artwork was improving all the time from the initial stipple effect to experiments with embossed paper.

In 1977 Litany broke up and I joined a local folk band named The Wassailers, it was meant to be temporary but the sound we produced was surprisingly good so we decided to carry on and fill already booked guest spots, and see where it went.

In April 1978 just twelve months after forming the revamped band we made a record with Fellside records. I asked Jim if he would like to produce a full-colour cover for the album. He agreed and produced a wonderful piece of artwork, the other guys in the band thought it was the best cover they had ever seen.

As the 1970s ended I became rather busy with the band and work. I had moved house to the other end of the town and Jim and I saw less of each other, although each time we met we always felt we should get together. I've enjoyed my friendship with Jim he is always interesting, adventurous and keen to learn more about the things that interest him. I have always rated him among my favourite artists and a good friend.

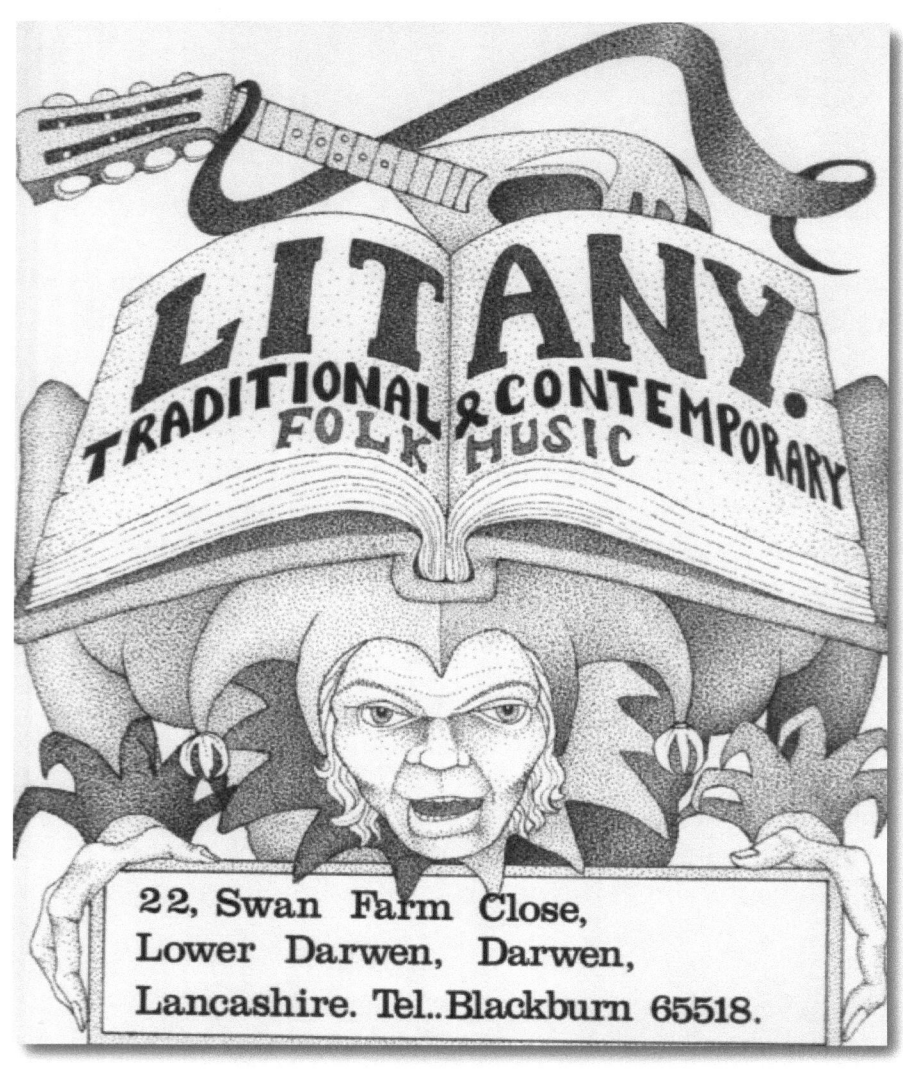

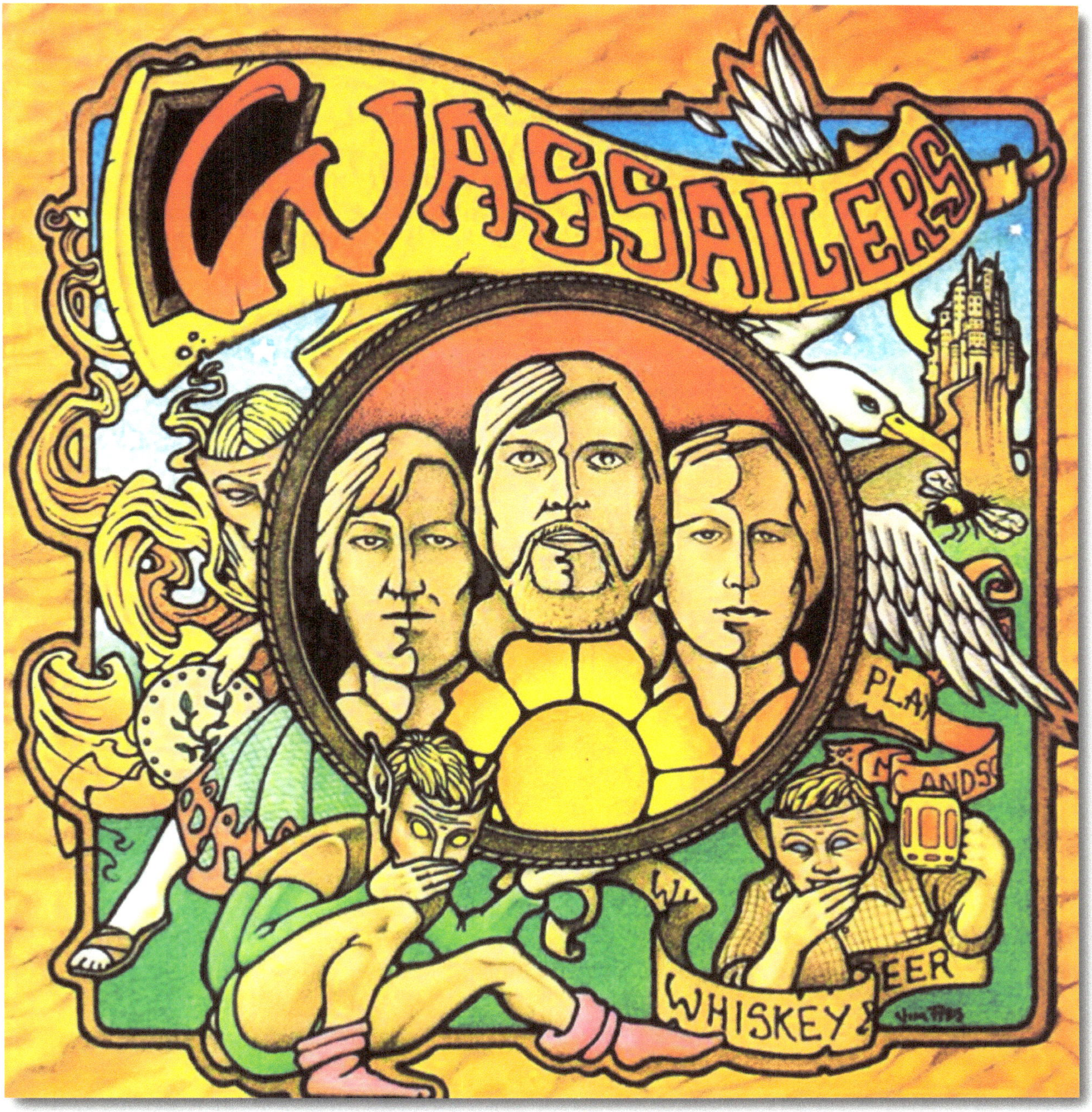

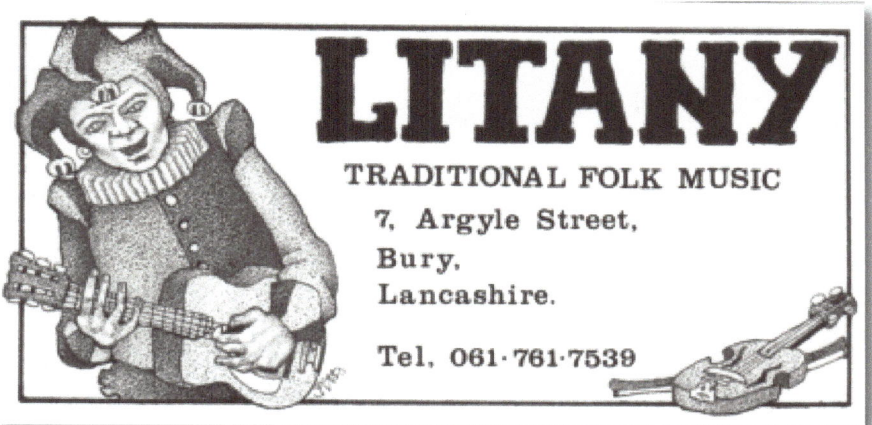

LITANY

TRADITIONAL FOLK MUSIC

7, Argyle Street,
Bury,
Lancashire.

Tel. 061-761-7539

Above is a record sleeve designed by Jim for the folk group The Wassailers. Jim's friend, Nick Caffrey, was its lead singer.

On the left and on the facing page are ads for Litany, a duo comprising Nick Caffrey and Ed McGurk.

WORLD OF HORROR - 1975

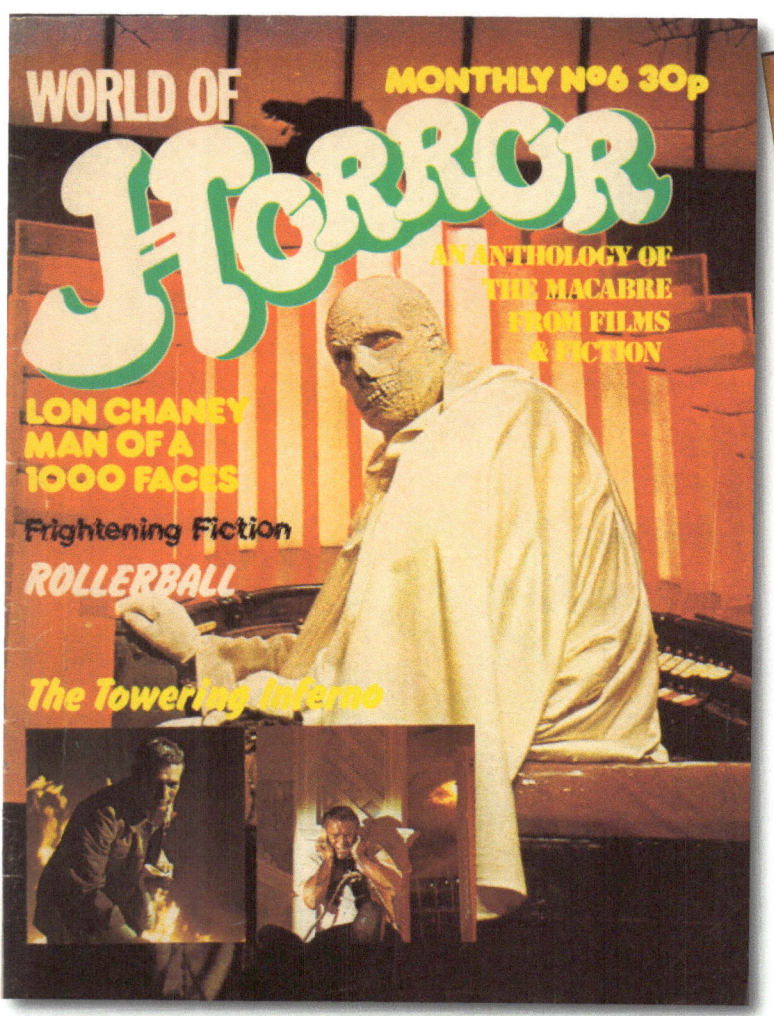
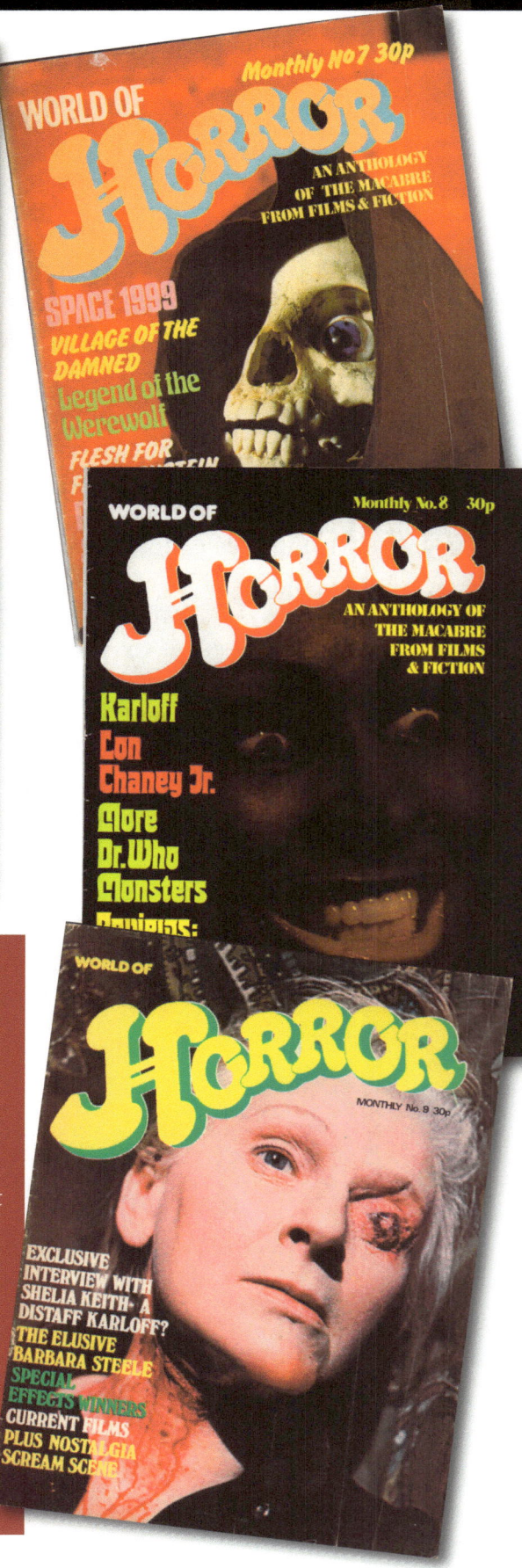

World of Horror was a professional British horror magazine that ran for 10 issues in 1975, a mix of sf and horror films and TV series, spiced up with a couple of short stories. Although Jim never worked on any of the covers (these were made up of photographs, mostly from horror films), he did illustrate four stories from issue 6 onwards, starting with *The Shade of Apollyon* by David A. Riley, where he provided a full-page title piece and a spot illo. Issue 7 saw two more illustrations for another David A. Riley story: *Terror on the Moors*. The next issue Jim illustrated *The Bestwick Papers* by David A. Sutton. It was the only one for which he didn't have a spot illo as well. In the penultimate issue Jim provided the usual two illustrations, this time for Frank Belknap Long's classic horror story, *The Brain-Eaters*.

The next issue was, unfortunately, the last.

The Shade of Apollyon by David A. Riley

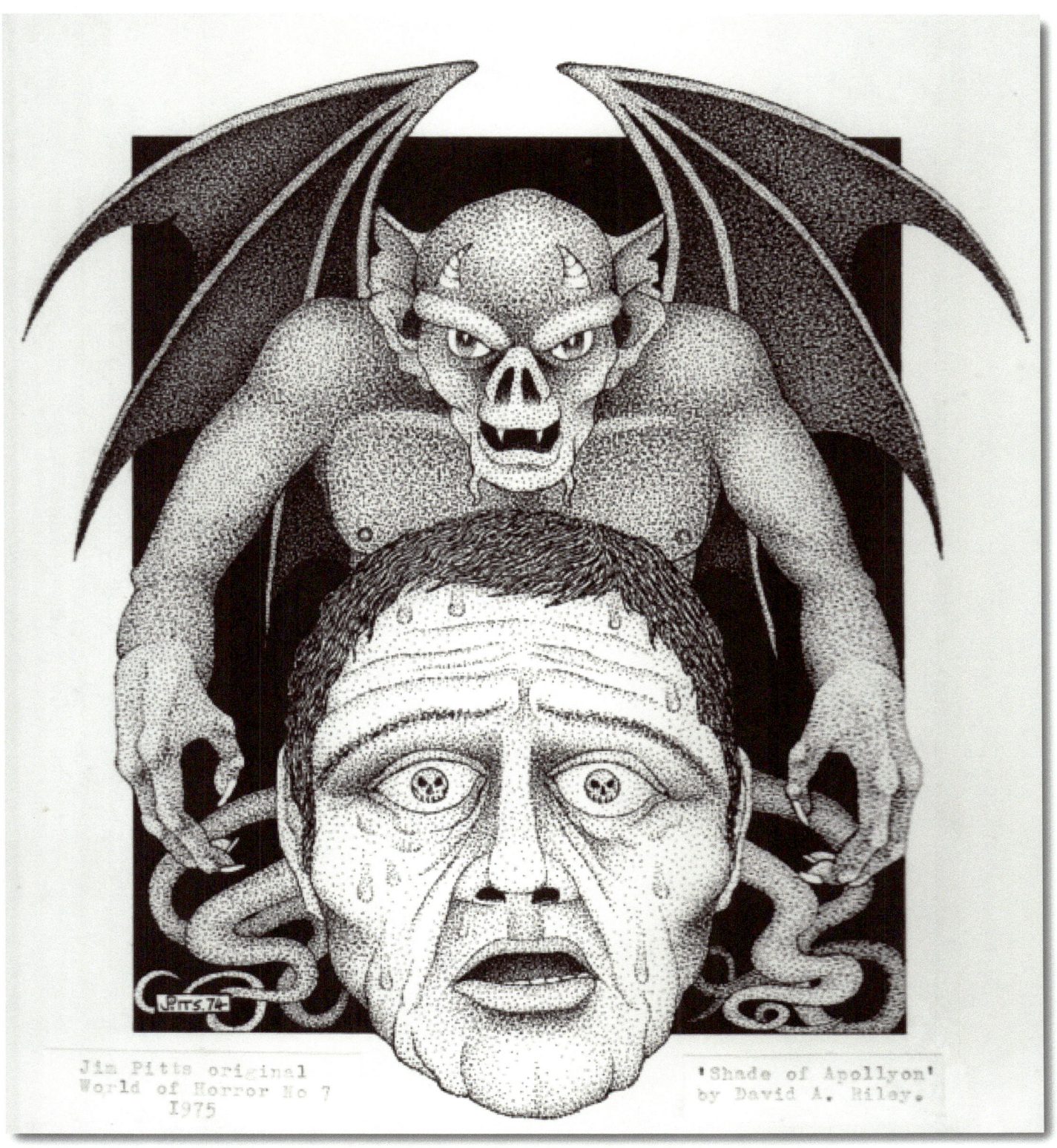

Frank Belknap Long's classic horror story, *The Brain-Eaters*

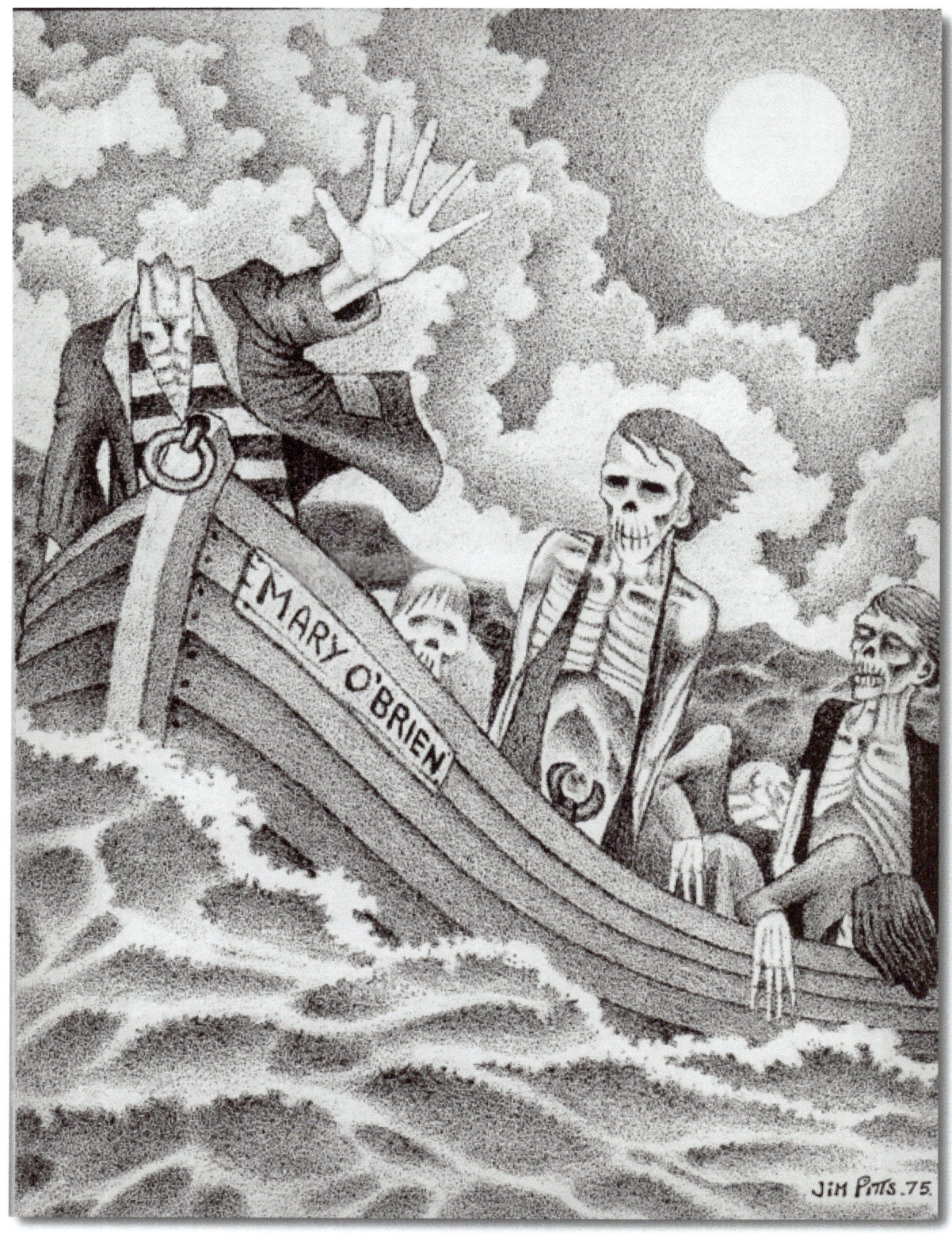

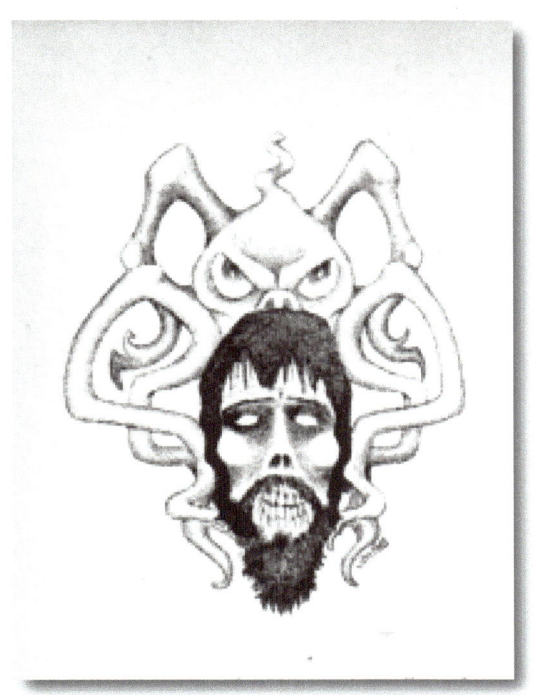
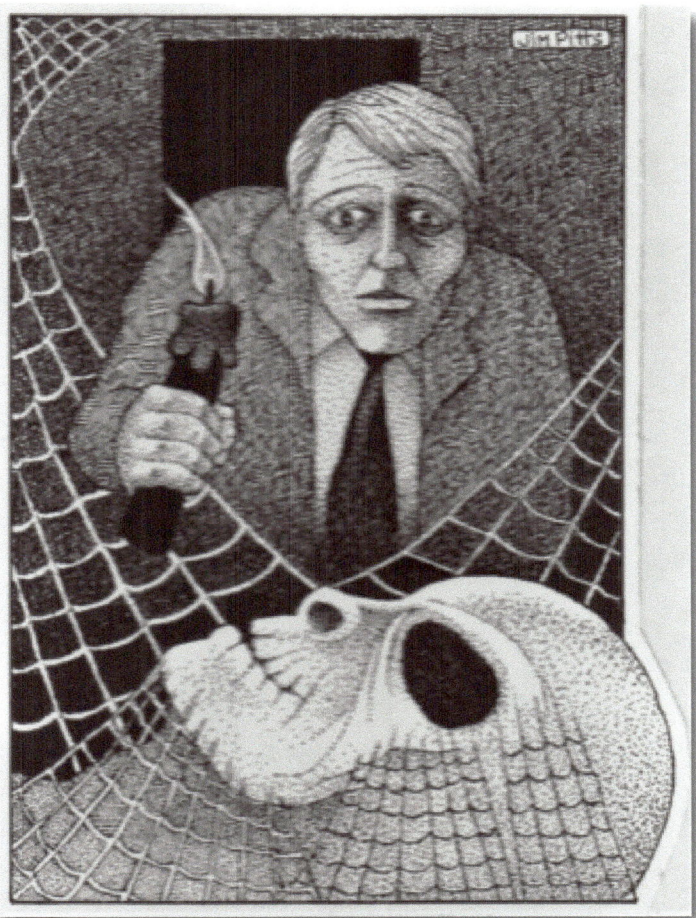
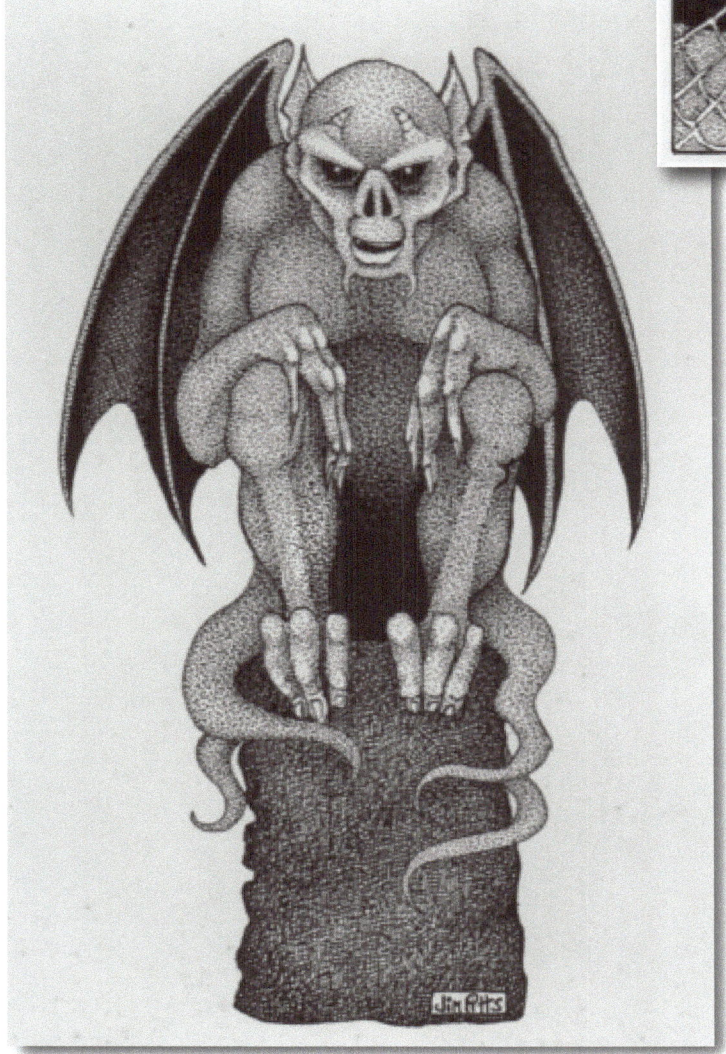

Three spot illustrations:
The Brain-Eaters
Terror on the Moors
The Shade of Apollyon.

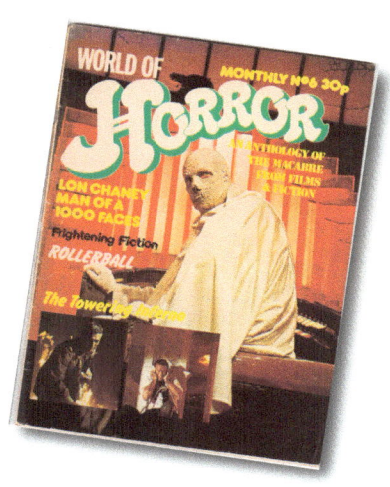

David A. Riley's story: *Terror on the Moors*

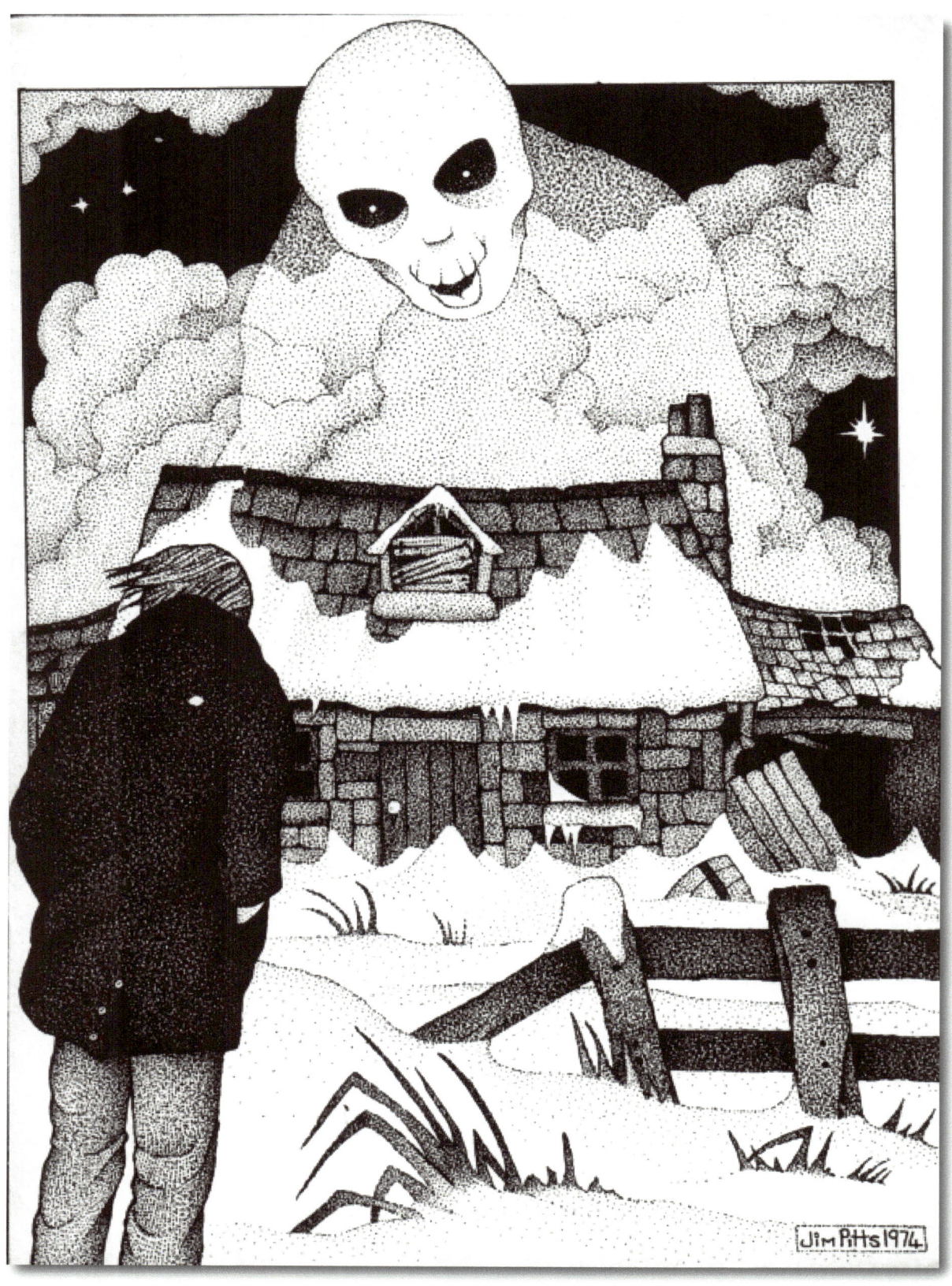

48

The Bestwick Papers by David A. Sutton

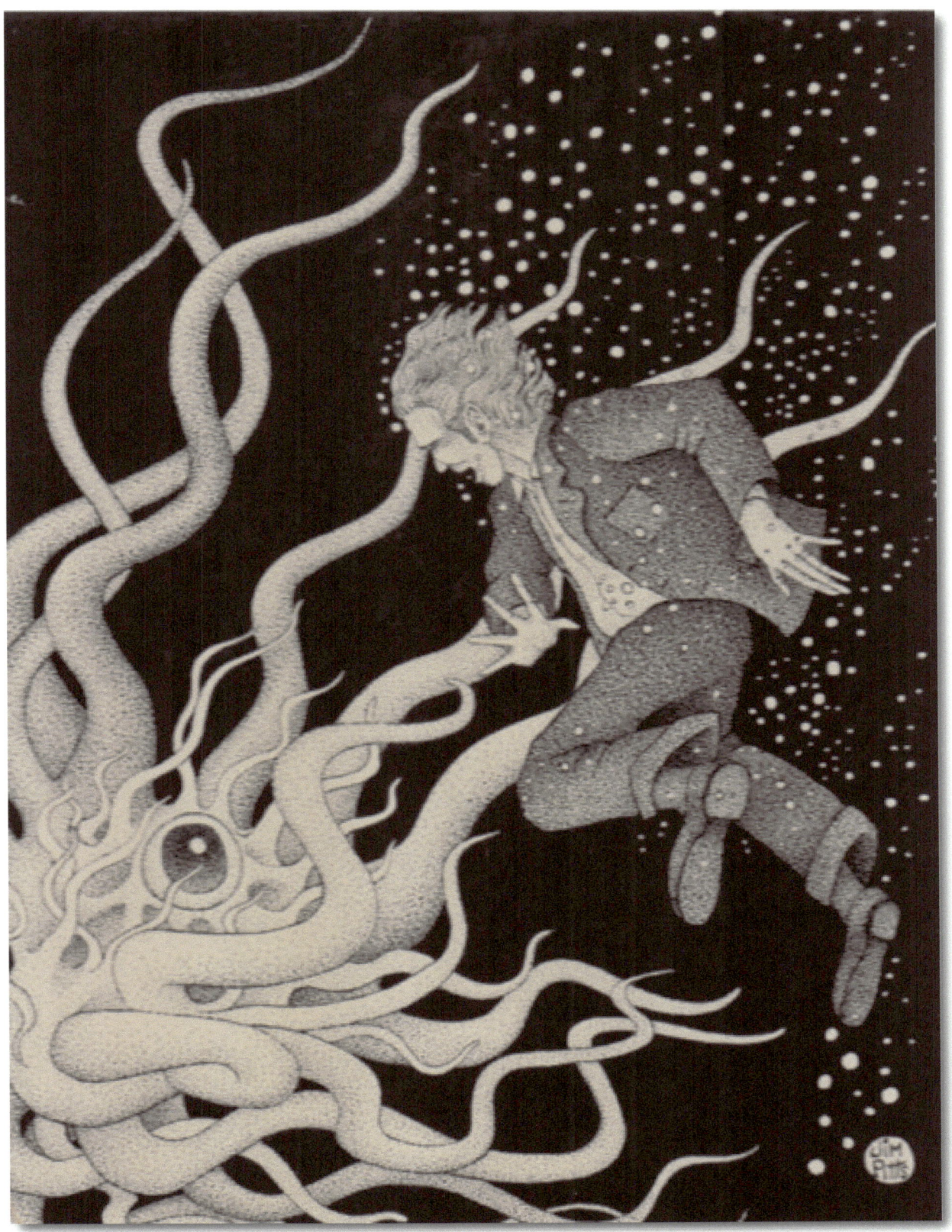

SPACED OUT
edited by Michel Parry

Spaced Out, edited by Michel Parry, was published by Panther Books in 1977. The front cover was the work of Brian Froud. The first illustration by Jim is for *The Deep Fix* by Michael Moorcock. *The Roger Bacon Formula* was by Fletcher Pratt. *Smoke of the Snake* was by Carl Jacobi. The next to the last is *Melodramine* by Henry Slesar. And the final picture is *Sky* by R. A. Lafferty.

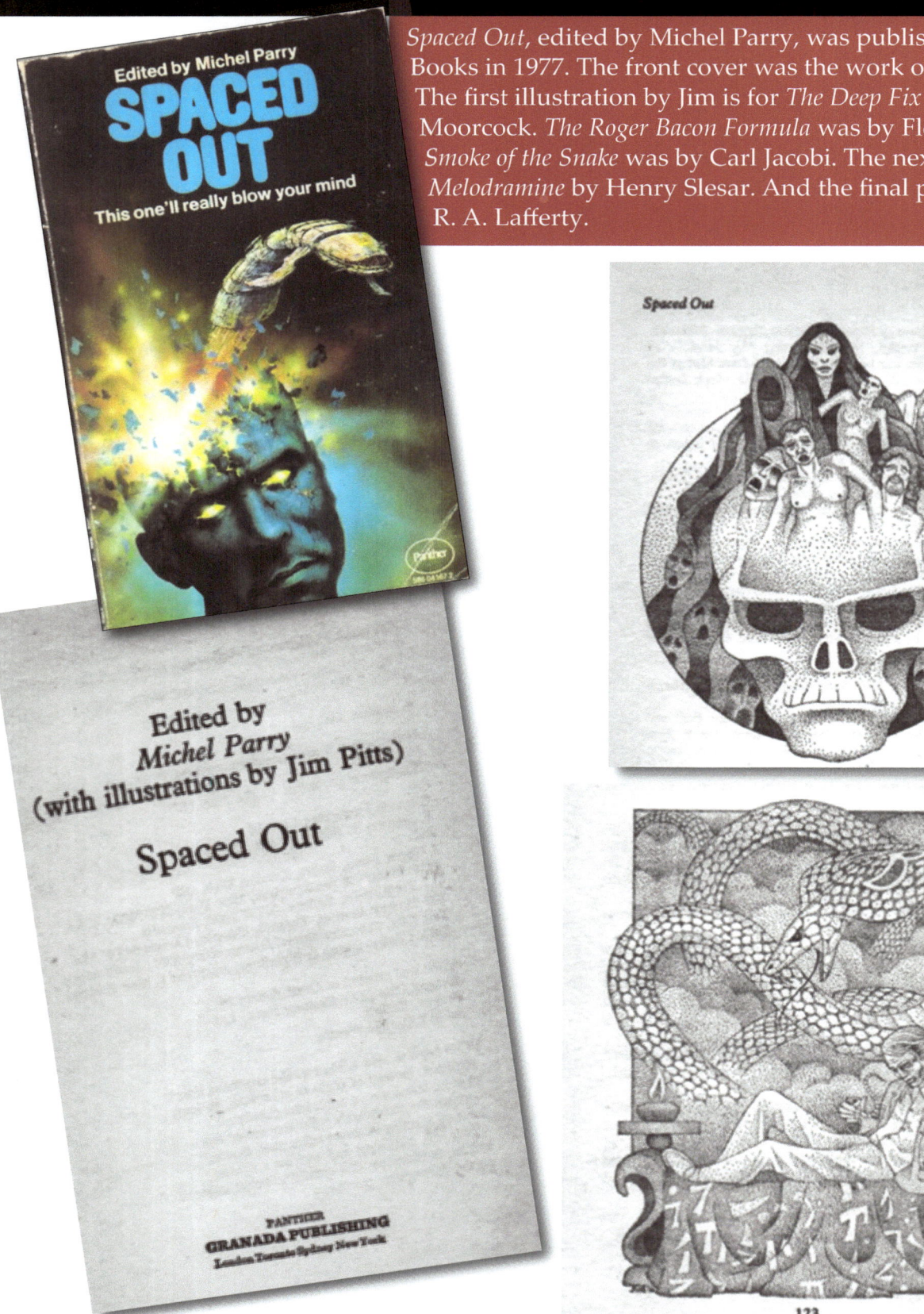

The Roger Bacon Formula

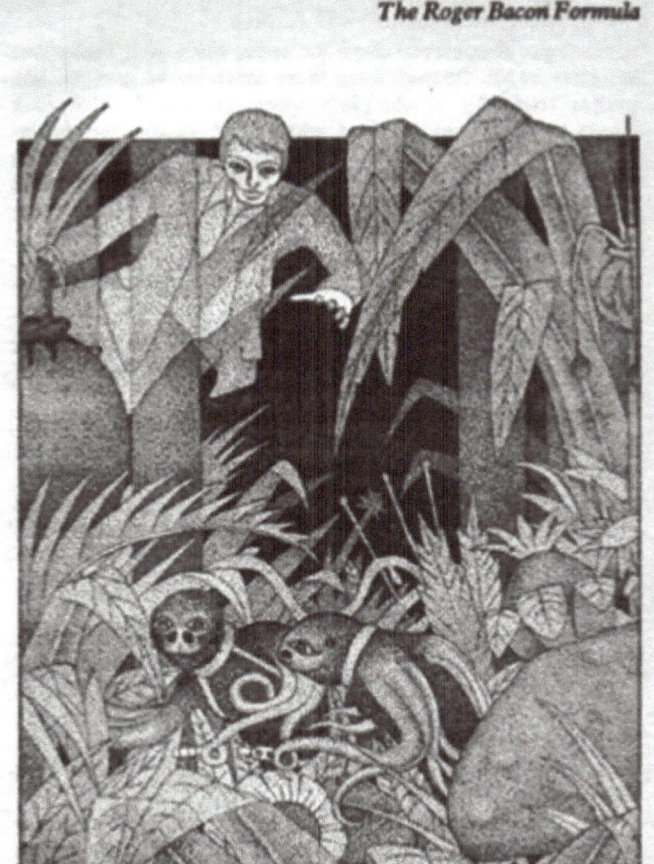

Spaced Out

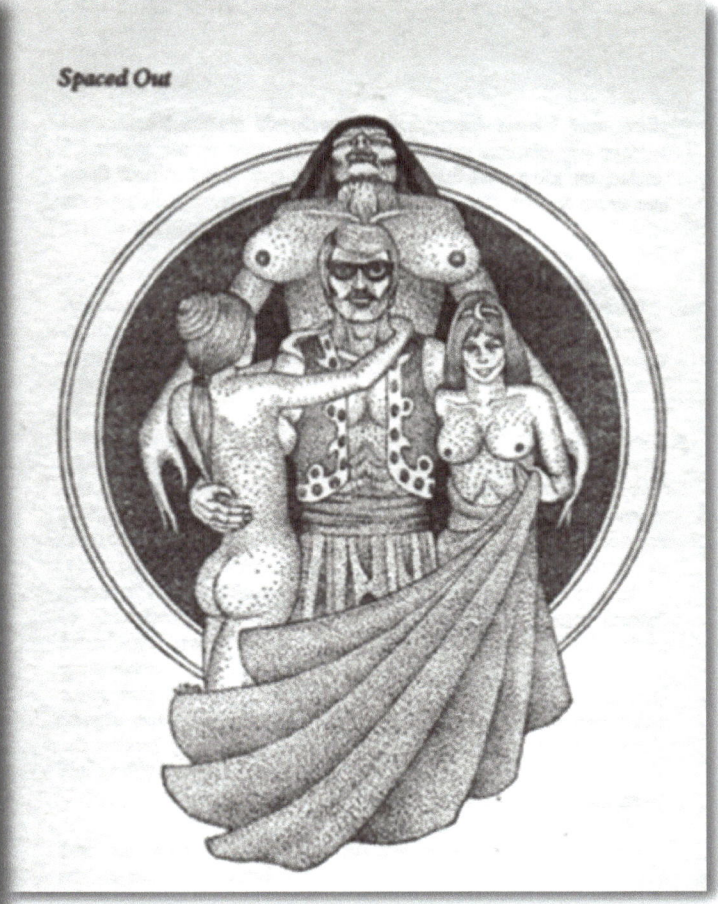

Spaced Out

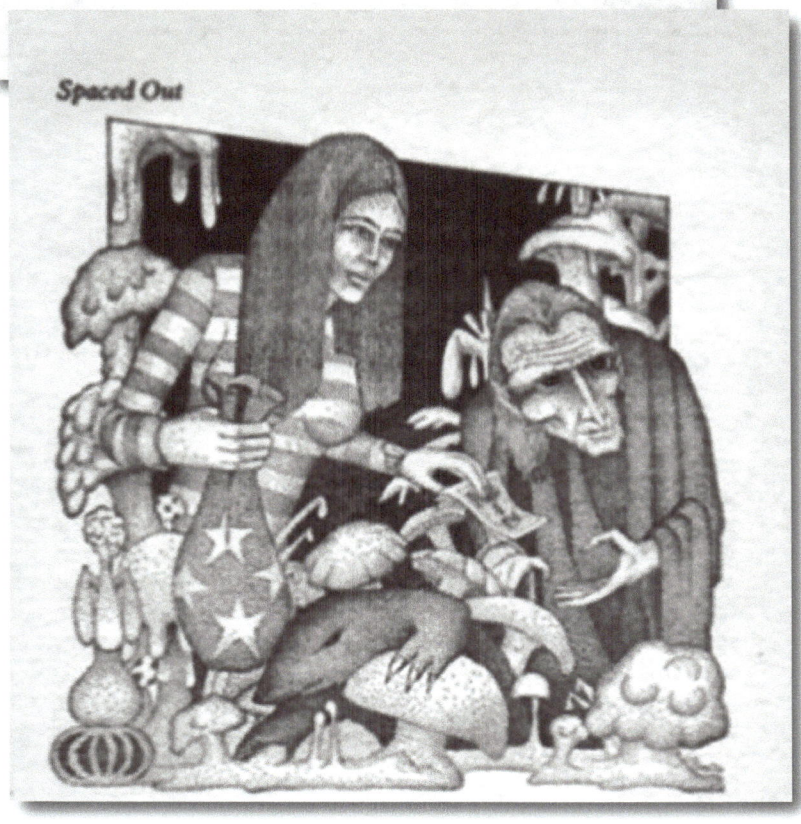

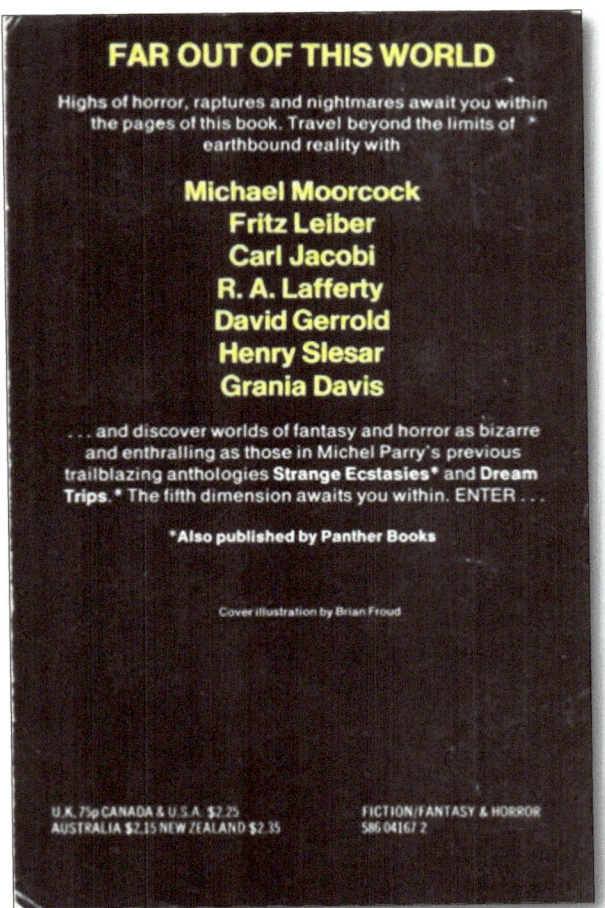

FAR OUT OF THIS WORLD

Highs of horror, raptures and nightmares await you within the pages of this book. Travel beyond the limits of earthbound reality with

**Michael Moorcock
Fritz Leiber
Carl Jacobi
R. A. Lafferty
David Gerrold
Henry Slesar
Grania Davis**

...and discover worlds of fantasy and horror as bizarre and enthralling as those in Michel Parry's previous trailblazing anthologies **Strange Ecstasies*** and **Dream Trips.*** The fifth dimension awaits you within. ENTER...

*Also published by Panther Books

Cover illustration by Brian Froud

U.K. 75p CANADA & U.S.A. $2.25
AUSTRALIA $2.15 NEW ZEALAND $2.35

FICTION/FANTASY & HORROR
586 04167 2

SAVAGE HEROES
edited by Eric Pendragon (Michel Parry)

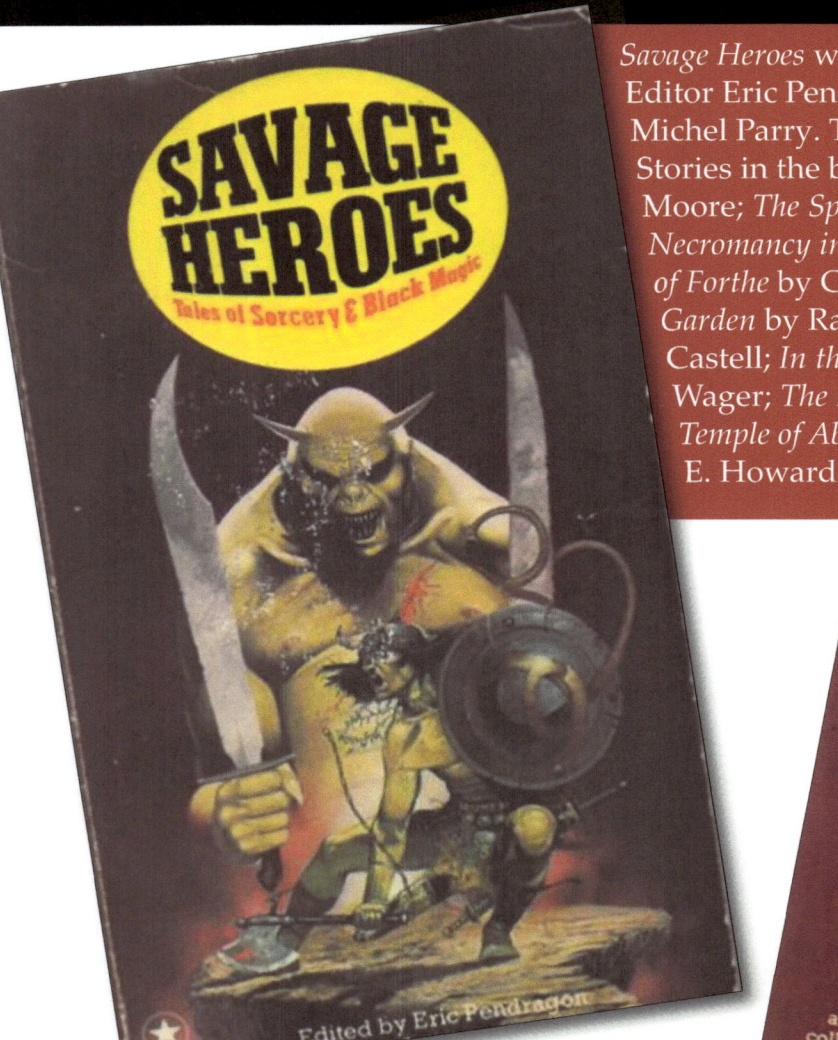

Savage Heroes was published by Star Books in 1975. Editor Eric Pendragon was another nom de plume of Michel Parry. The front cover was by Les Edwards. Stories in the book were: *Jirel Meets Magic* by C. L. Moore; *The Spawn of Dagon* (Elak) by Henry Kuttner; *Necromancy in Naat* by Clark Ashton Smith; *The Thief of Forthe* by Clifford Ball; *The Song at the Hub of the Garden* by Ramsey Campbell; *Alma Mater* by Daphne Castell; *In the Lair of Yslsl* (Kane) by Karl Edward Wager; *The Barrow Troll* by David A. Drake; and *The Temple of Abomination* (Cormac Mac Art) by Robert E. Howard.

CONTENTS

Acknowledgements	7
Introduction – Eric Pendragon	9
JIREL MEETS MAGIC – C. L. Moore	13
THE SPAWN OF DAGON – Henry Kuttner	50
NECROMANCY IN NAAT – Clark Ashton Smith	70
THE THIEF OF FORTHE – Clifford Ball	91
THE SONG AT THE HUB OF THE GARDEN – Ramsey Campbell	116
ALMA MATER – Daphne Castell	130
IN THE LAIR OF YSLSL – Karl Edward Wagner	147
THE BARROW TROLL – David A. Drake	165
THE TEMPLE OF ABOMINATION – Robert E. Howard	178

A World Where Magic Works...

is a brilliant realm of the imagination, full of thrills, menace and action where monsters lurk, where demons dwell, where maidens cry out to be rescued and where young men, mighty warriors all, are happy to oblige them.

**HENRY KUTTNER
CLARK ASHTON SMITH
RAMSEY CAMPBELL
KARL EDWARD WAGNER
ROBERT E. HOWARD**

are among the magical masters included in this collection, all of whom can conjure up this world of swords and sorcery at will. A world that will bewitch you and hold you spellbound until the last page!

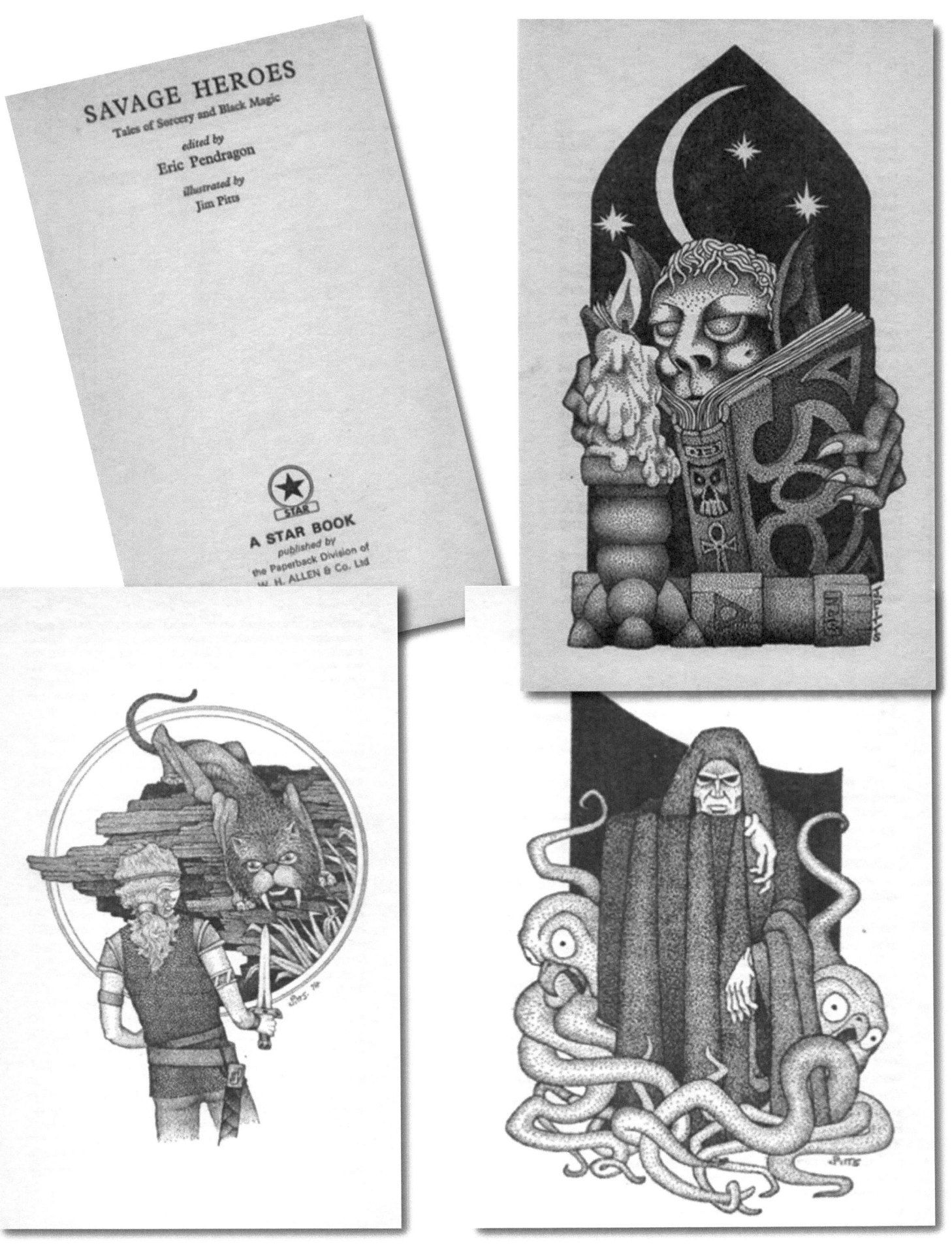

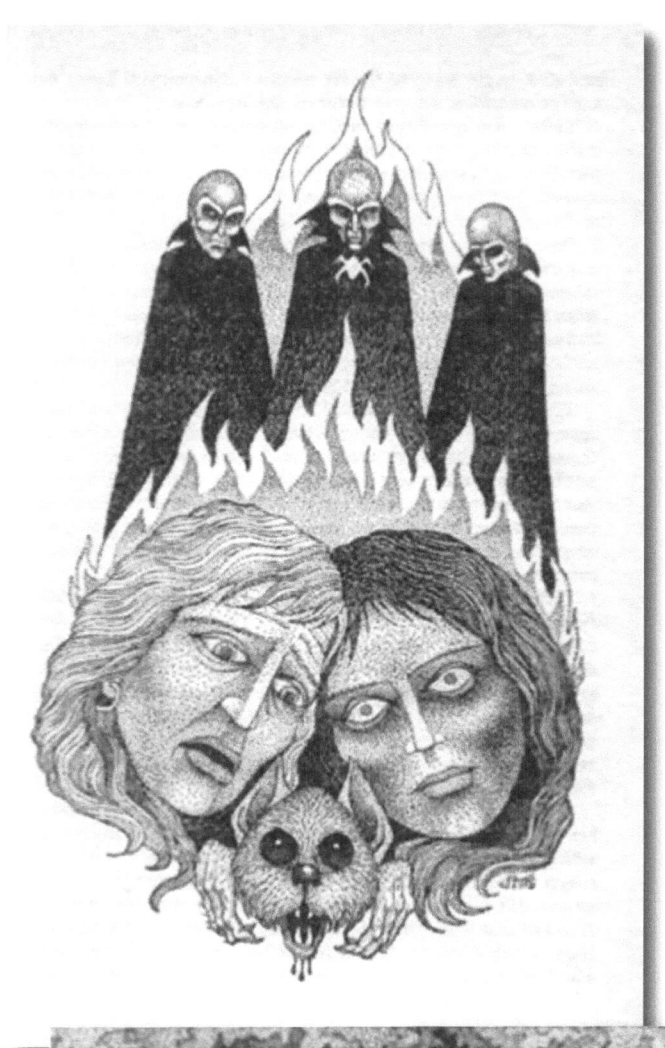
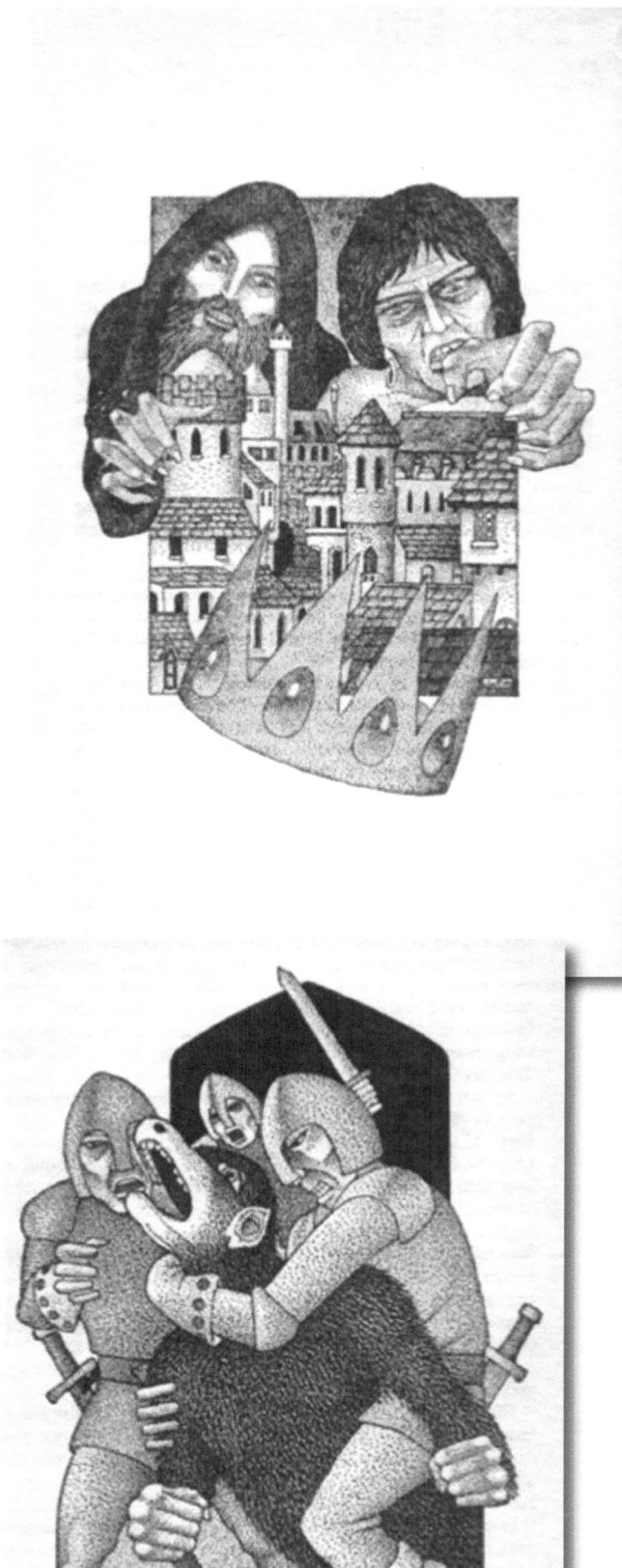
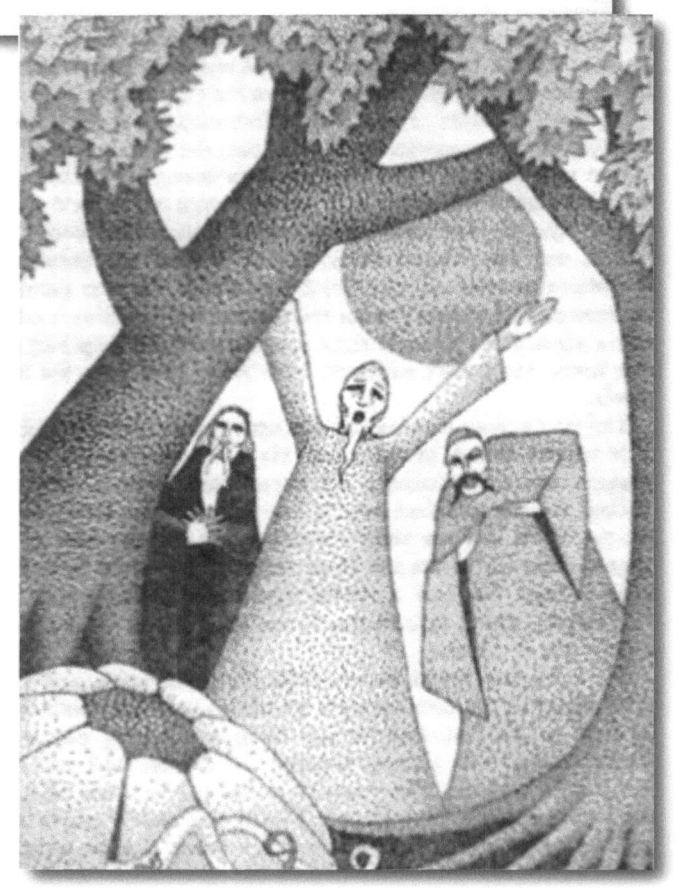

'There was a curious story of a long brown thing ...'

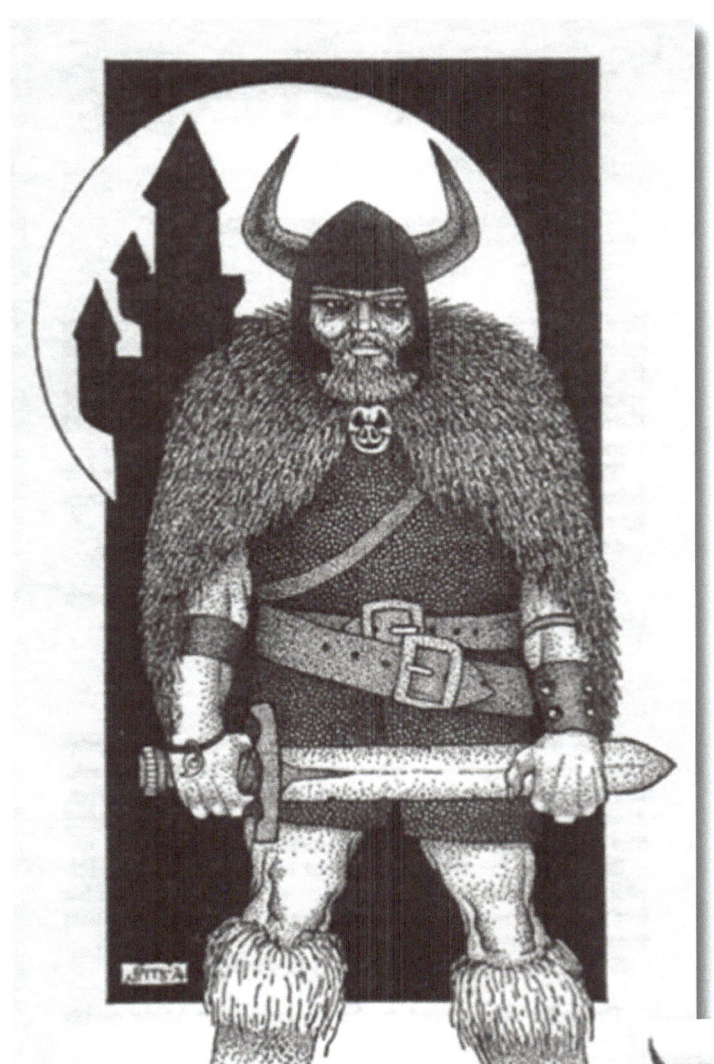
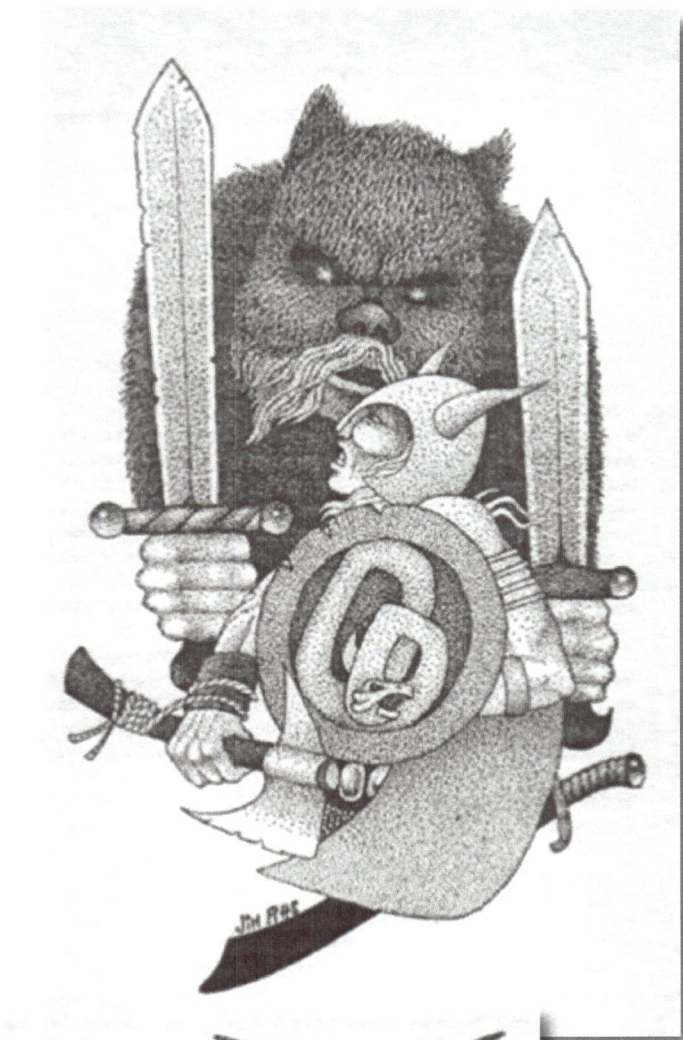
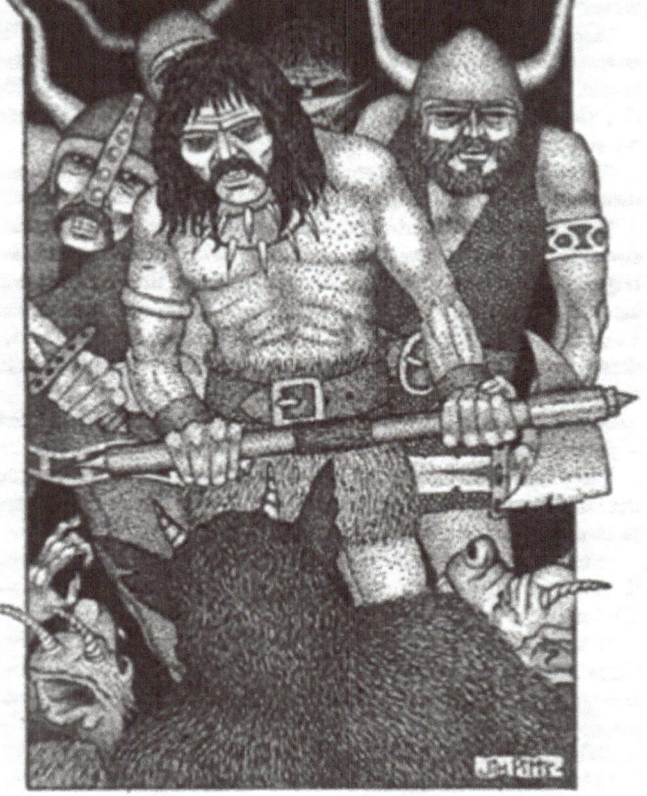

Three pages of "barbarians", including Karl Edward Wagner's anti-hero "Kane"

The American edition of *Savage Heroes* not only had interior illustrations by Jim Pitts but the front and back covers were by him too.

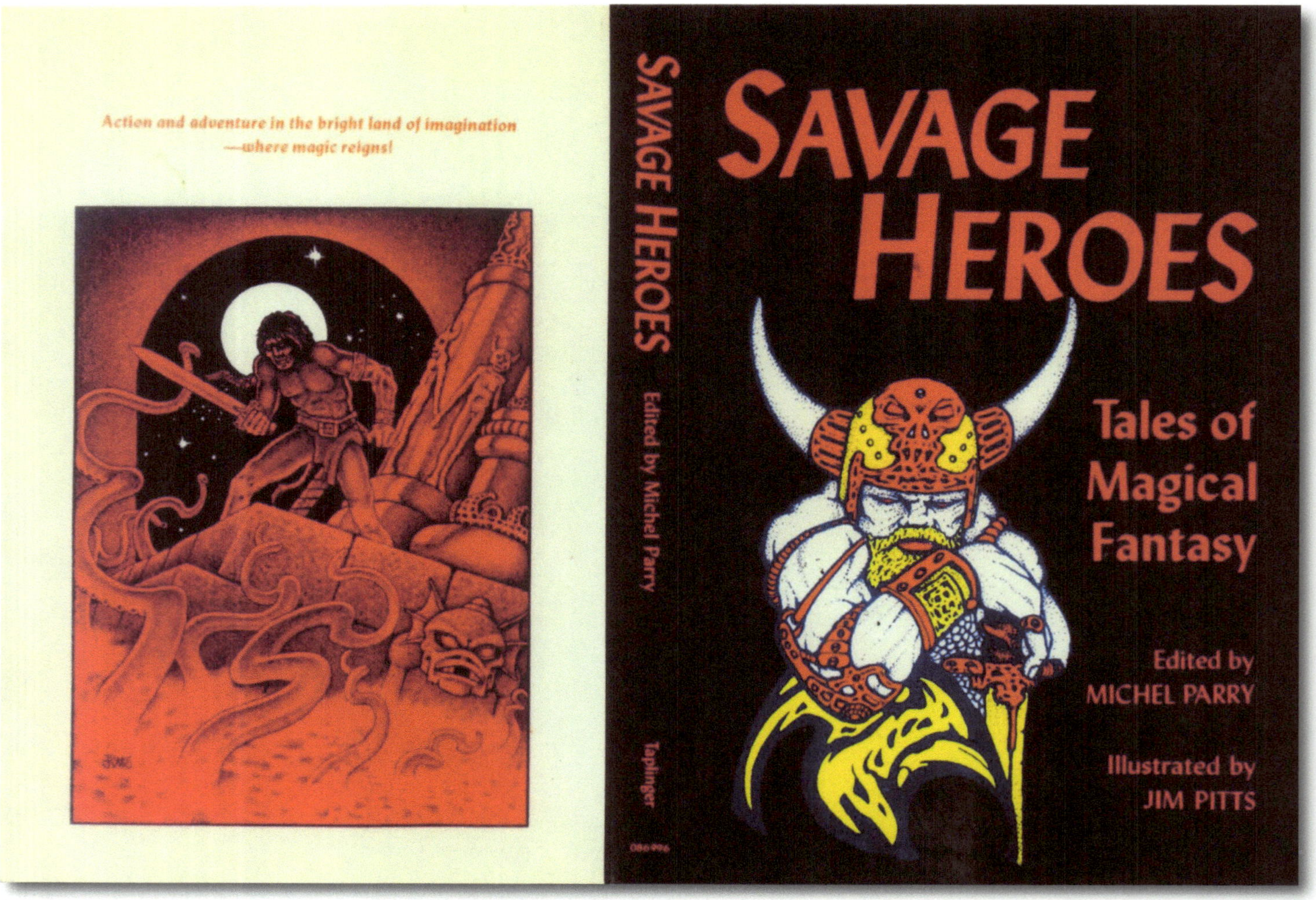

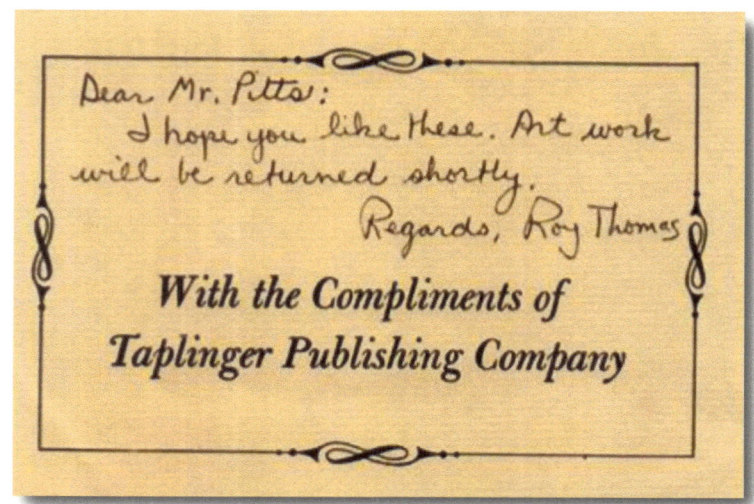

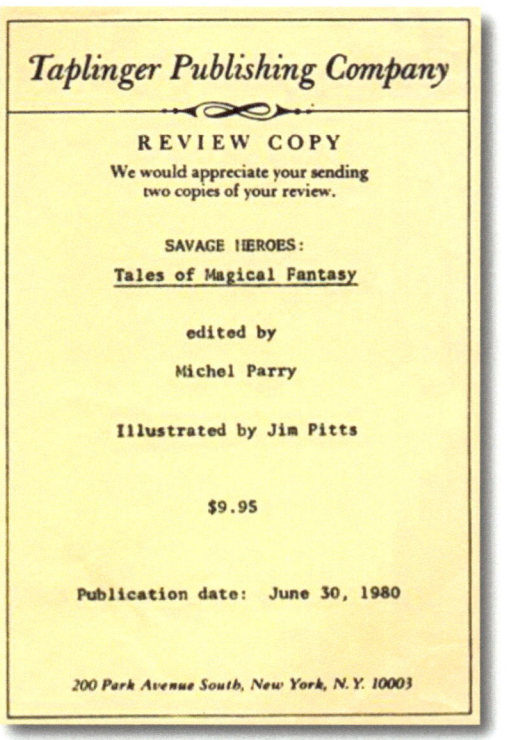

To be used as the cover for the collected *Cthulhu: Tales of the Cthulhu Mythos* from Spectre Press.

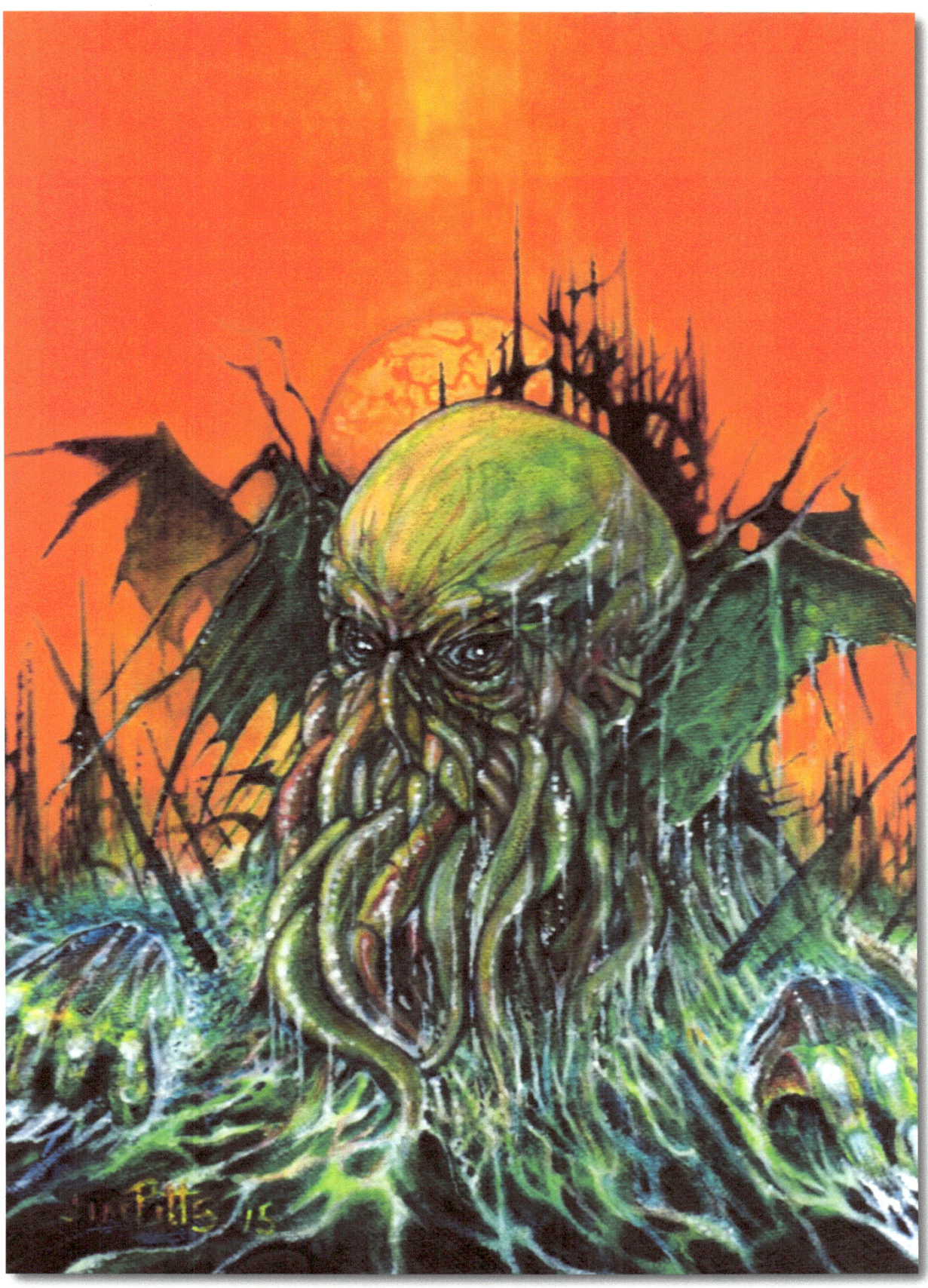

JIM PITTS AND SPECTRE PRESS

by Jon M. Harvey

In 1971 I started up my own publication called *Balthus*. It was meant to publish both stories and articles of fantasy and folklore. The first issue was rather bereft of illustrations. I did the stipple front cover of Icarus and Trevor Goring did the reverse of the character for the back cover.

Between *Balthus* 1 and 2 I received a suitable cover by Jim Pitts. Jim didn't do another cover for *Balthus*, but illustrated the interiors for a poem by a friend – Nick Caffrey – and a story, "Sang the Stone" by Gordon Larkin. Jim, Gordon and I decided to produce a book of Gordon's stories and poems, all illustrated by Jim. I got the book typeset – a difficult task in those days - Jim illustrated one of Gordon's stories . . . Then Gordon pulled the plug on the project. He didn't want to be remembered by such 'childish' stories. There is another reason which I will not go into here. Anyway, the story that Jim had illustrated I published in *Worlds of the Unknown*, volume 2.

Over issues 2 to 4 of *Balthus* a number of very decent artists contributed. Also, I had a number of stories and articles that I published . . . but, I was running out of steam. The folklore side of the magazine was dying on its feet. I needed to do something more to keep the magazine going. No such luck. All I got was a small cry of "Would you publish my portfolio for me, please?"

I was very lucky to have another good friend as an artist: David Lloyd (of *V for Vengeance* fame). David created the logo for Spectre Press. I was in contact with Dr Dirk Mosig who was well into Lovecraft and, between the two of us, we produced a 4-page booklet to fit in with Jim Pitts' "Lovecraftian Characters and Other Things".

Goodbye *Balthus* and hello Spectre Press. Jim has illustrated every issue of my magazine *Cthulhu: Tales of the Cthulhu Mythos* and, hopefully be there at the end when I publish the 'Collected' stories published in the magazine, plus several new stories. We also produced Adrian Cole's *The Coming of the Voidal*.

Jim and I met up quite often over the years. I visited him at home in Blackburn a couple of times, at FantasyCon each year and at David and Sandra Sutton's place in Birmingham.
I then joined the Royal Navy . . . for an easy life, which is what most of my intake had. For me, my abilities were quickly spotted. Out went murder and horror in magazines and books as they became an every-day part of reality in my life in the Navy . . . and afterwards.

Then I became close to retirement and ever closer to death.

"Sod this" I thought. I used to have loads of 'Fantasy' friends. I went to a single day of a 'FantasyCon' in Brighton and found myself swamped by 'old friends'. I was amazed!

Although I tried to ease my way back into publishing via a portfolio of artwork that I already had – Jim's work stood out as the only colour art-

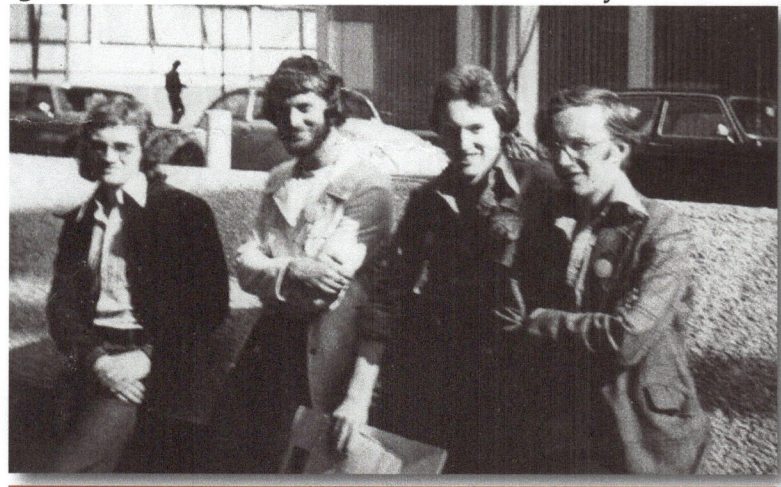

London, 1975: left to right: Jim Pitts, Jon Harvey, Stephen Jones, and David A. Riley

work in the portfolio - it was Adrian Cole who offered me a Nick Nightmare story for the restart of *Cthulhu* . . . if I could get Jim to Illustrate it. That was the hard part. A wrap-around cover and two interior illustrations. That was all very hard work and I commend Jim for his perseverance to his work as well as the work's beauty.

Jim's partner Joyce has thanked me so much for bringing Jim back 'life' as it was. Without Jim, Adrian Cole, Peter Coleborn, Mike Chinn and others, maybe I would still be out there in the wilderness myself. I have described Jim as a friend. It would take well over a thousand words to describe Jim as an artist, a very friendly artist.

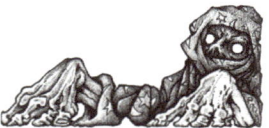

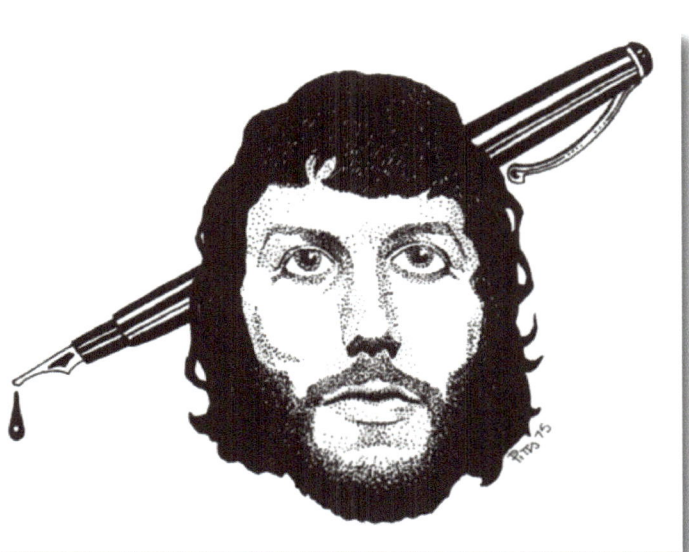

Jon Harvey as drawn by Jim in 1975

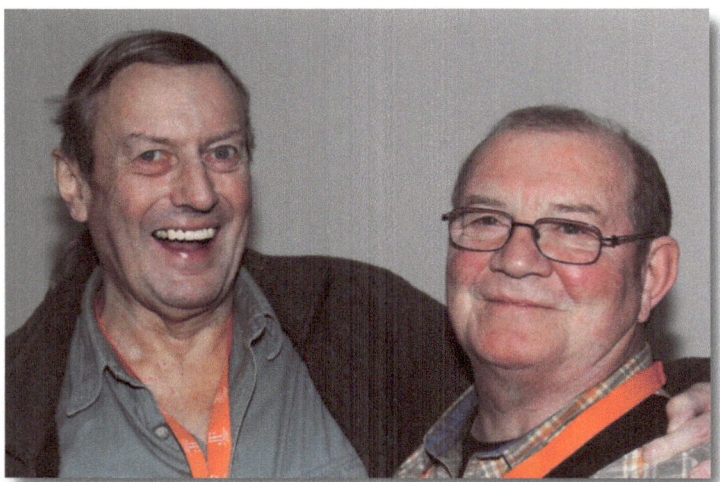

Jon Harvey and Jim in more recent times, still working together nearly fifty years on.

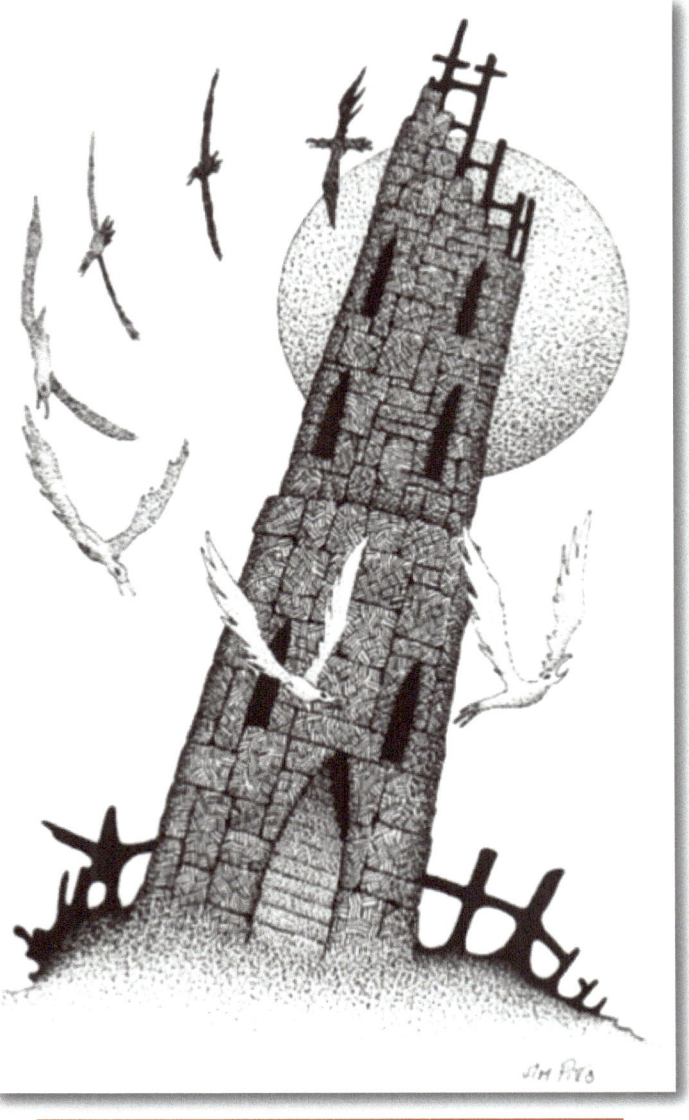

The above illustration was created for Gordon Larkin's story *Seagulls of Senecd* which was published in Jon Harvey's *Worlds of the Unknown* Volume 2

SPECTRE PRESS
Lovecraftian Characters and Other Things

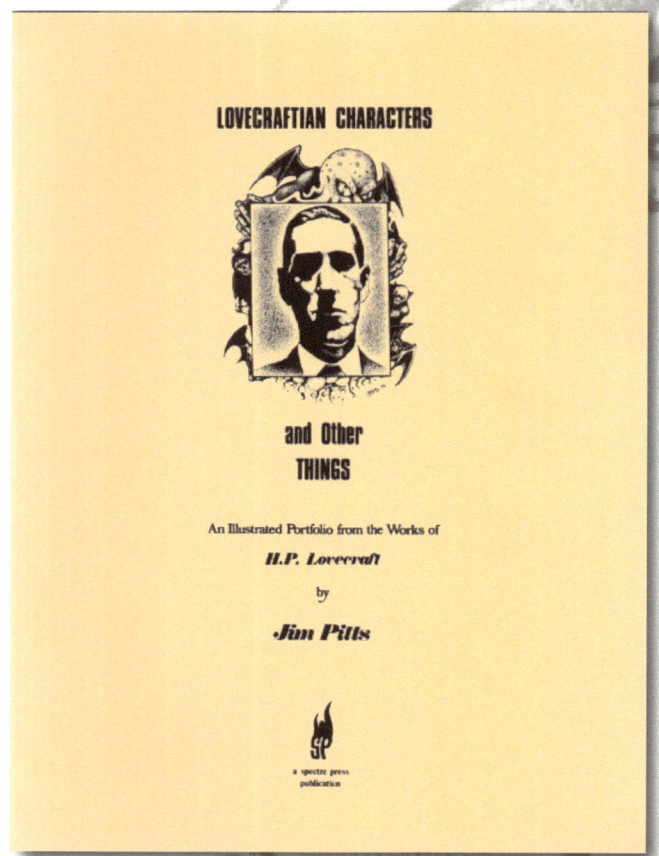

In 1976 Jon Harvey's Spectre Press produced a portfolio of Jim Pitts' artwork, *Lovecraftian Characters and Other Things*.

Accompanying the prints was a 4-page booklet containing articles by Dr Dirk W. Mosig and Dr Jon M. Harvey.

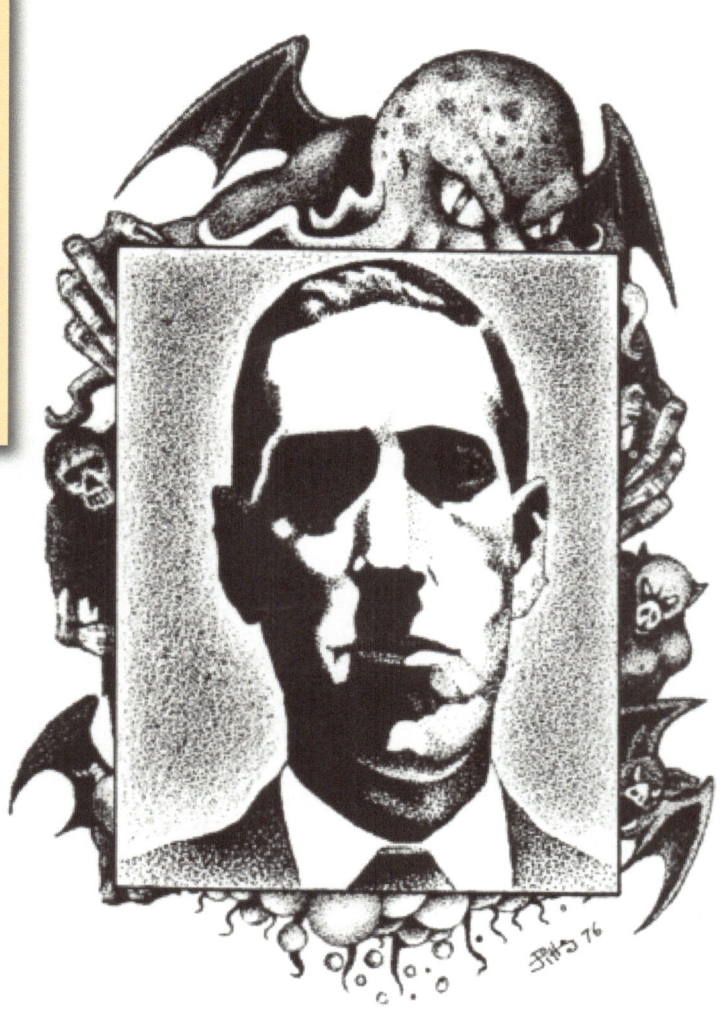

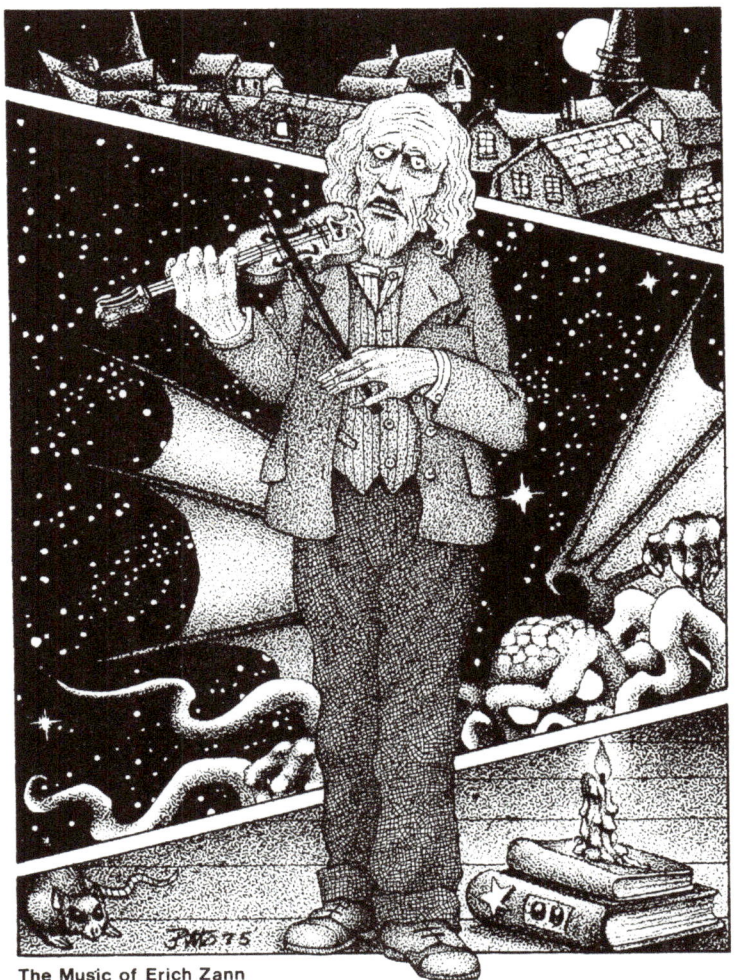
The Music of Erich Zann

"There is also that feeling of grim caricature which may suggest humour but portrays horror. The look on the face of Erich Zann backed by that of the winged creature, the devilish features of the Deep One in Innsmouth or the stance of the Outsider as he climbs those stone steps. Each could be labeled typically Hannes Bok, but each could equally be labeled *Jim Pitts*."
Dr Jon M. Harvey

The Call of Cthulhu

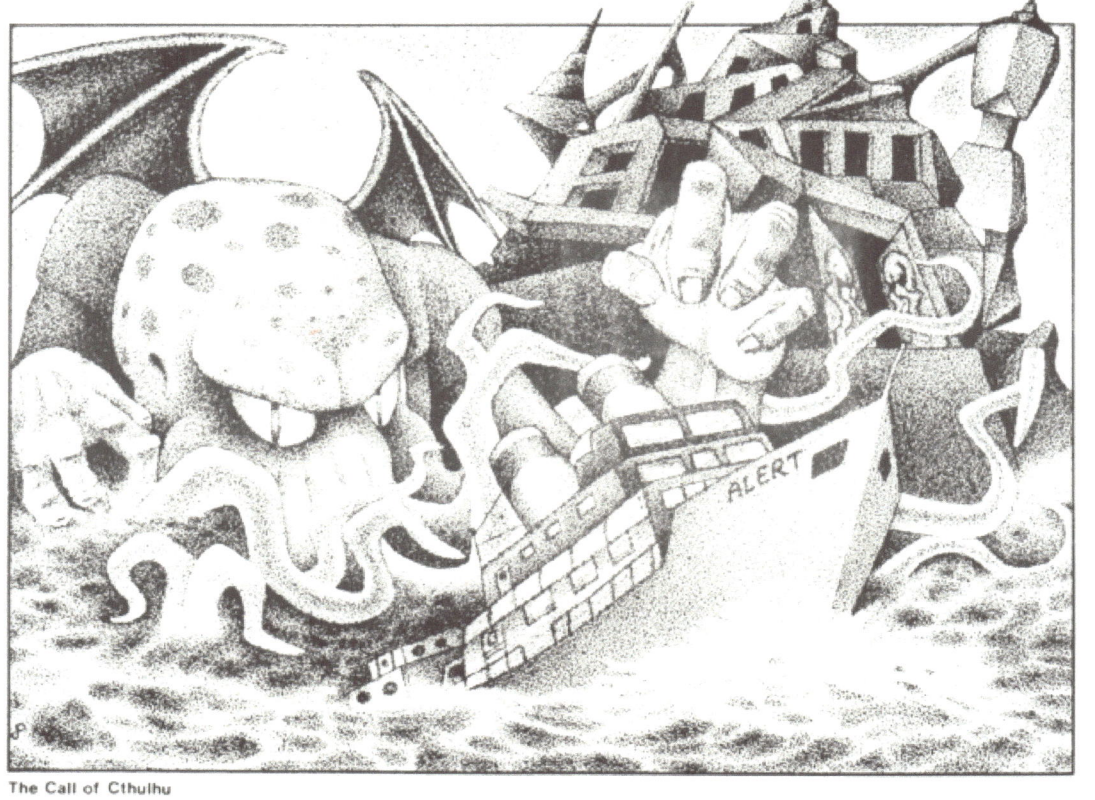
The Call of Cthulhu

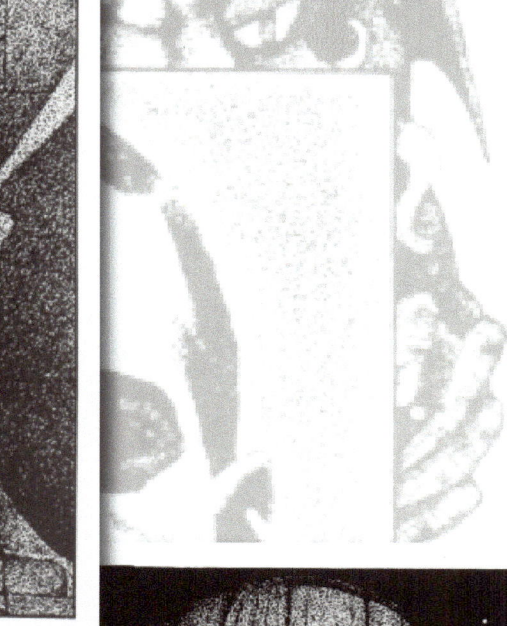

The Outsider

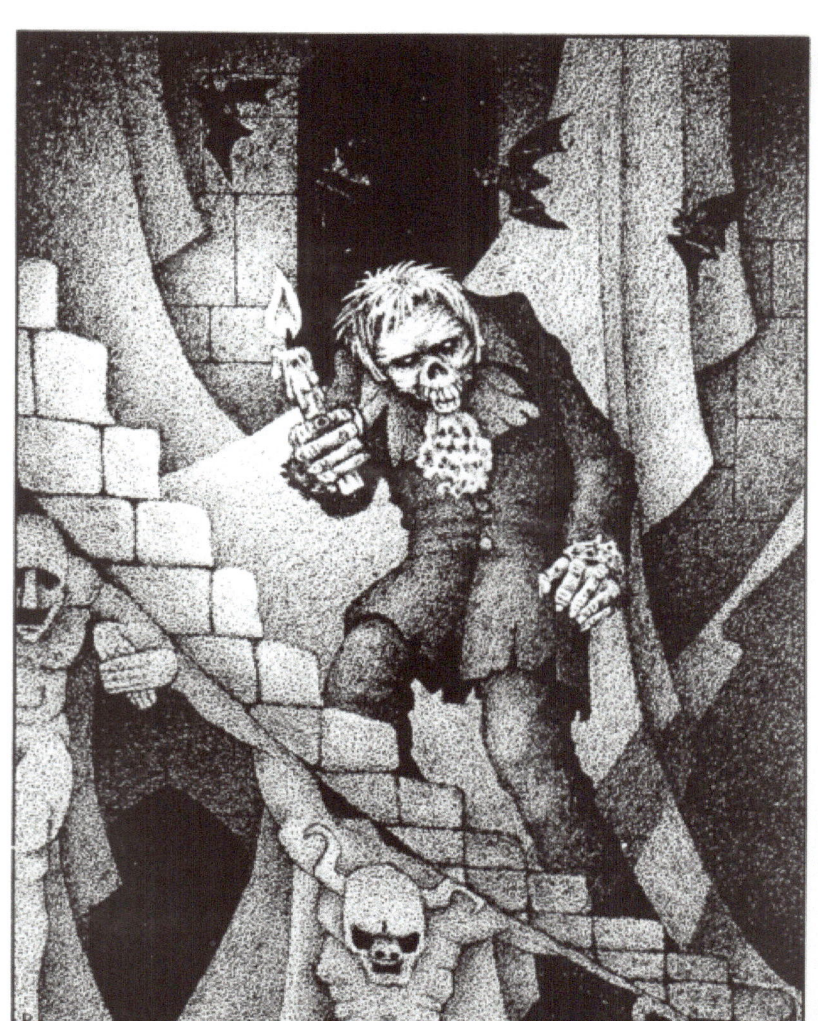

The Outsider

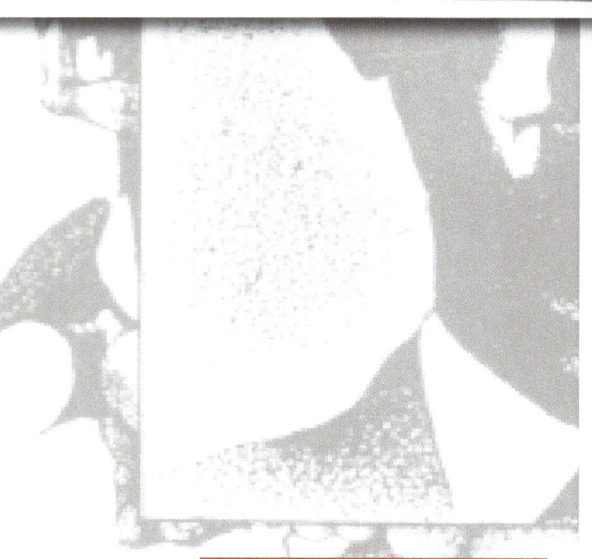

The Terrible Old Man

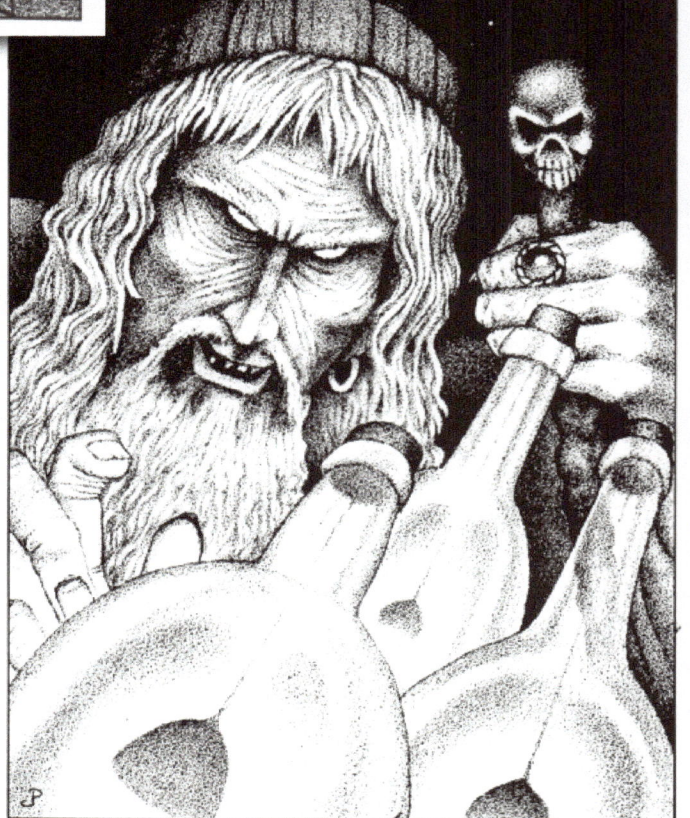

The Terrible Old Man

Night Gaunts

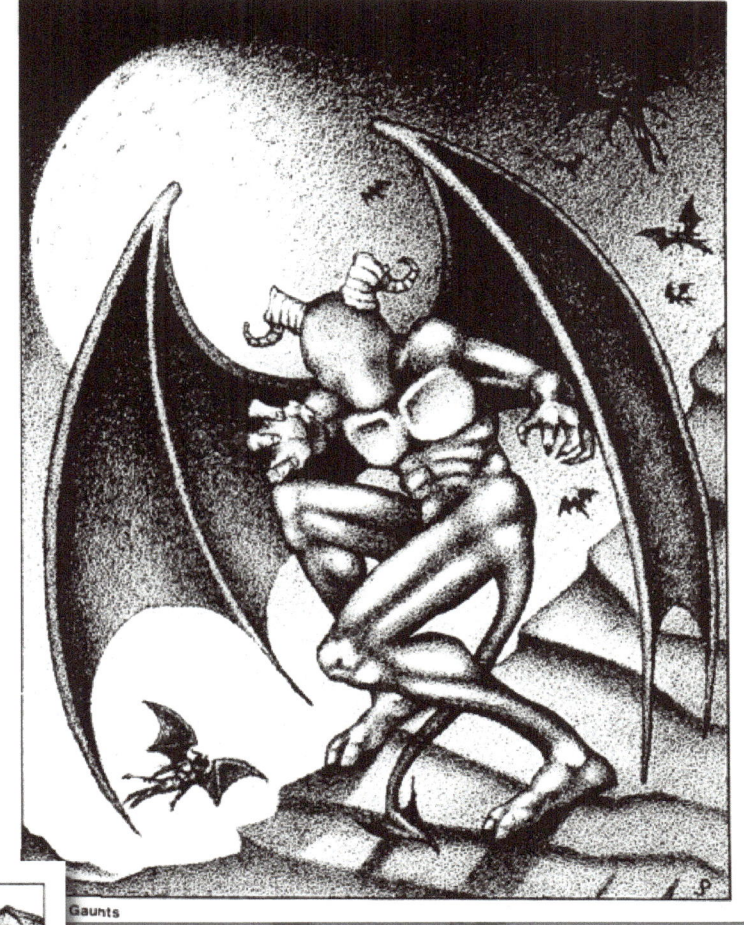
Gaunts

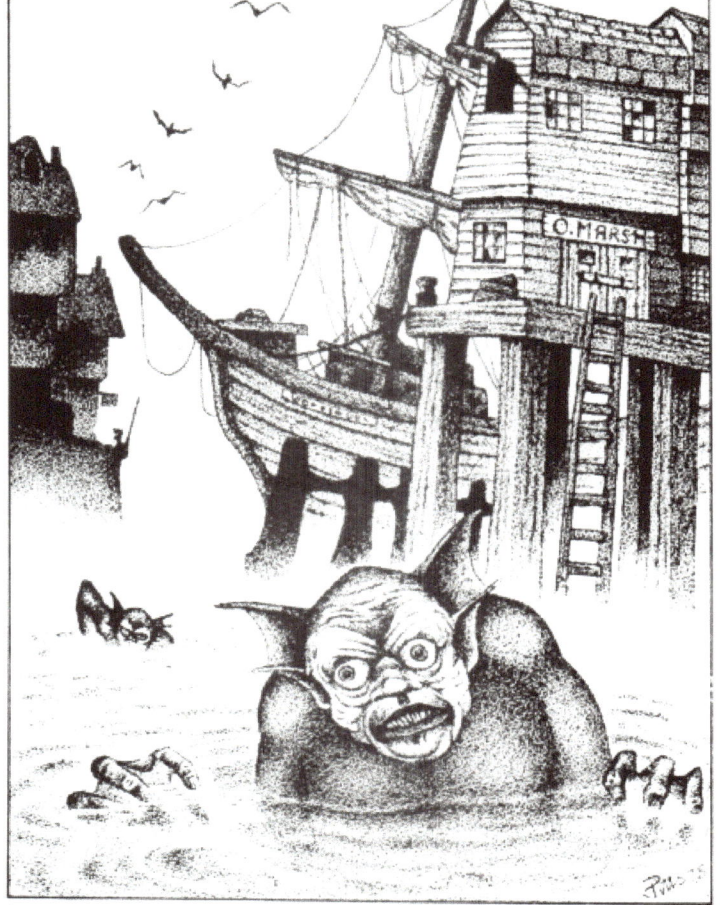
Innsmouth

The Shadow Over Innsmouth

THE WEIRD AND THE WONDERFUL PORTFOLIO 1
SPECTRE PRESS

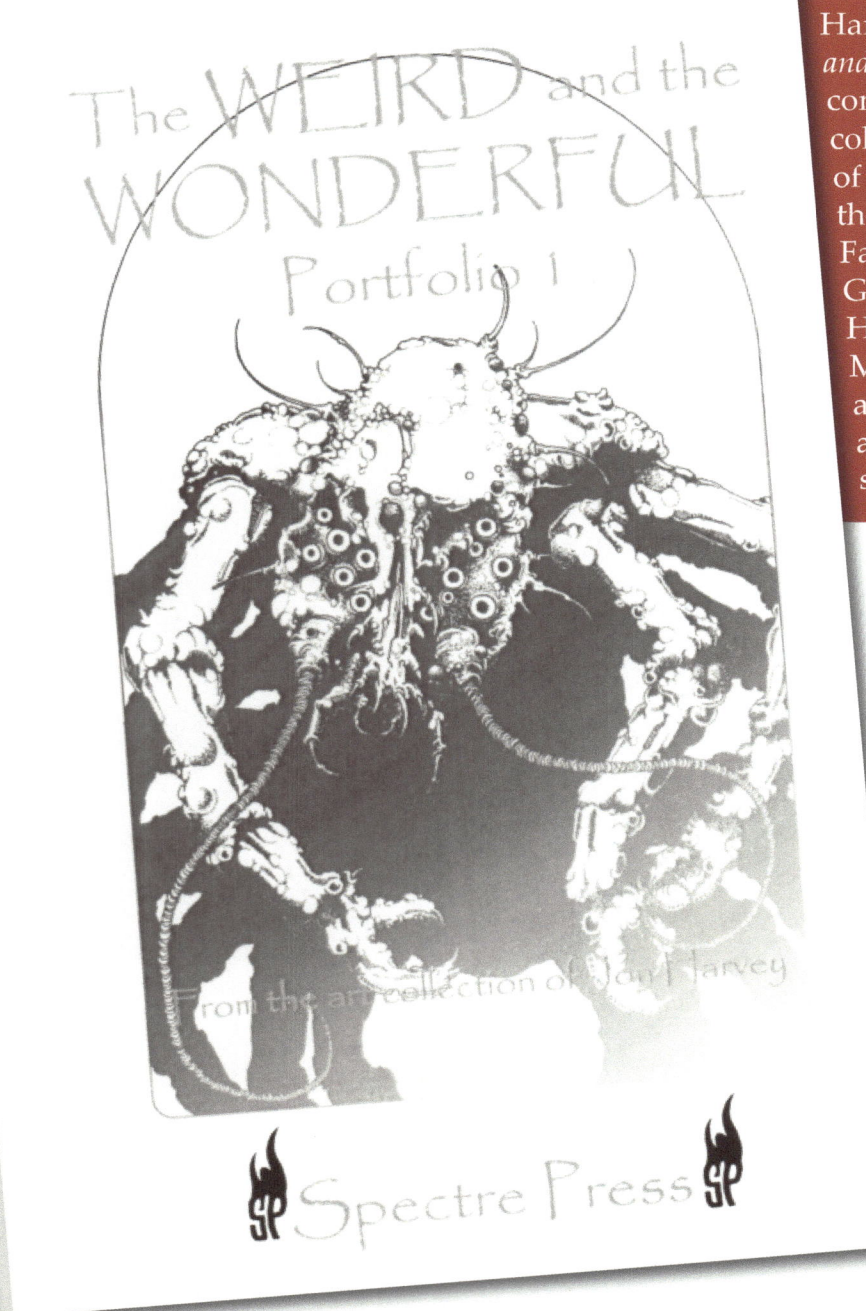

Published for charity by Jon Harvey's Spectre Press, *The Weird and the Wonderful - Portfolio 1* comprised ten top quality full-colour plates of artwork by some of the best fantasy/SF artists in the field, including Stephen E. Fabian, Brian Frost, Dallas Goffin, Jon Harvey, Alan Hunter, David Lloyd, Martin McKenna, SMS, John Stewart and, of course, Jim Pitts, whose artwork from this collection is shown opposite.

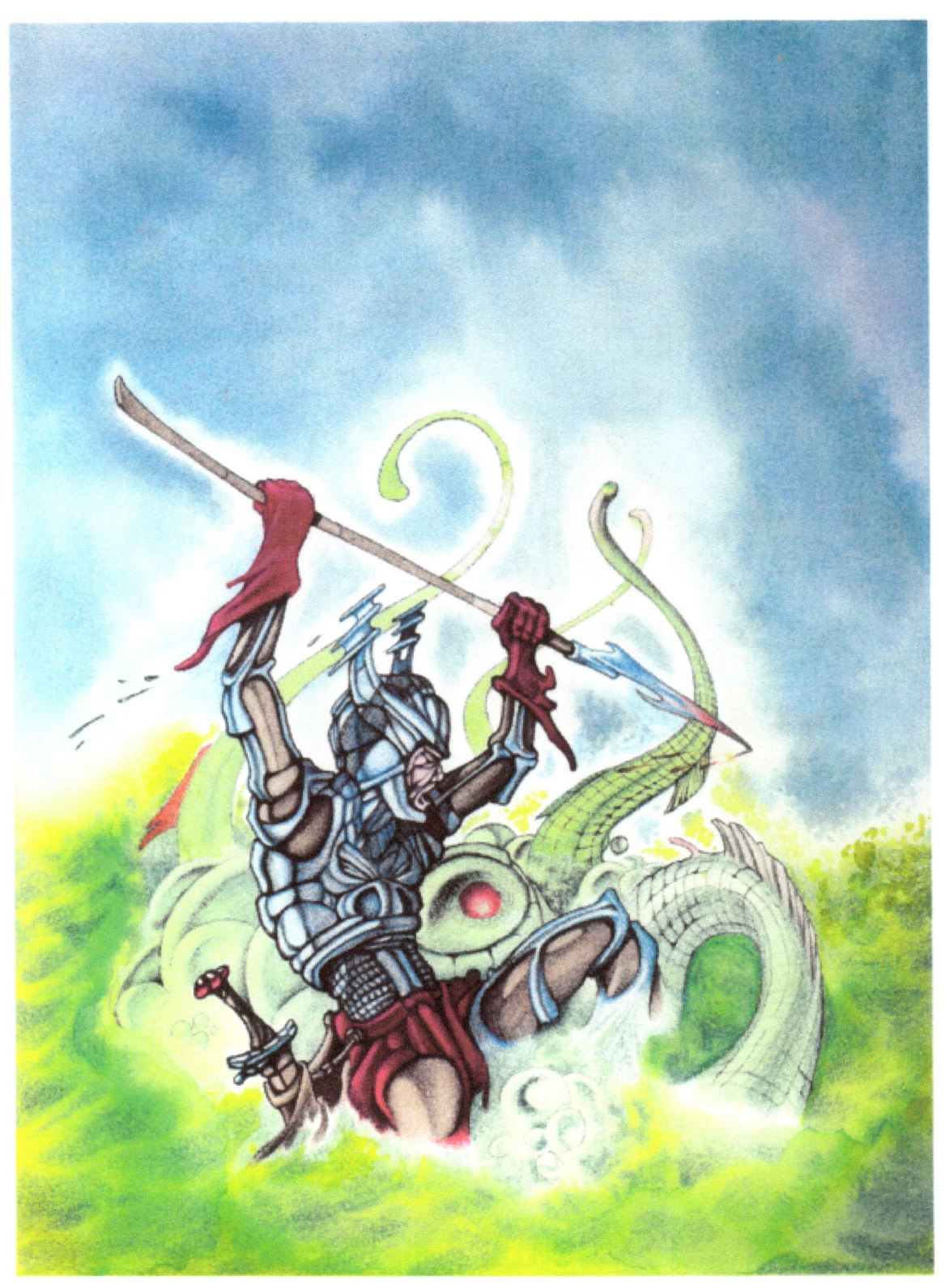

Plate 8 - Jim Pitts

Latest illustration for Cthulhu magazine
Adrian Cole's story *The Place of Unutterable Names*

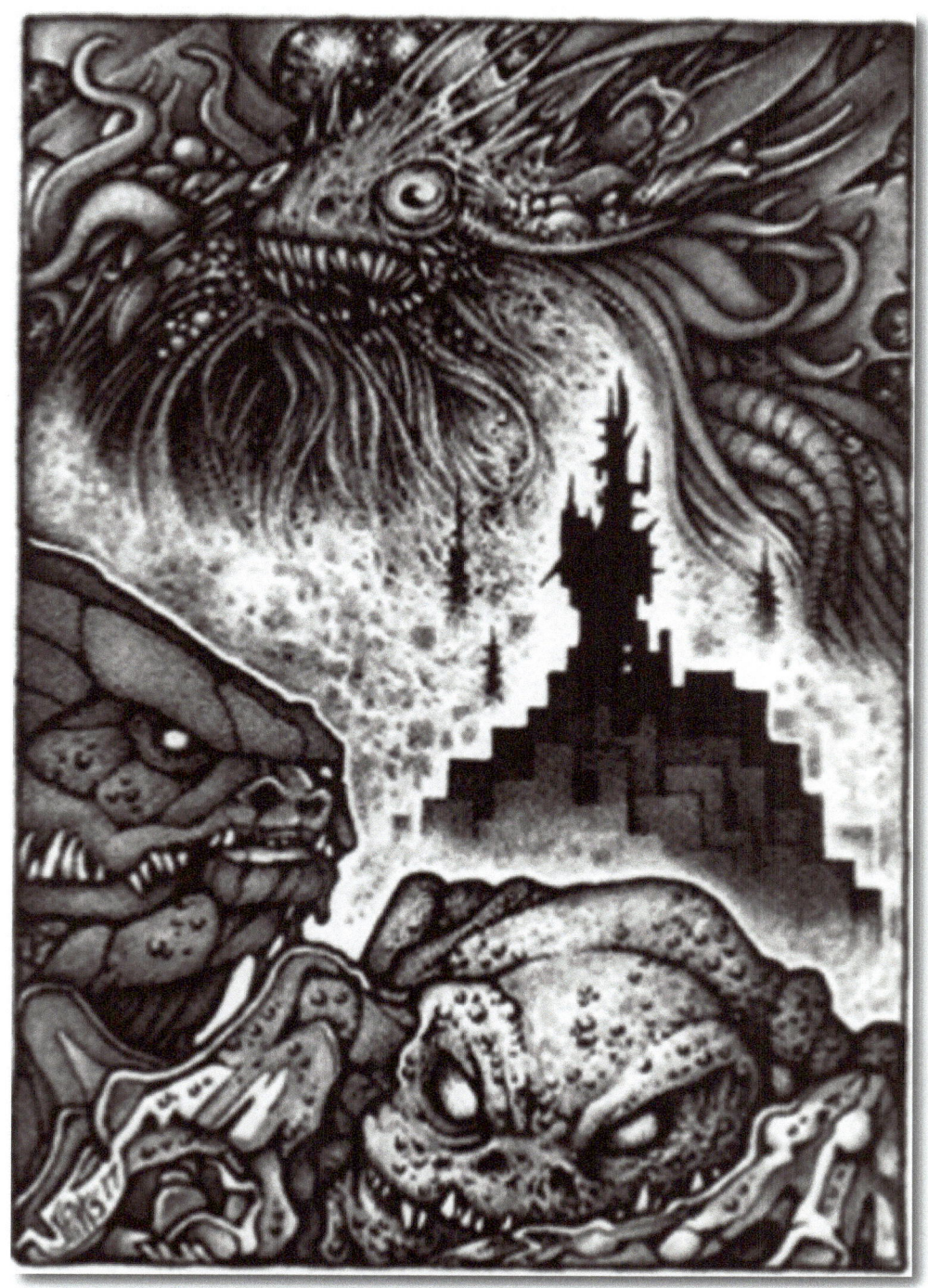

Cthulhu: Tales of the Cthulhu Mythos published by Spectre Press

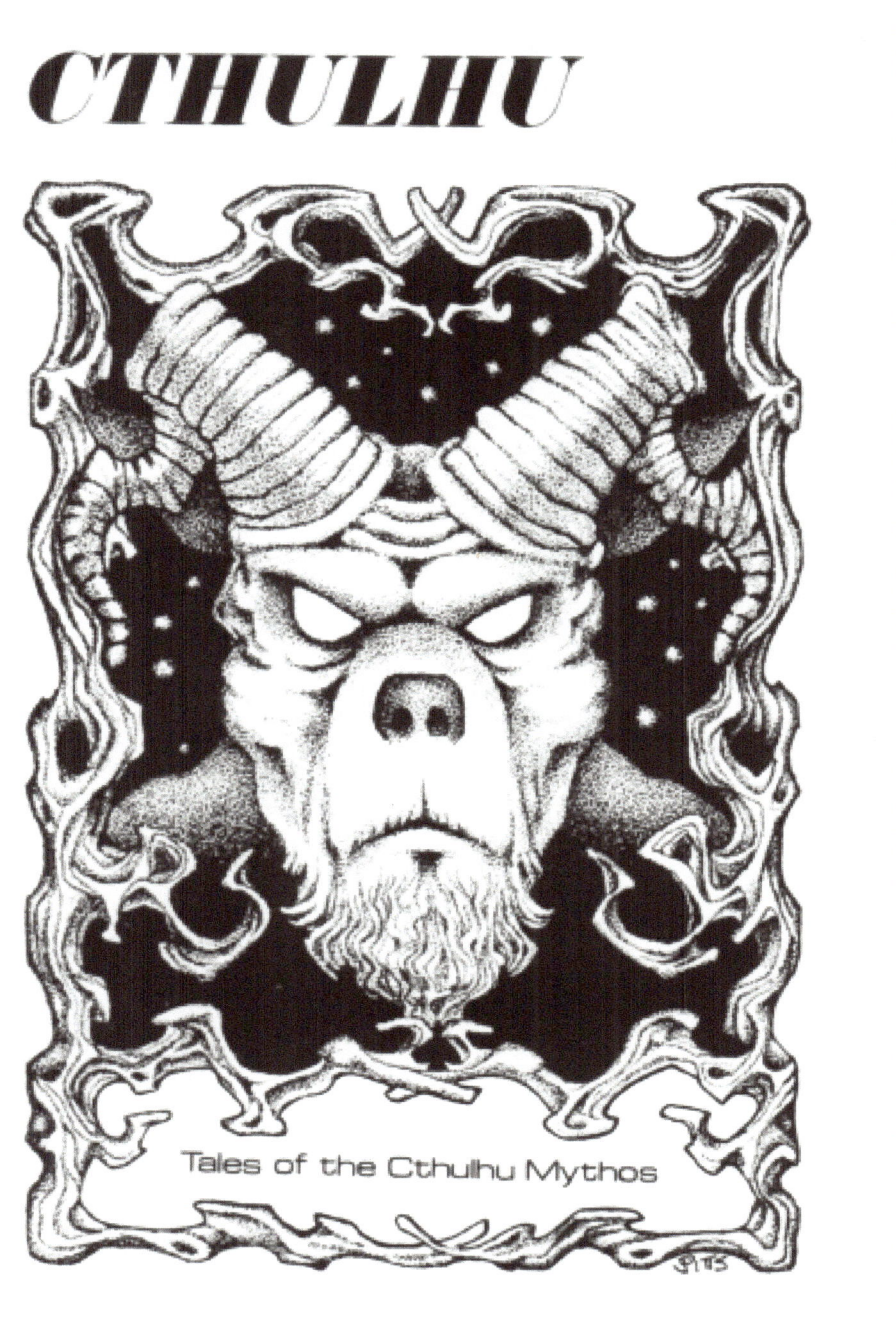

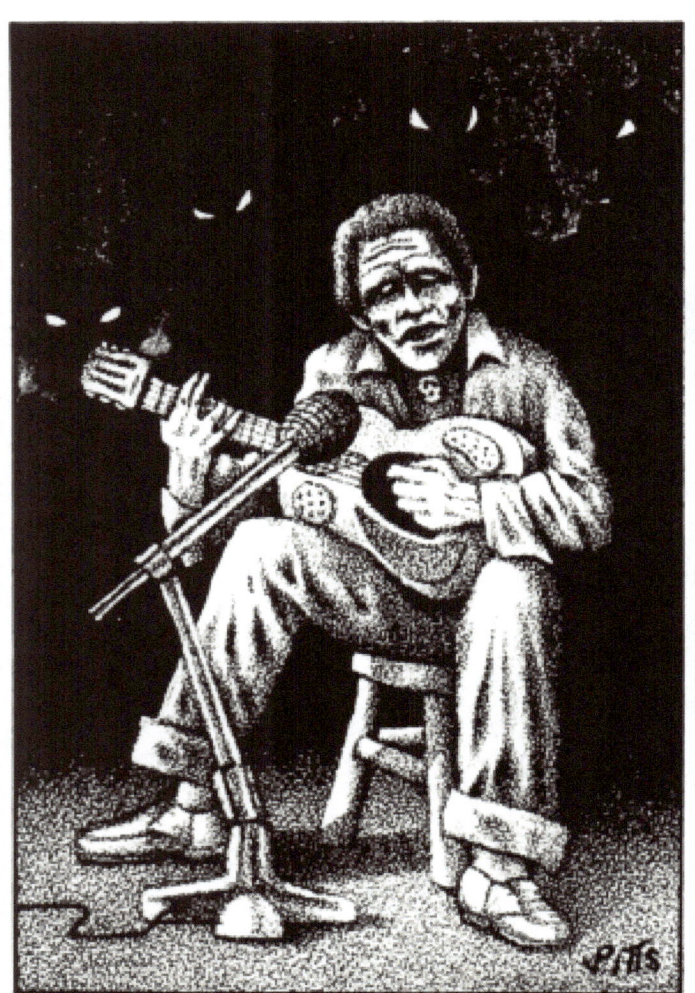

Cthulhu: Tales of the Cthulhu Mythos interior artwork illustrating *Harold's Blues* by Glen Singer

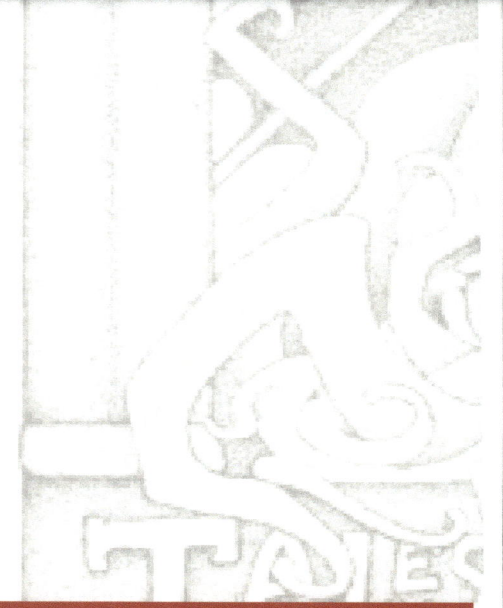

Cthulhu 2: Tales of the Cthulhu Mythos Interior artwork illustrating Brian Mooney's *The Guardians of the Gates*

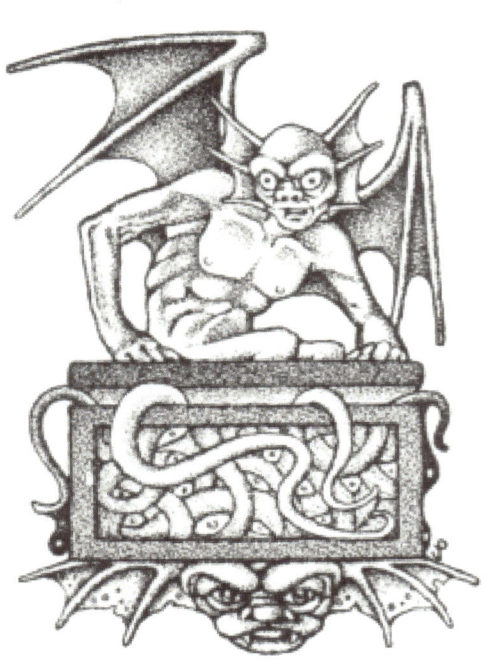

'It was a writhing intricacy, with neither an apparent beginning nor an apparent ending. I feel that nothing describes it as well as comparing it with a huge serpent huddled in a complexity of coils, a serpent which crawled and twisted its way across the surface. At each convolution in each monstrous carving was a madly glaring eye.'

– "The Guardians of the Gates"
– Brian Mooney

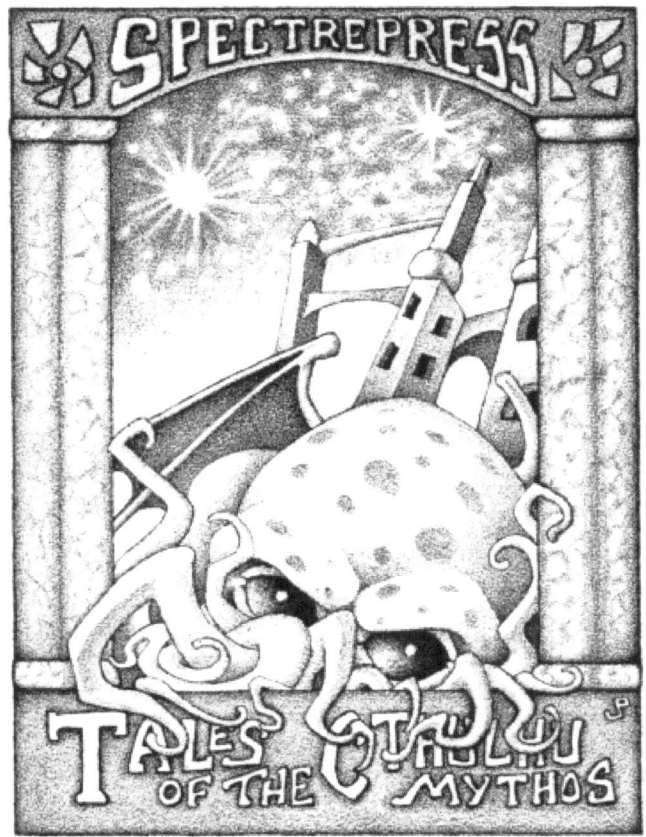
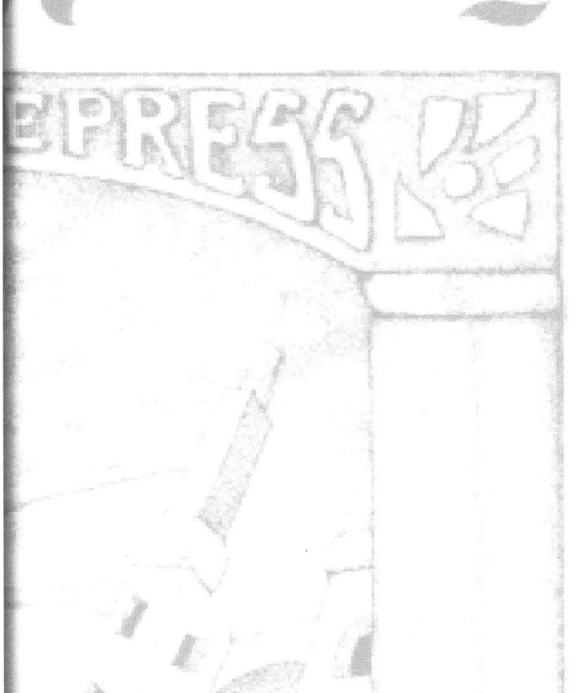
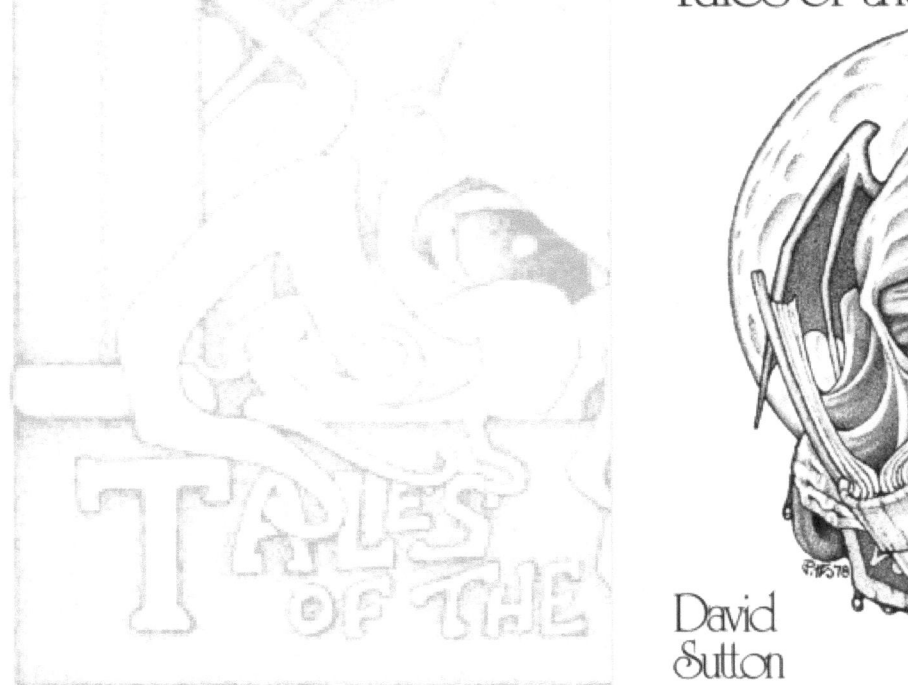
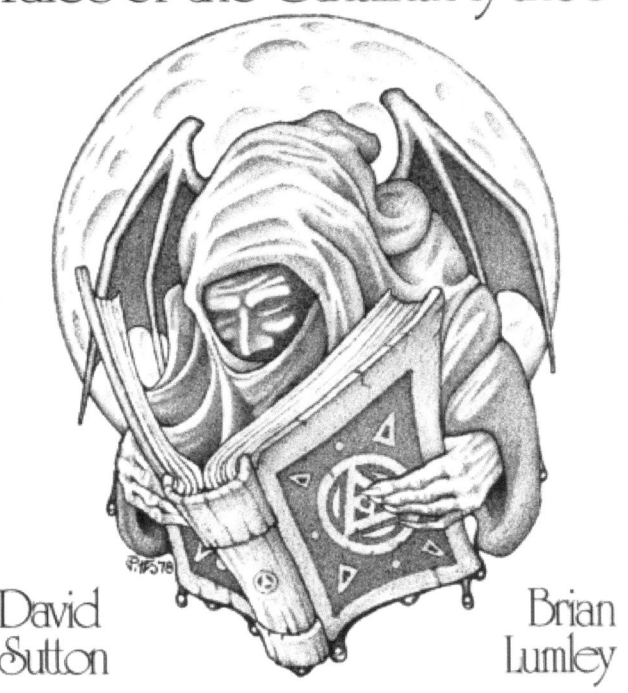

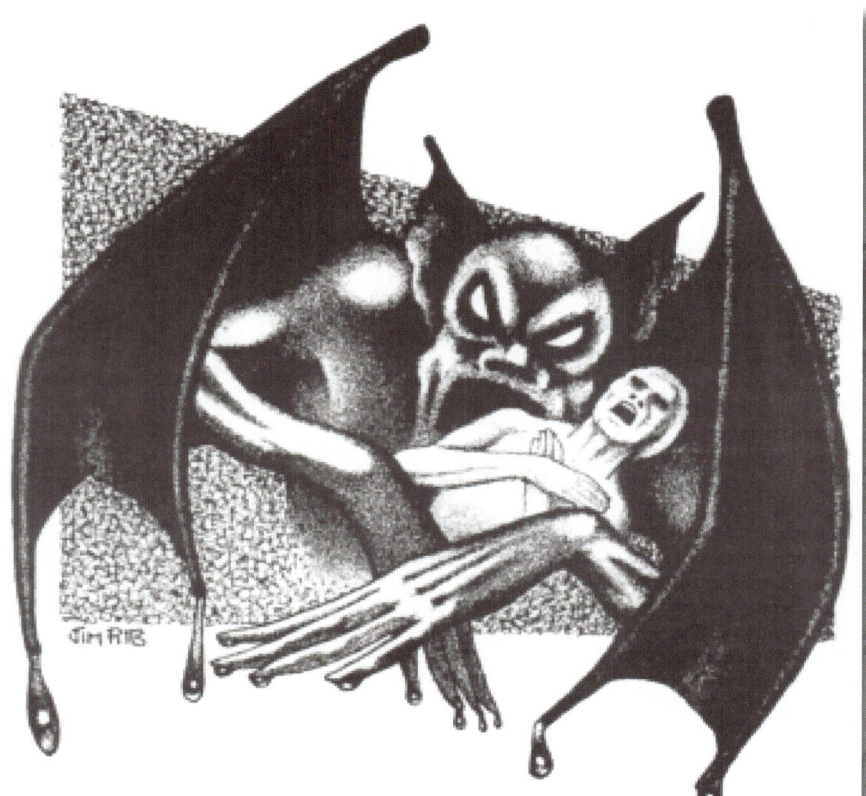
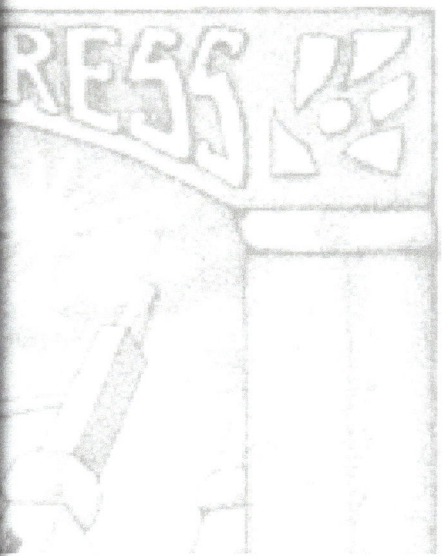

Cthulhu 3: Tales of the Cthulhu Mythos published by Spectre Press.
Interior art illustrating *Demoniacal* by David Sutton

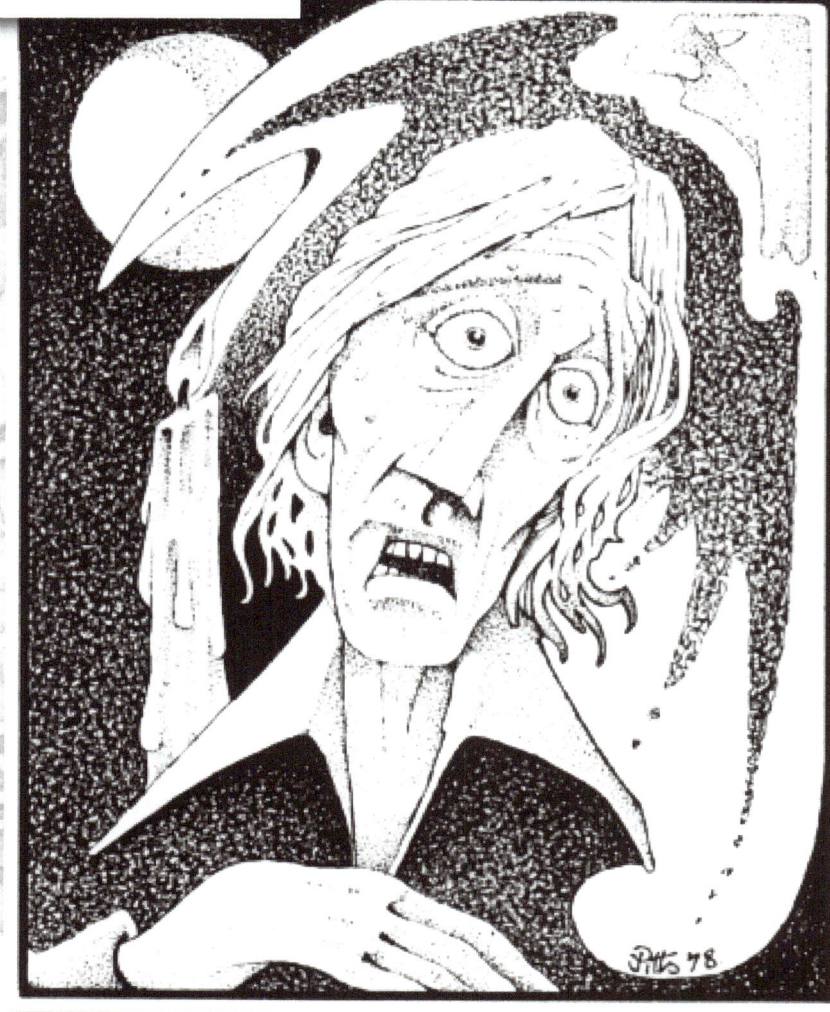

Cthulhu 3: Tales of the Cthulhu Mythos.
Interior artwork illustrating *The Kiss of Bugg-Shash* by Brian Lumley

Cthulhu 4 interior art

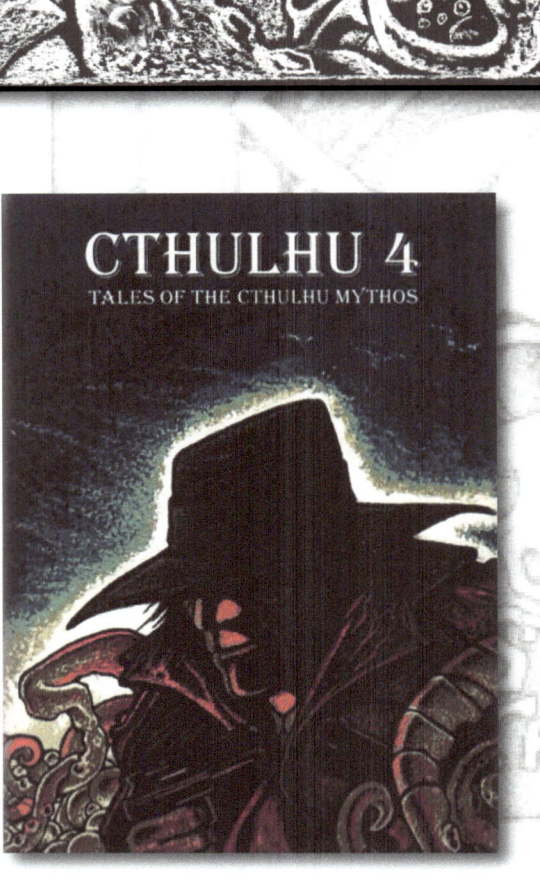
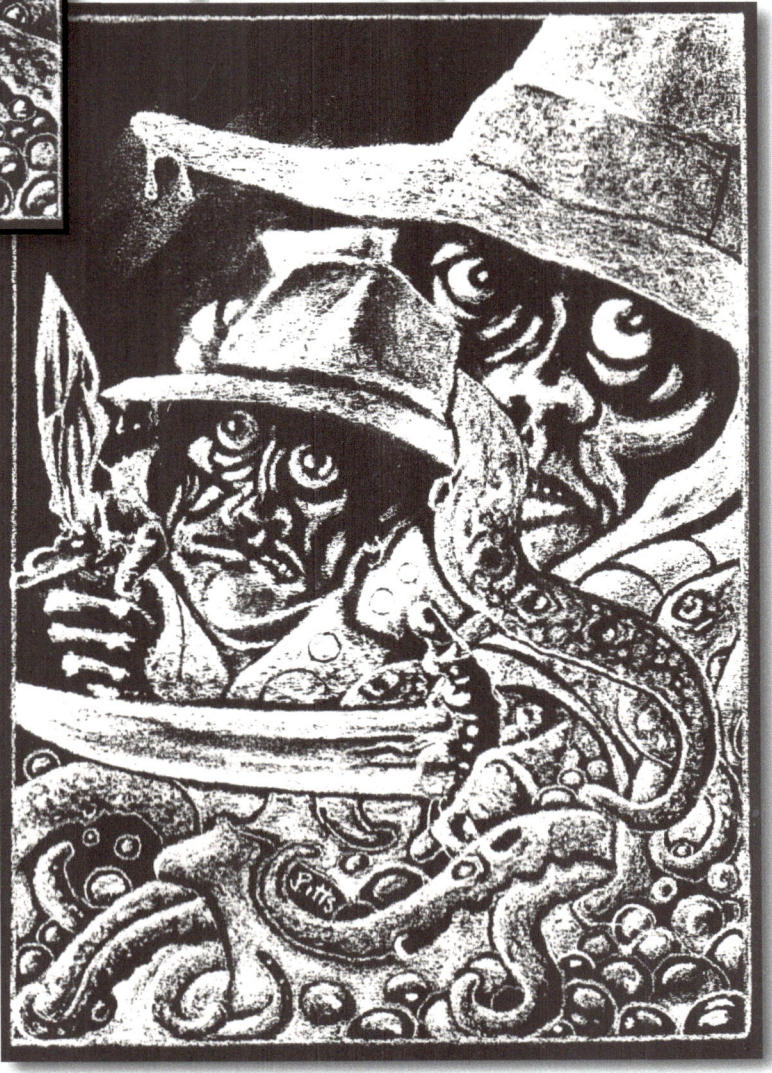

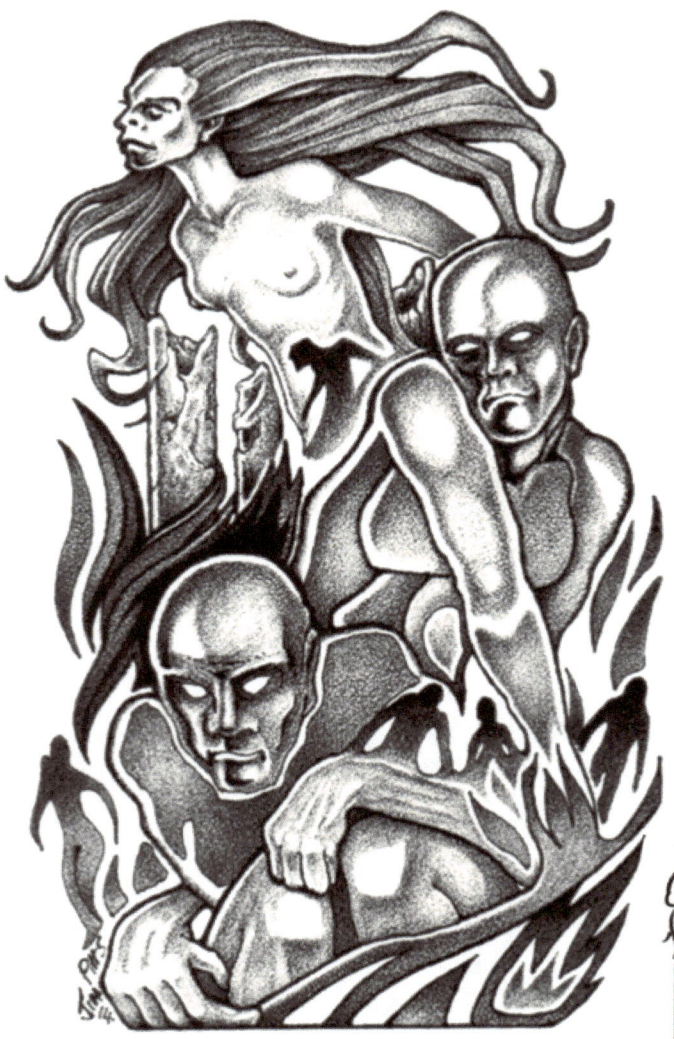

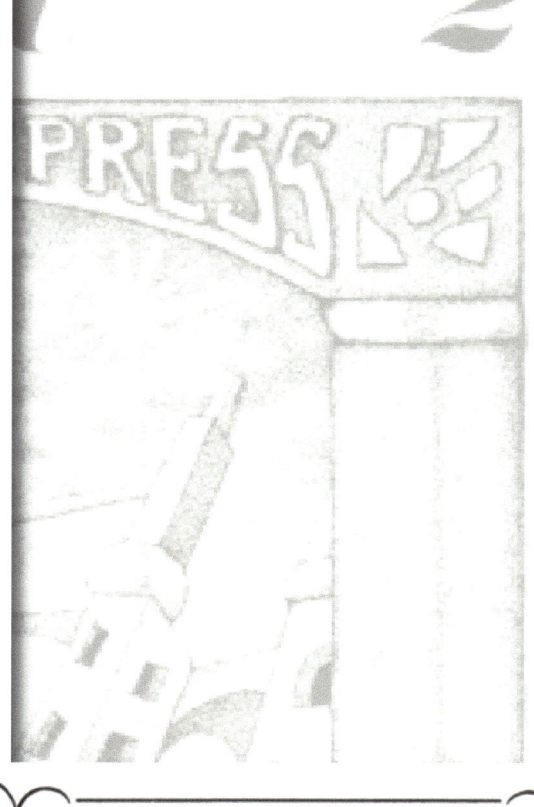

Original art used for cover of *Cthulhu 5*

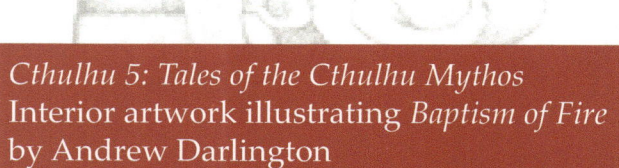

Cthulhu 5: Tales of the Cthulhu Mythos
Interior artwork illustrating *Baptism of Fire* by Andrew Darlington

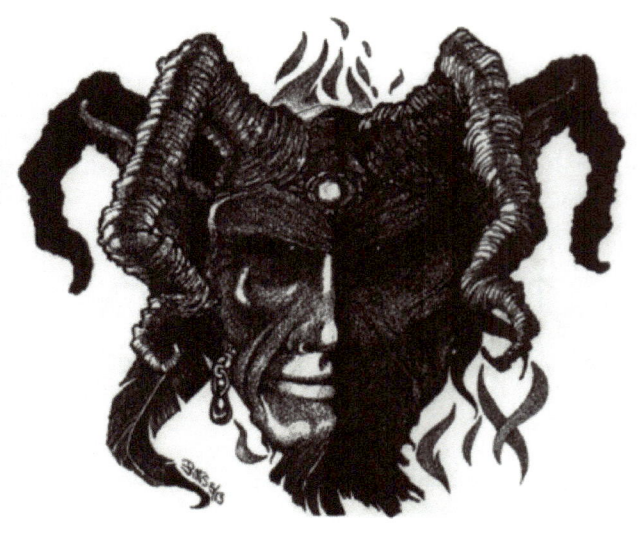

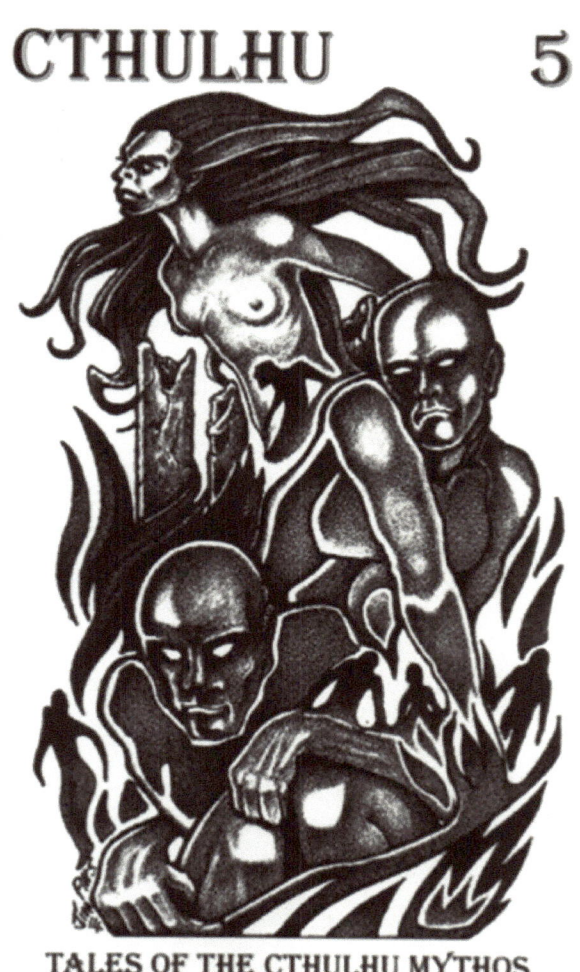
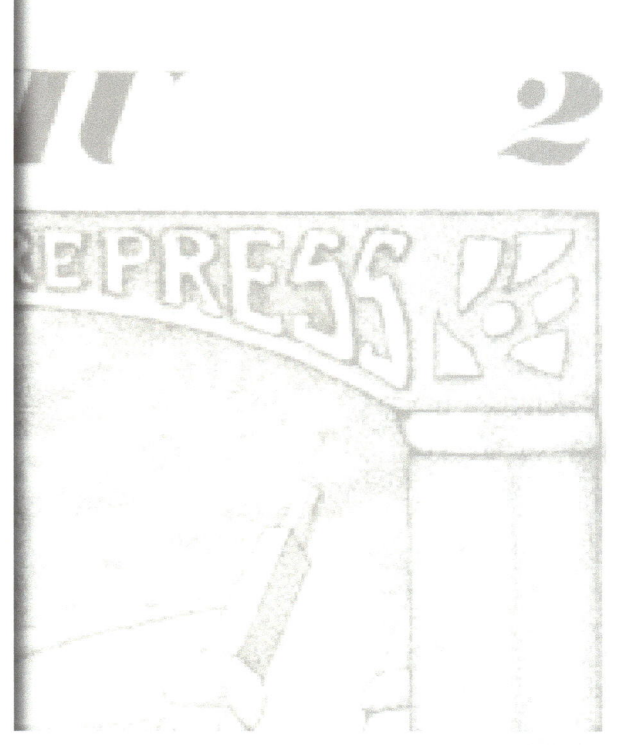
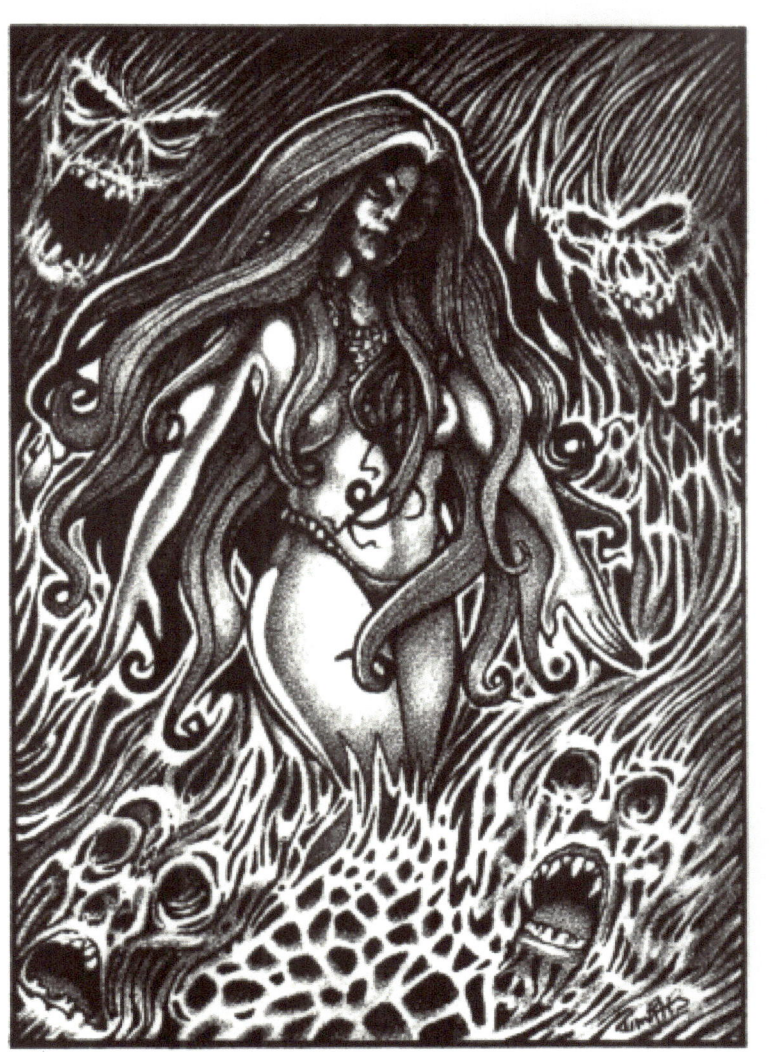

Cthulhu 5: Tales of the Cthulhu Mythos
Interior artwork illustrating *Baptism of Fire* by Andrew Darlington

CTHULHU 6

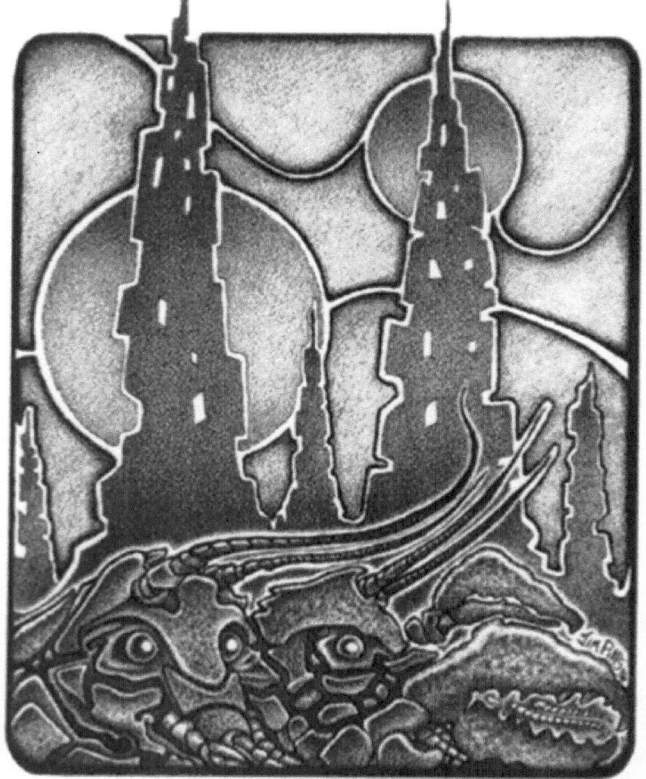

TALES OF THE CTHULHU MYTHOS

CTHULHU 7

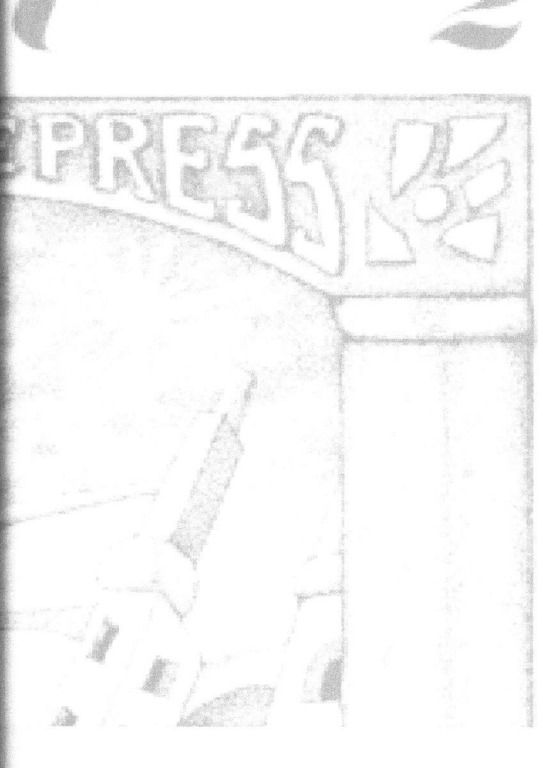

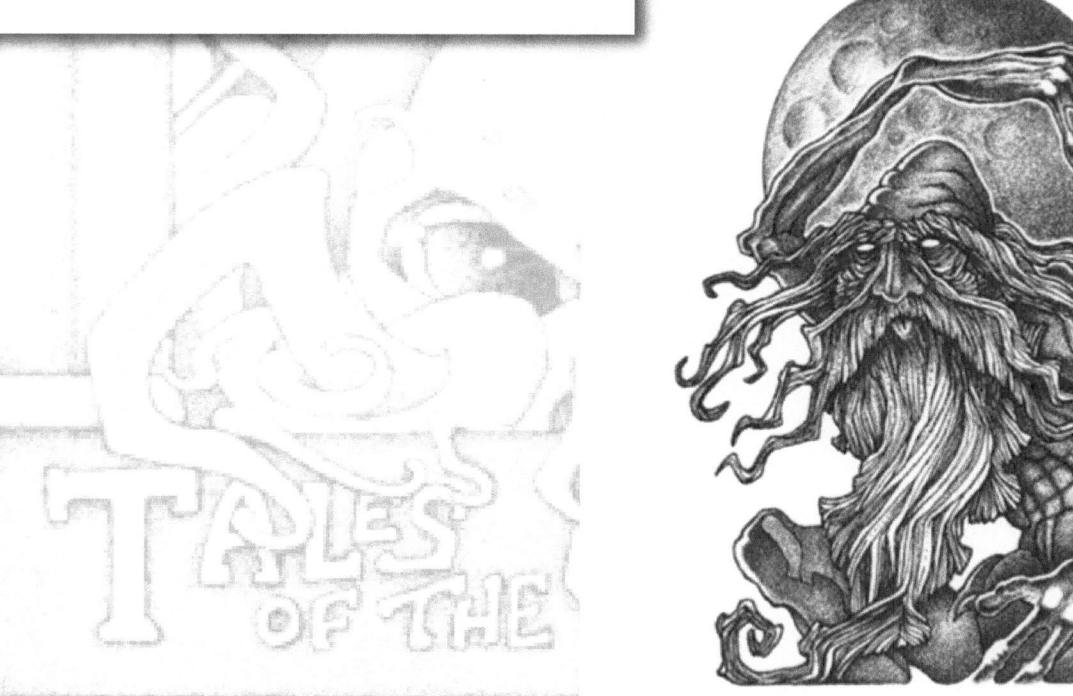

TALES OF THE CTHULHU MYTHOS

Cthulhu 6: Tales of the Cthulhu Mythos
Interior artwork illustrating
Fallout by D J Tyrer

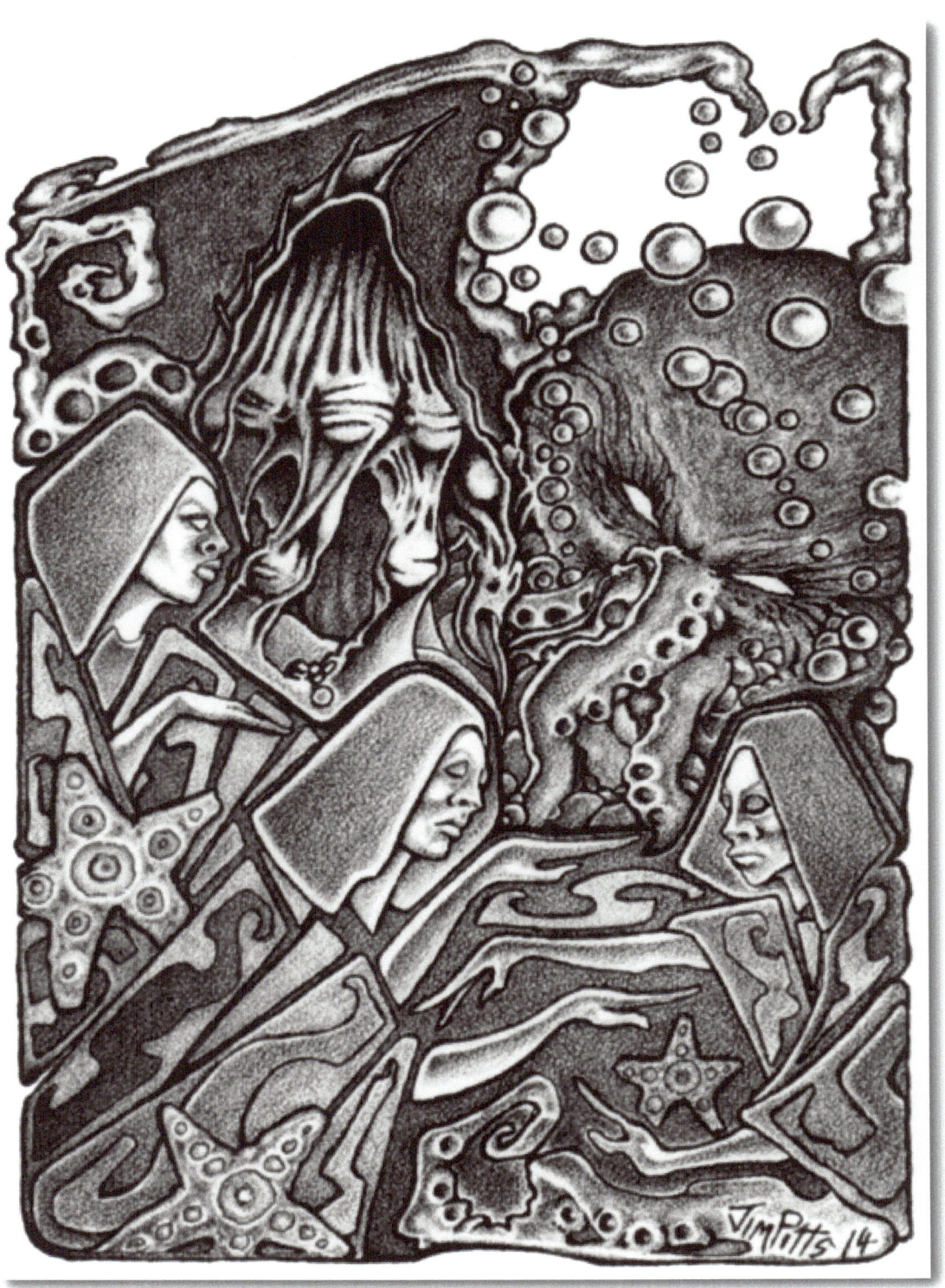

Cthulhu 7: Tales of the Cthulhu Mythos
Interior artwork illustrating *Game of Nine Pinns* by Don Webb

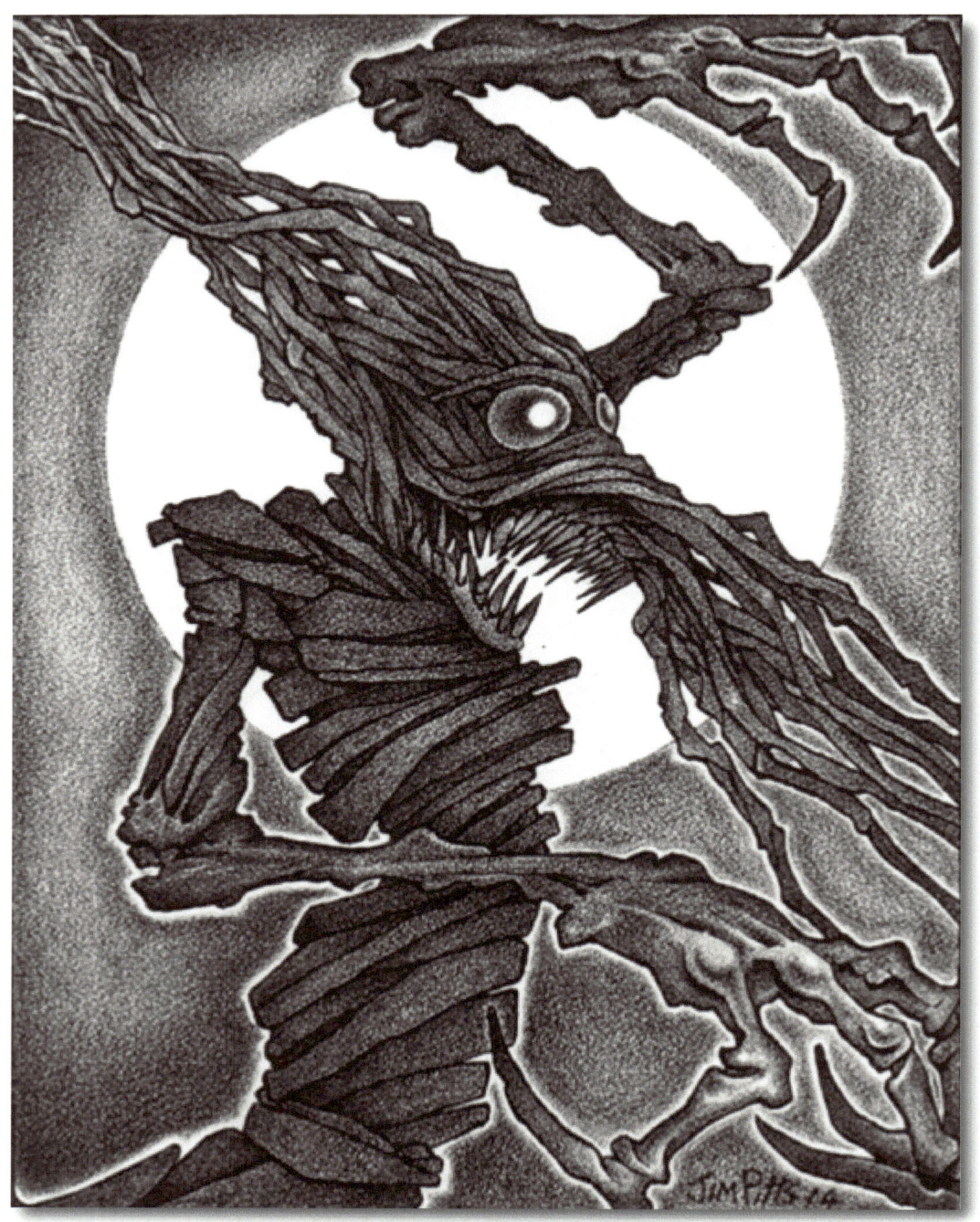

Front cover artwork for *Cthulhu 8*
Illustrates *The Furies from Boras* by Anders Fager

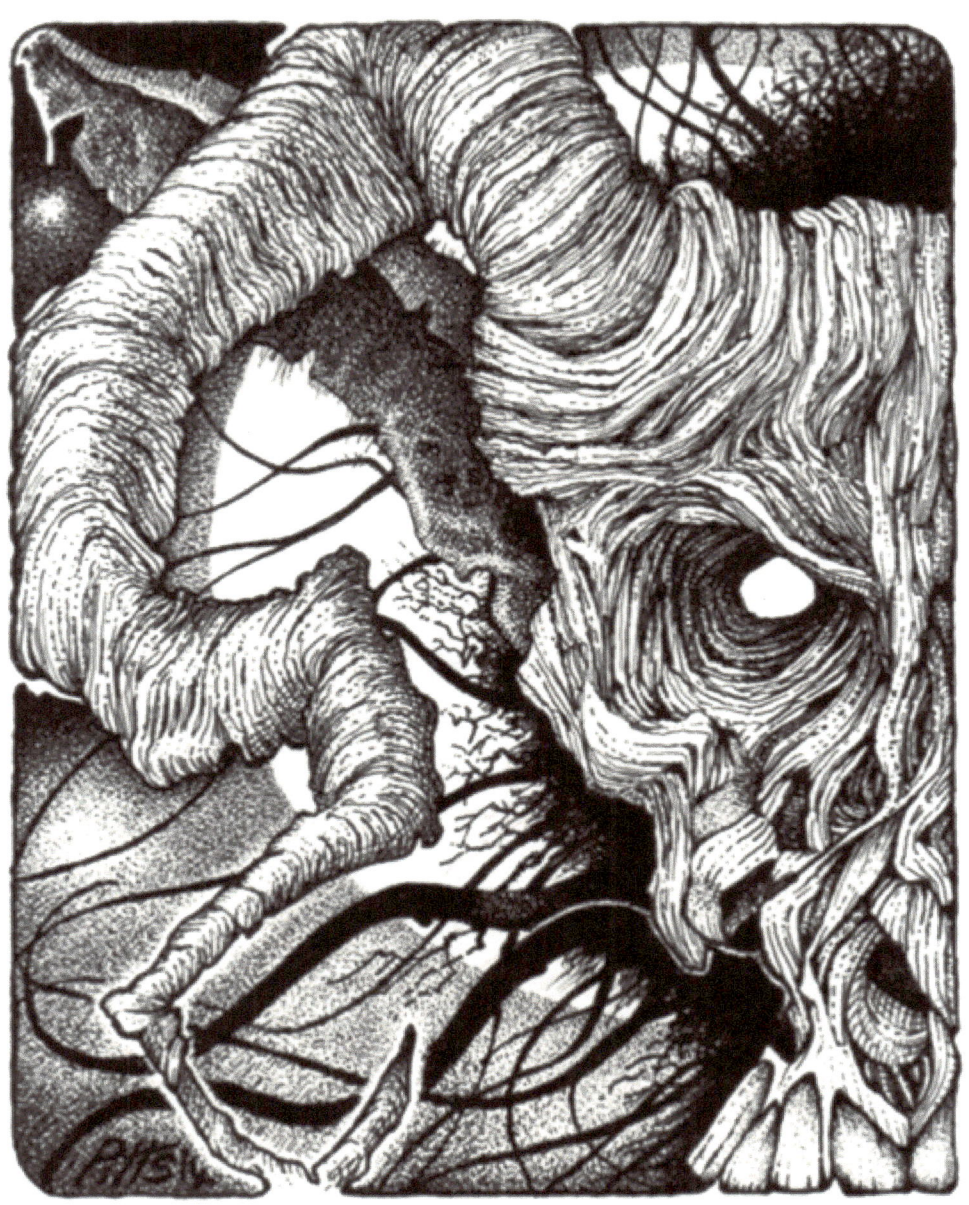

Front cover artwork for *Cthulhu 8*
Illustrates *The Furies from Boras*
by Anders Fager

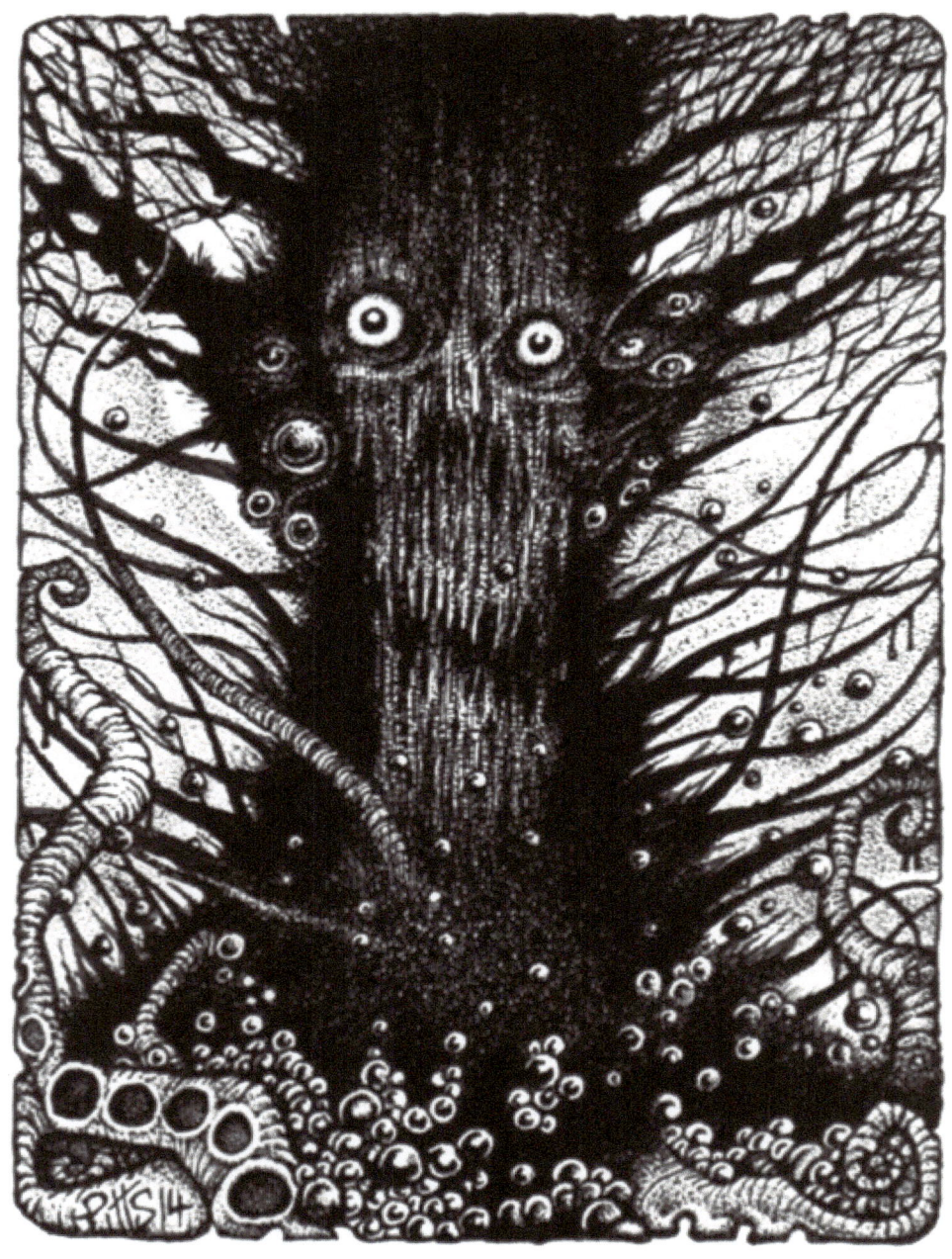

CTHULHU SCULPTURE

The photographs below originally appeared in *Skeleton Crew*.

The figure of Cthulhu was Jim's second attempt at sculpting, the cowled figure that was used by the BFS for its British Fantasy Award being the first.

He used DAS modelling clay and coloured with Acrylics and then varnished. It sold at its first showing at a FantasyCon in the 1990's.

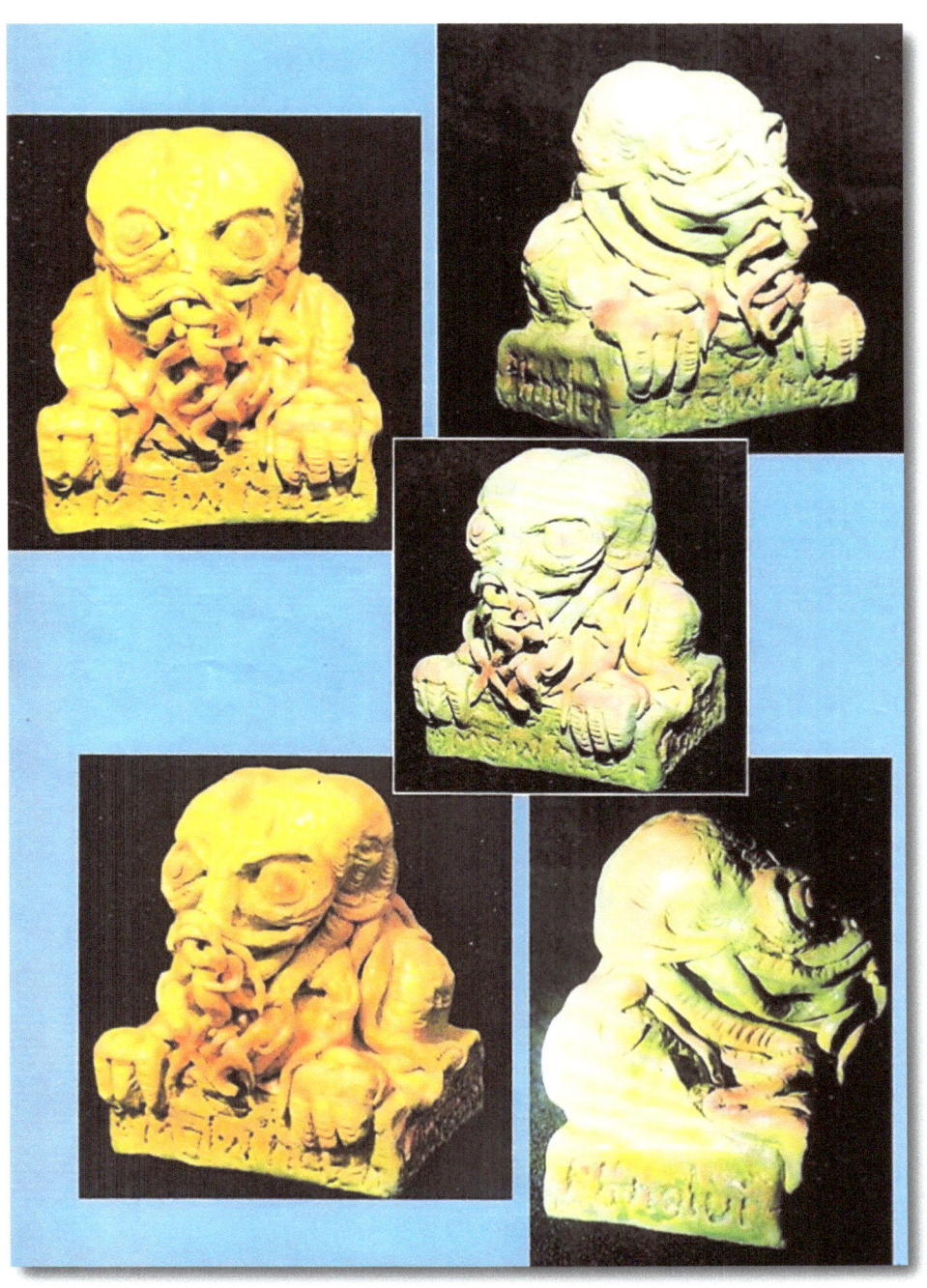

JIM PITTS AND *FANTASY TALES*
by Stephen Jones

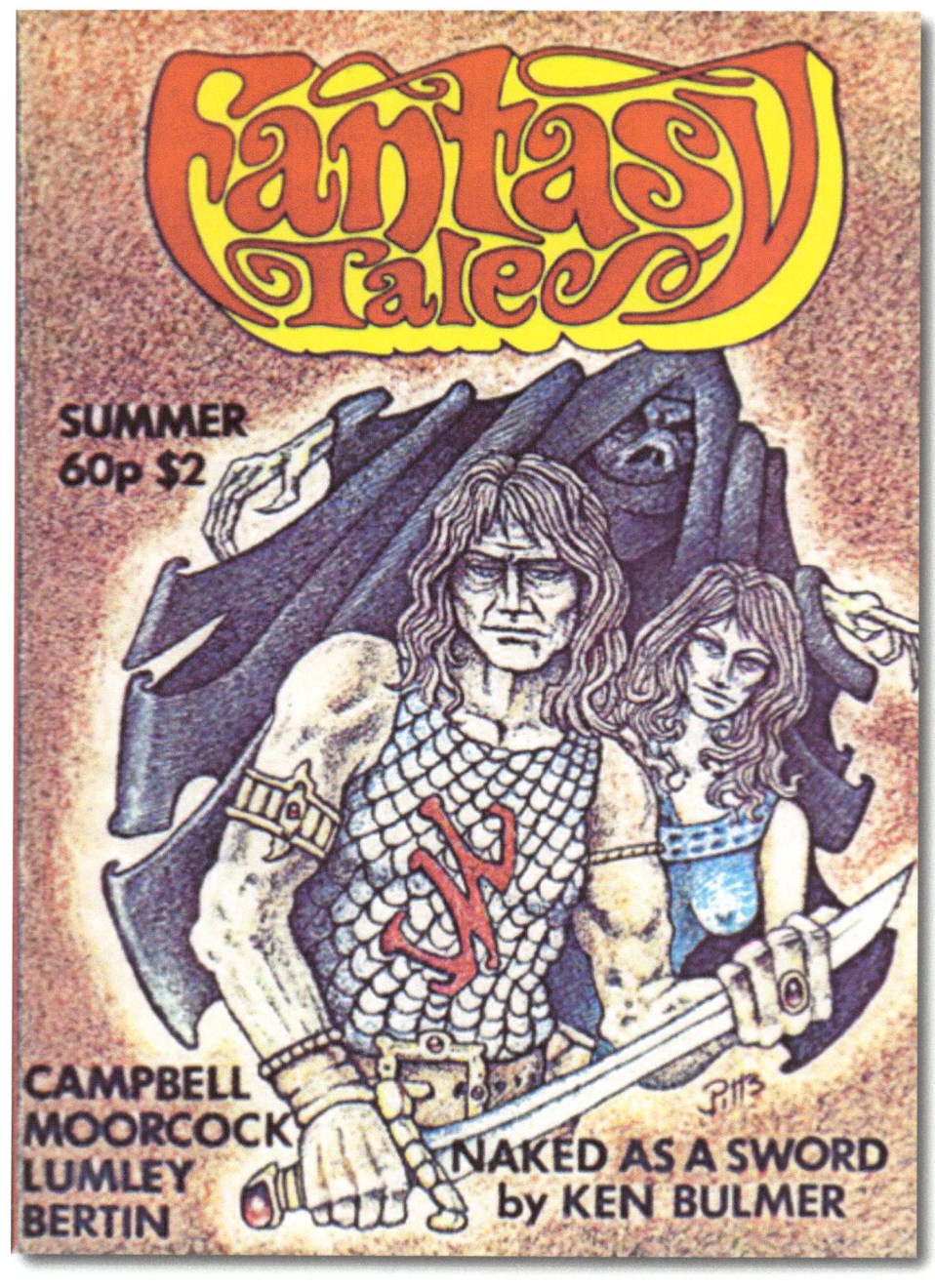

Cover for the first issue of *Fantasy Tales*

As I explained in my Introduction to his portfolio *Olde Horrors* (The British Fantasy Society, 1989), I first became aware of Jim's artwork when I came across an issue of David Sutton's seminal fanzine *Shadow* during the summer of 1972.

It was issue #17, and Jim's cover depicted a demon reading an arcane tome by the wavering flame of a much-used candle. I had barely heard of Virgil Finlay or Hannes Bok in those days but, as something of an amateur illustrator myself, I was fascinated by Jim's meticulous pen-and-ink stipple technique. So I purchased the magazine, and obtained my introduction to British fantasy fandom at the same time.

I soon began to search for other magazines featuring Jim Pitts' artwork – *Balthus*, *Mallorn* and *Anduril*, to name but a few – and, inspired by his example, I made my own genre debut with a piece of derivative sword and sorcery art on the back cover of *Shadow* #19 the following year. Of course, my minor illustration was completely eclipsed by Jim's superb front cover interpretation of William Hope Hodgson's *The House on the Borderland*.

By now I had also joined The British Fantasy Society, and discovered that Jim and David Riley were editing the bi-monthly *B.F.S. Bulletin*, which supplied news and reviews to the membership. One of the high points of this publication for me was that each issue would include various spot-illustrations by Jim. So it made sense that when I took over the editorship of the Society's journal, *Dark Horizons*, with issue #9 (summer 1974), it would boast a cover and interior artwork by Jim, along with an interview with the artist and a portfolio of his work.

After corresponding for some time, we finally met in person at the British Fantasy Society's first Fantasycon, a one-day event held in Birmingham on February 22nd, 1975. We were both on a panel about "Fantasy Art in Fanzines" along with George Locke, and our artwork graced the minimalist programme book put together by David Sutton.

Jim contributed artwork to the next five issues of *Dark Horizons* that I edited, but by 1976 I was beginning to think that I had done all I could with the format. At this time in Britain there were few, if any, magazines specifically devoted to fantasy and horror fiction, and David Sutton and I had begun talking about producing our own semi-professional publication along the same lines as Stuart David Schiff's *Whispers* in America.

Colour printing was still hugely expensive, but I had found a small printer in London's West End who could turn out colour photocopies at a price that made the process economical. I therefore decided that my final issue of *Dark Horizons* would be a test-run for this new colour-cover process, and it would also serve as a "pilot" for the ambitious fantasy periodical that David and I were planning.

Dark Horizons #15 appeared in winter 1976 with a colour cover by Jim depicting a

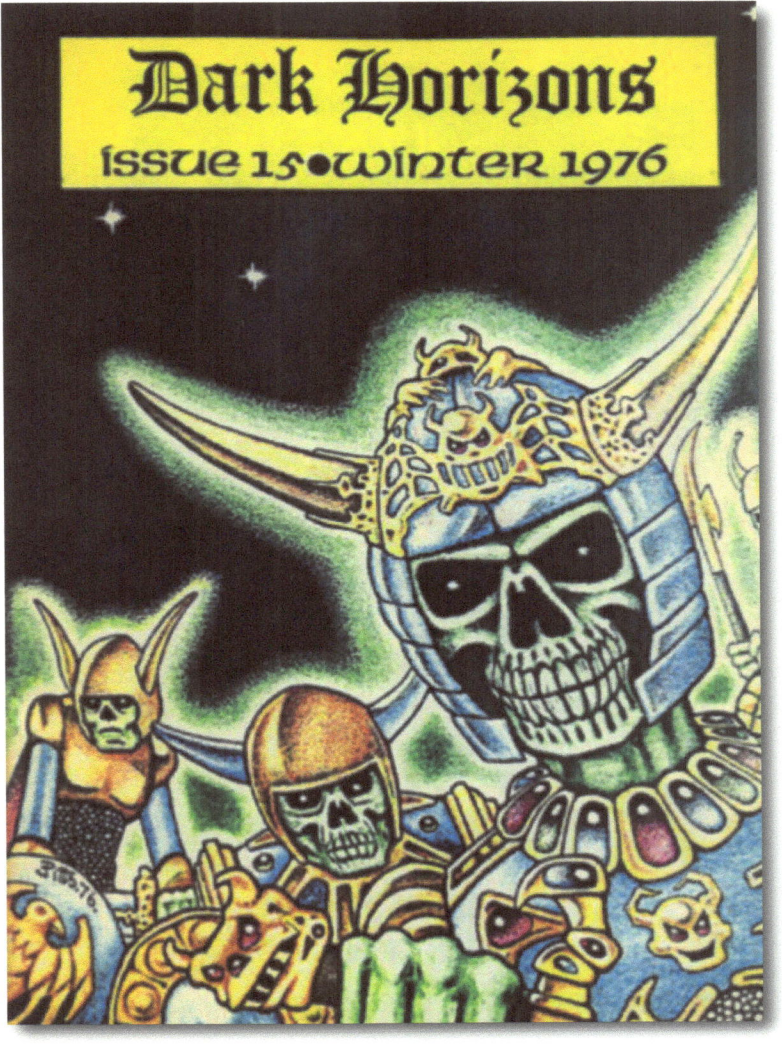

trio of eerily glowing warrior liches in armour wielding jewel-encrusted swords and emblazoned shields. The printing effect didn't do justice to the vibrant colours of Jim's original artwork, but it was good enough to make an impact and, more importantly, it was relatively affordable.

David and I moved ahead with our plans for the new magazine.

We contacted a number of professional writers that we knew through the British Fantasy Society and told them what we were contemplating. We explained that due to the colour copying we needed to produce 1,000 copies, and although we couldn't afford to pay for the first issue (all our money was going on the production costs), we hoped that we would have a small budget for fiction from the second issue onwards.

You have to remember that there was really nothing quite like this in the UK at the time, and the US only had Stuart's *Whispers* and Paul W. Ganley's *Weirdbook*, so we were basically offering a completely new fiction market.

The response was overwhelmingly positive, and the first square-bound issue of *Fantasy Tales* appeared in summer 1977 with stories by, amongst others, Kenneth Bulmer, Ramsey Campbell, Brian Lumley, Eddy C. Bertin and even Michael Moorcock!

We had decided to base the design of the magazine on the old *Weird Tales* pulp, and a colleague of mine working in ITN's graphic design studio created the distinctive red-and-yellow logo on an acetate overlay. As there was only one version of this, we re-used it on every edition. There was never any doubt that Jim would contribute the first cover, and we based it around the two recurring characters, Torr and Tara Vorkun, from Ken Bulmer's lead sword and sorcery tale, 'Naked as a Sword'. Jim also contributed a full-page illustration for that story and a piece of heading art for Brian Lumley's fantasy short, 'Mylakhrion the Immortal'.

A modest advertising campaign, along with relentless promotion to specialist dealers and at UK conventions, meant that we all but sold out of the first issue. Despite positive word-of-mouth, it was a while before we recouped our initial investment (and in at least one case we were never paid by a disreputable American dealer who took a tenth of our print-run), but David and I pressed ahead with the second issue anyway.

Fantasy Tales #2 was dated winter 1977, and the cover was once again by Jim, illustrating Adrian Cole's demonic novelette 'Scars'. He also contributed the double-page heading art for the story, along with a small splash illustration for the first UK publication of Karl Edward Wagner's evocative tale, 'The Last Wolf'.

We had always budgeted for a second issue, and with the money starting to roll in from our debut edition, we kept our promise and began paying the authors a small stipend. Unfortunately, we were never affluent enough to reimburse the artists as well, which was something that we had hoped we might be able to do.

Stephen E. Fabian took over the cover duties on *Fantasy Tales* #3 (summer, 1978), and Jim was only represented with a heading illustration for a poem by Pat McIntosh. This was because he was working on something much more lavish for the following issue. It appeared in spring 1979 with Jim's impressive cover for Adrian Cole's 'First Make Them Mad', a new novelette featuring the author's fantasy character, the Voidal. He also contributed a full-page illustration and four fillers for the story.

Fantasy Tales #4 marked the last issue that we used the photocopy covers. Although the colour reproduction was at best variable, there is no doubt that they gave the magazine a distinctive appearance. However, our printer in Holborn hated them – because of the square-blocked spines the covers had to be glued on by hand, and the glossy paper surface meant that they were always getting jammed in the trimming machines. In the end they simply refused to handle them any longer.

So we had to work out a compromise, and from #5 (winter, 1979) the covers reverted to black and white with a printed two-colour logo and saddle-stitched spine, which could all be done by machines. For that issue, Jim created a beautiful full-column illustration for Frances Garfield's rare *Weird Tales* reprint, 'Don't Open the Door'.

Jim's decidedly feline heading art graced another story by Frances, 'The Elementals', in the following issue (summer, 1980). This time, however, it was an original story and not a reprint. The artist also contributed a back cover illustration after the style of Hannes Bok, one of his favourite artists.

Incidentally, a small run of *Fantasy Tales* #6 was signed by Frances and her husband, veteran pulp author Manly Wade Wellman (who had the cover story), for the London specialist bookseller Fantasy Centre. Copies of these inscribed issues are a rare find nowadays.

Jim was back on the cover of issue #7 (spring, 1981) with his depiction of Kane, the Mystic Swordsman, for Karl Edward Wagner's 'The Other One'. Although the original art was produced in pastel pencils, we could only use it in black and white on the magazine, and it was later reprinted in colour on the cover of *Kadath* #6-7 (1984). Jim also created two interior illustrations of Kane to go with the story.

Jim contributed a fine heading illustration for James Glenn's 'The Legacy' in *Fantasy Tales* #8 (summer, 1981), but he outdid himself with the magazine's first and only wraparound cover on issue #9 (spring, 1982), illustrating David Malpass' story 'The Grey Horde', for which he also did the heading art.

By the early 1980s, Jim was refining his style – his compositions were tighter and more "designed", and he was now using a textured paper rather than a pen to create his stippling effect. His artwork had certainly come a long way since those early *Shadow* days. Jim's heading drawing for the first UK publication of Manly Wade Wellman's story 'A Witch for All Seasons' graced the tenth issue of *Fantasy Tales* (summer, 1982), and he contributed the cover to #11 (winter, 1982) illustrating H. Warner Munn's classic *Weird Tales* story 'A Sprig of Rosemary', for which he also produced an even more effective piece of heading art.

His full-page illustration for 'In the Labyrinth' by Simon R. Green appeared in *Fantasy Tales* #12 (winter, 1983). This was the last issue of the magazine to use a black and white cover. Offset technology had moved on, and our printer found a supplier who could produce full-colour glossy covers at a price that even we could afford (with a bit of help from our advertising revenue).

Fantasy Tales #13 (winter 1984) debuted this new look with front and back cover paintings by Stephen Fabian. Jim was represented inside with two column-breaking designs for Steve Rasnic Tem's 'The Bad People', including a particularly ugly-looking frog.

In retrospect, we really should have put the first publication of Clive Barker's 'The Forbidden' (the basis of the Candyman movie series) on the cover of *Fantasy Tales* #14 (summer, 1985), but instead we went with Jim's stylised interpretation of Ramsey Campbell's modern-day ghost story, 'The Sneering', for which he also did a full-page illustration.

Issue #14 also marked the last time Jim's work appeared on the cover of the magazine. However, he continued to be a reliable contributor, with art for no less than three stories and a poem in *Fantasy Tales* #15 (winter, 1985) and two further stories and another poem in issue #16 (winter, 1986).

Fantasy Tales #17 (summer, 1987) was not only our tenth anniversary edition, but also the final issue in the small-press run of the magazine. David Sutton and I no longer had the time to devote to it that we used to, and by the late 1980s the nature of the genre itself had changed in Britain, with many more outlets available for fiction than there had been a decade before.

We decided to go out in style with an "all-star" issue that welcomed back such original supporters of the title as Ramsey Campbell, Brian Lumley and Michael Moorcock. We also included work by Clive Barker and Robert E. Howard, and Jim produced a lovely splash illustration for William F. Nolan's Ray Bradbury tribute, 'The Dandelion Chronicles'. With this final contribution, Jim had the rare distinction of having appeared in every issue of the original run of *Fantasy Tales*.

But that wasn't the end. A year later Robinson Publishing re-launched the title as a short-lived paperback series, as well as producing a number of anthologies based around the name. Although Jim and many of our other regular contributors were involved with these professional revivals of *Fantasy Tales*, the restrictions of the publishing industry meant that they never quite recaptured the verve and style of the magazine version, which I used to put together on my mother's kitchen table.

It is strange to think back to those days now, and so much has happened in the interim. While many of those with whom David and I worked with have gone on to bigger and better things, there are others who are sadly no longer amongst us. But for a decade during the 1970s and '80s, *Fan-*

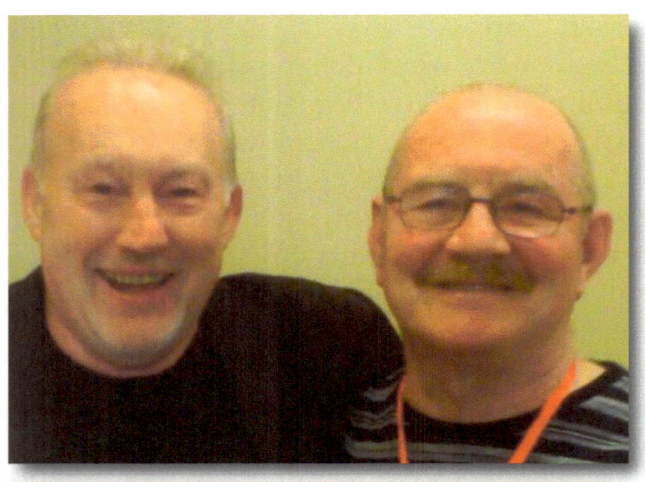
Stephen Jones and Jim Pitts

tasy Tales played an important role in laying the foundations for a genre publishing industry in the UK, and served as a stepping-stone for many of us who went on to have careers in horror and fantasy.

And when it comes to the artwork, there is no doubt that Jim Pitts was an integral part of all that.

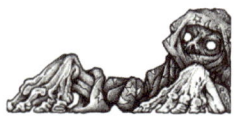

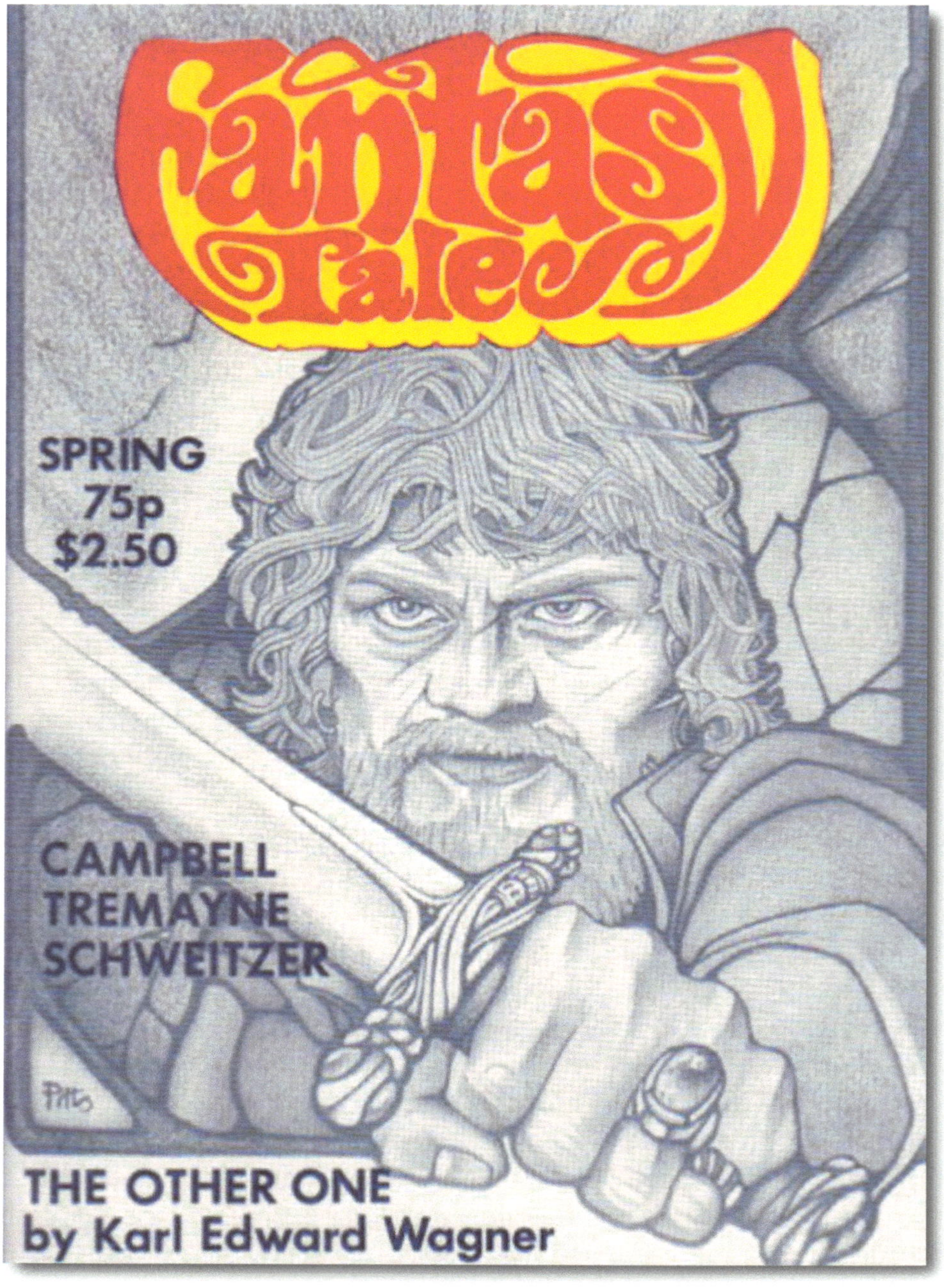

The original artwork for Karl Edward Wagner's character Kane, which was used not only as a cover for *Fantasy Tales* (in black and white) but also (in full colour) on the American fantasy magazine, *Kadath*.

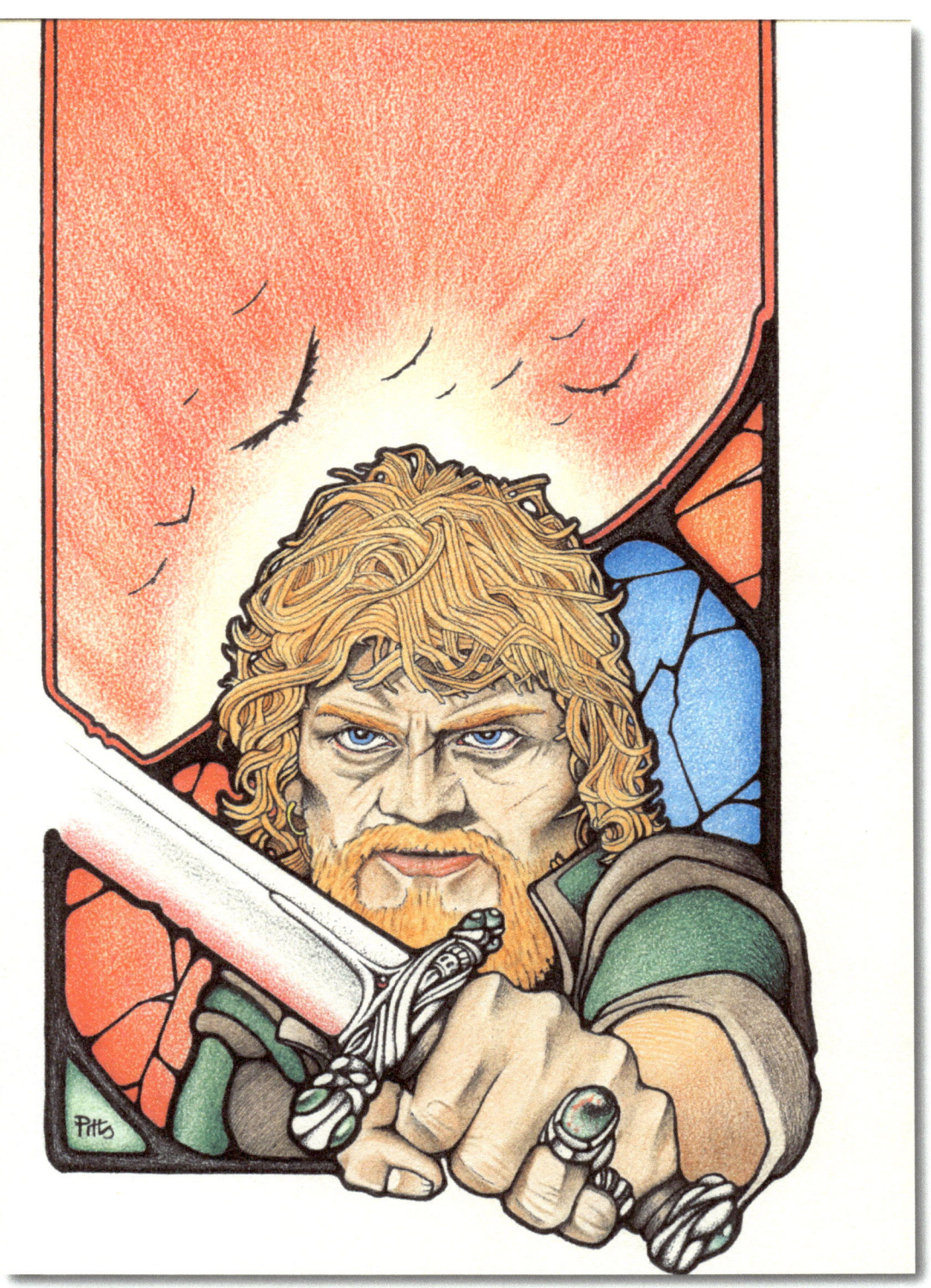

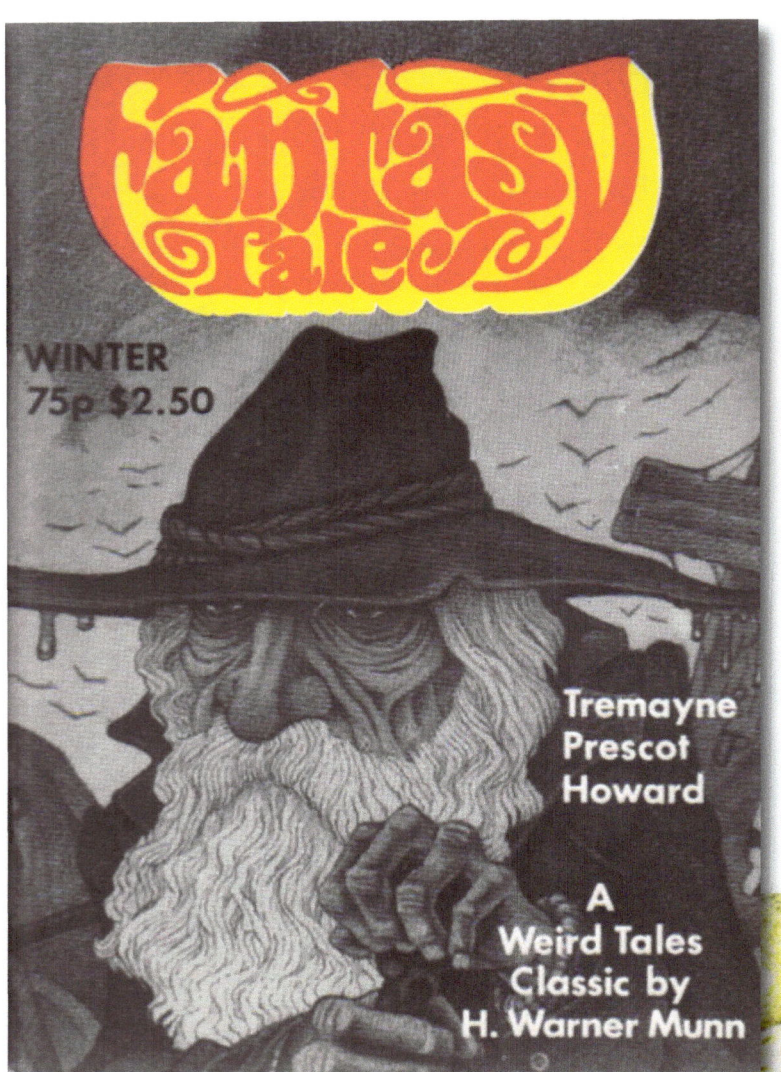

To the left: front cover design illustrating a scene from *A Sprig of Rosemary* by H. Warner Munn

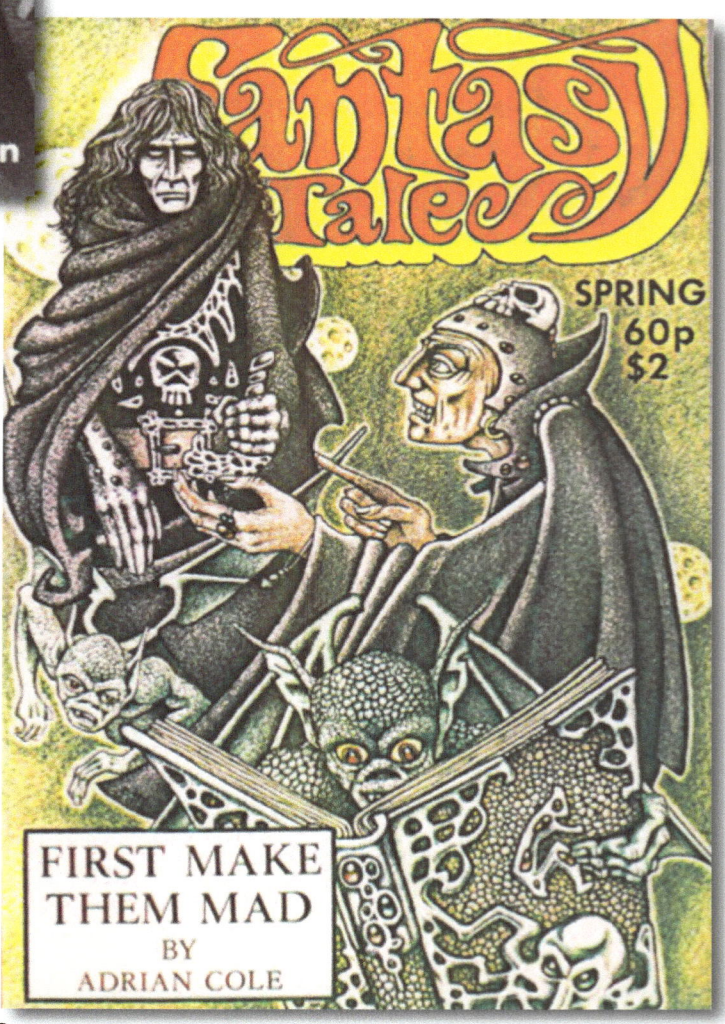

To the right: front cover design illustrating *First Make Them Mad* by Adrian Cole

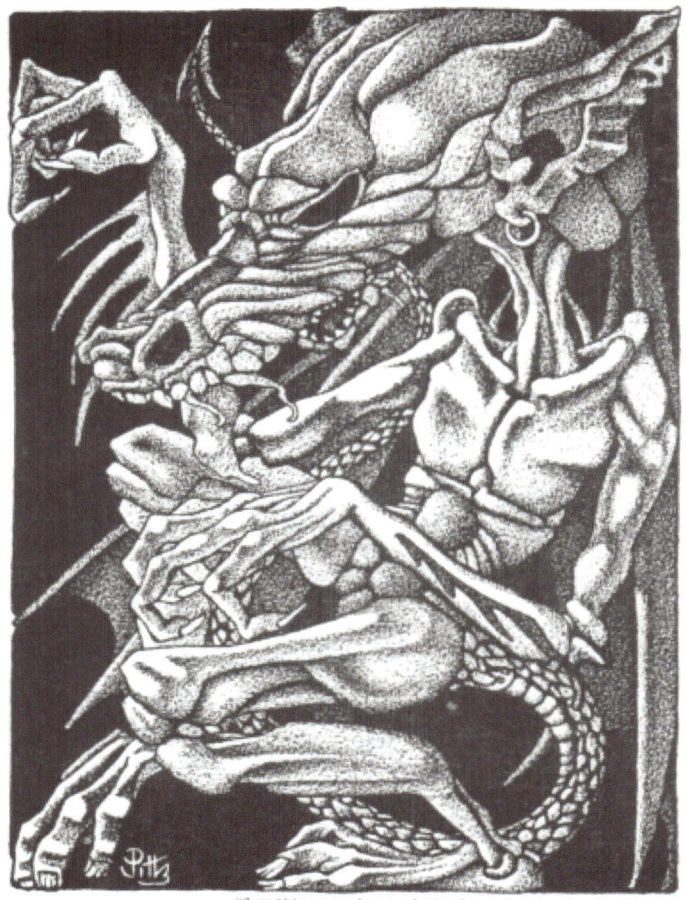

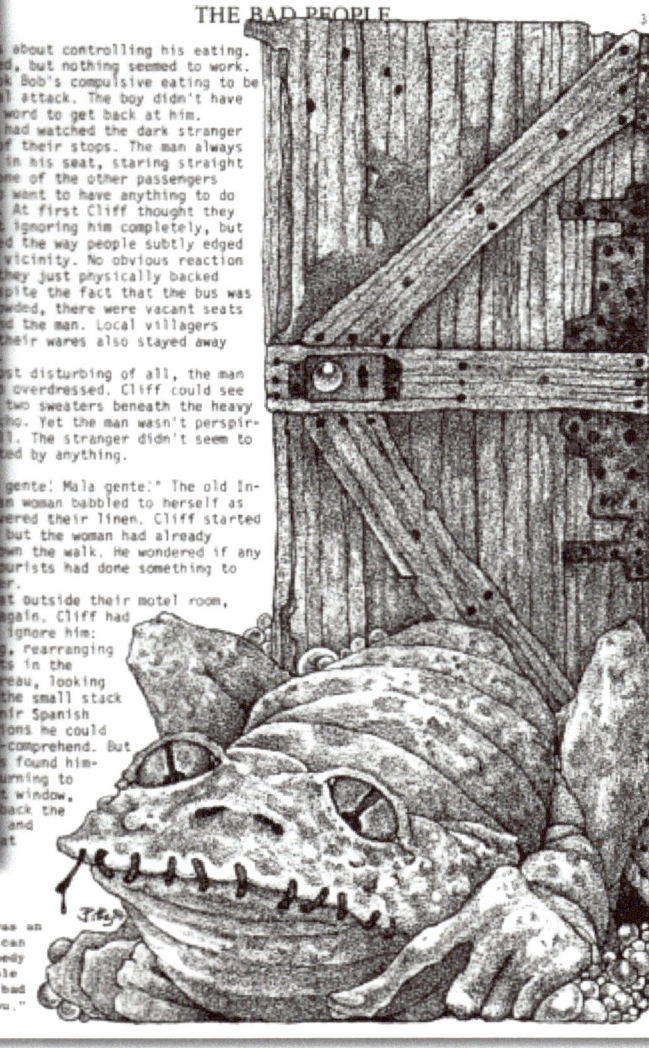

Above: *Fantasy Tales* Winter 1983, *In the Labyrinth* by Simon R. Green (the original is now in the collection of artist Andrew Smith)

Above: *The Bad People* by Steve Rasnic Tem, *Fantasy Tales* Winter 1984.

To the left: *A Witch for All Seasons* by Manly Wade Wellman, *Fantasy Tales* Summer 1982.

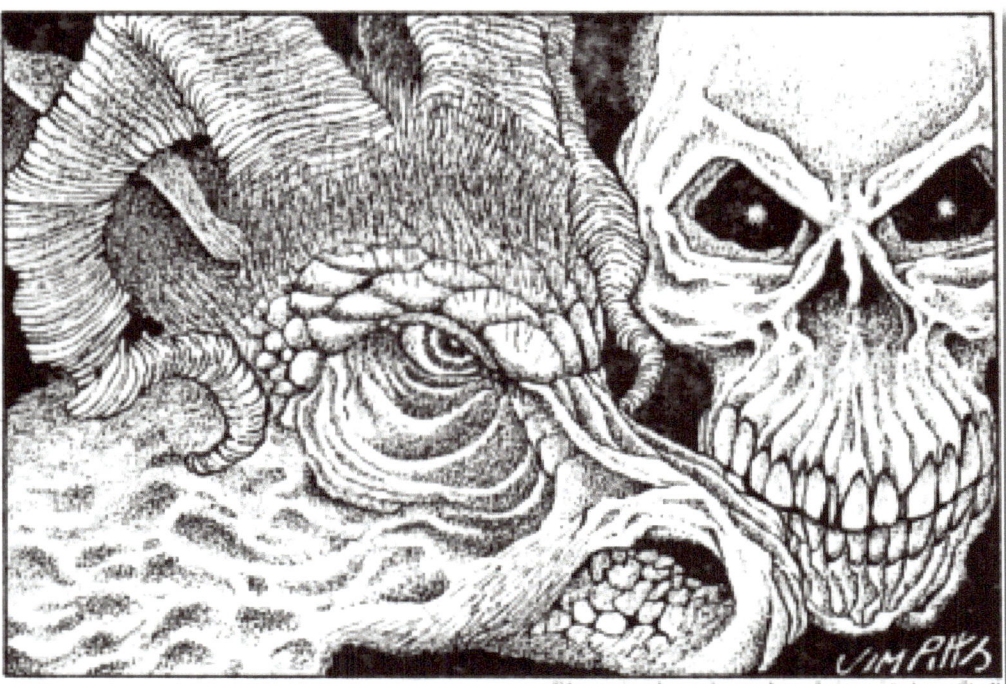

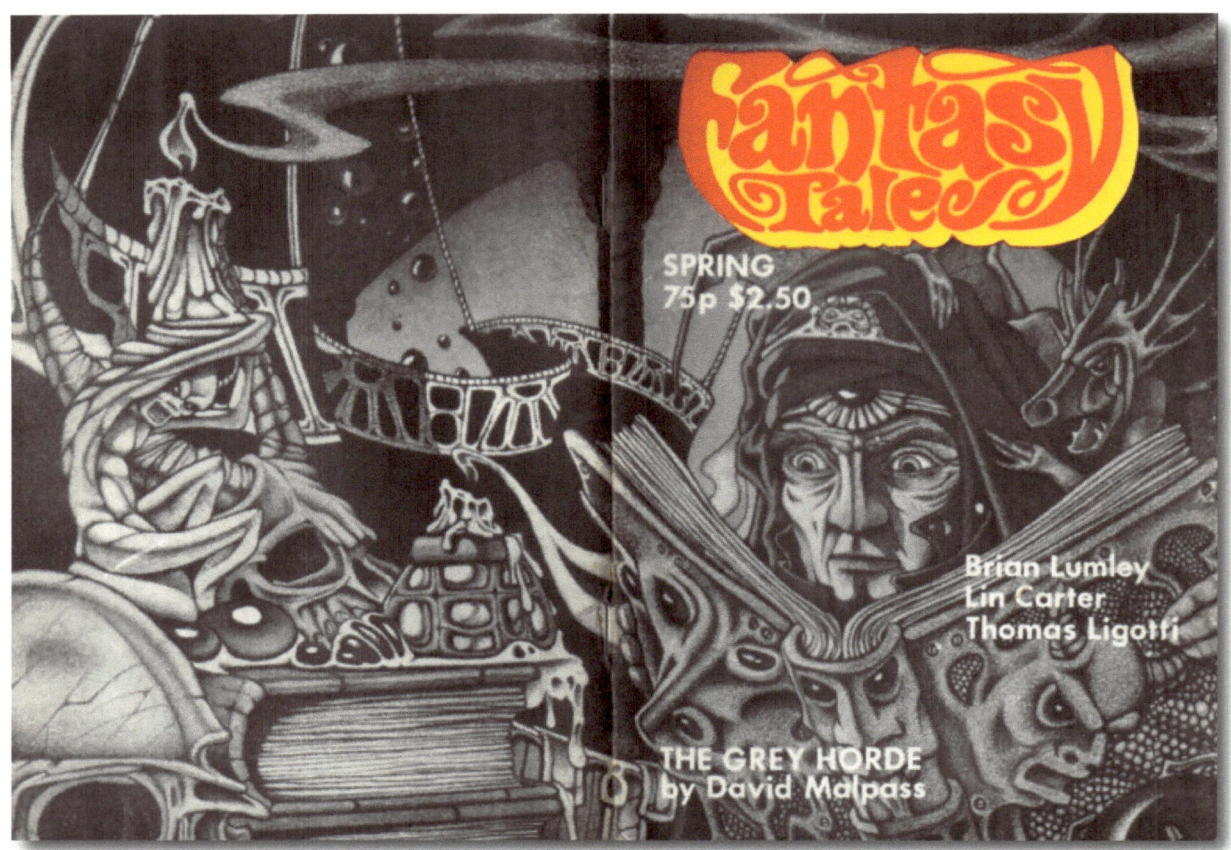

Wraparound cover design based on *The Grey Horde* by David Malpass

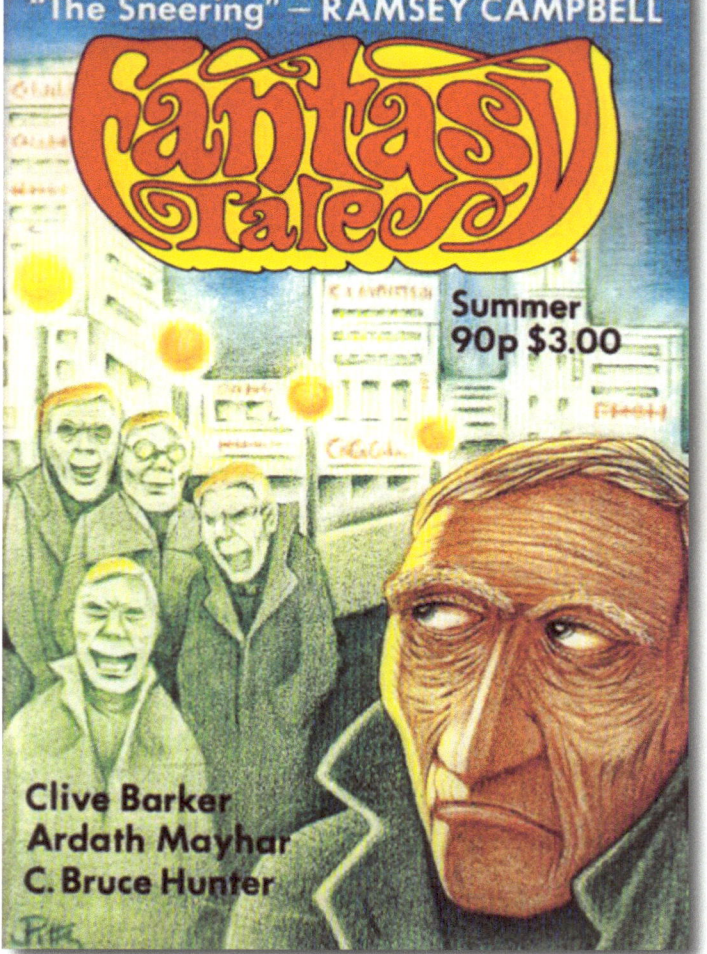

Cover design based on *The Sneering* by Ramsey Campbell

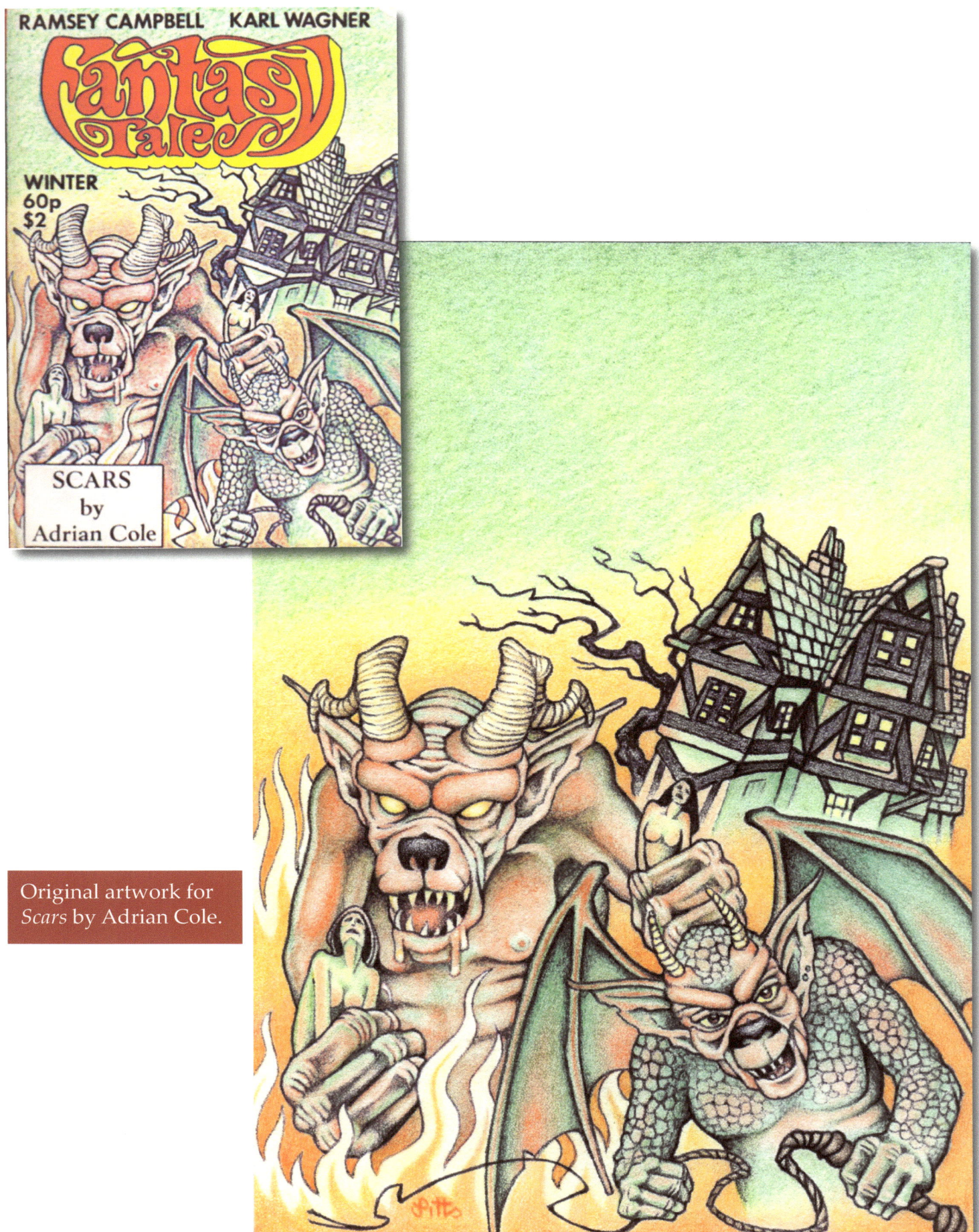

Original artwork for *Scars* by Adrian Cole.

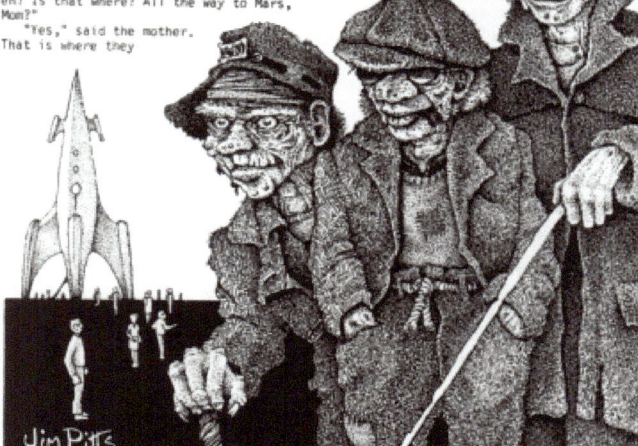

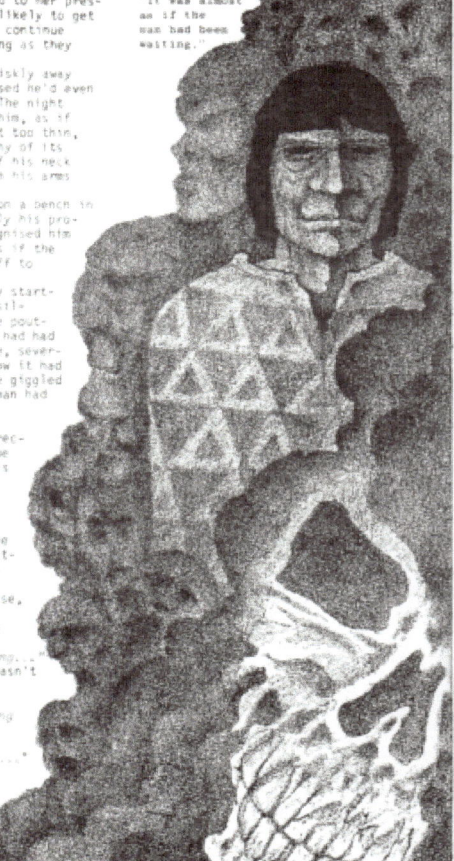

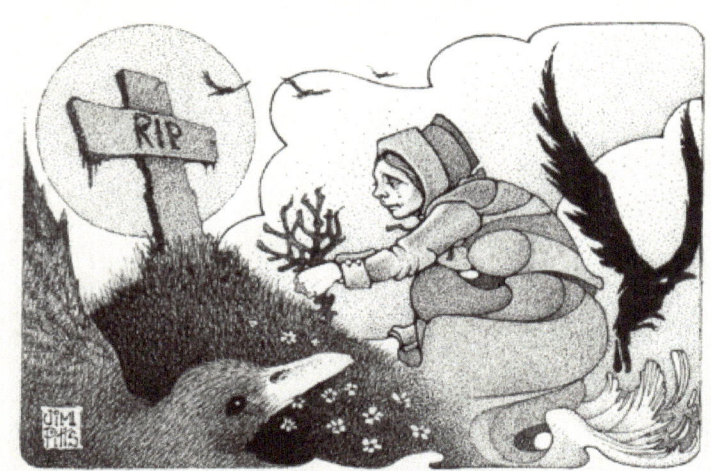

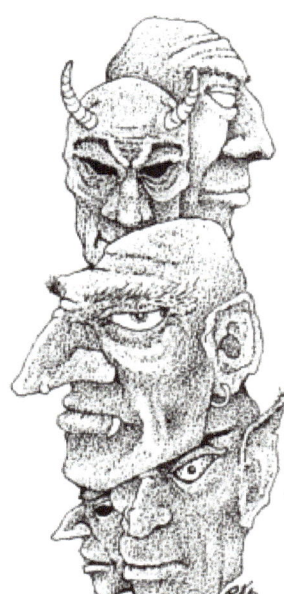

Top right: *The Bad People* by Steve Rasnic Tem, *Fantasy Tales* Winter 1984.

Above: *Fantasy Tales* Winter 1982, *A Sprig of Rosemary* by H. Warner Munn

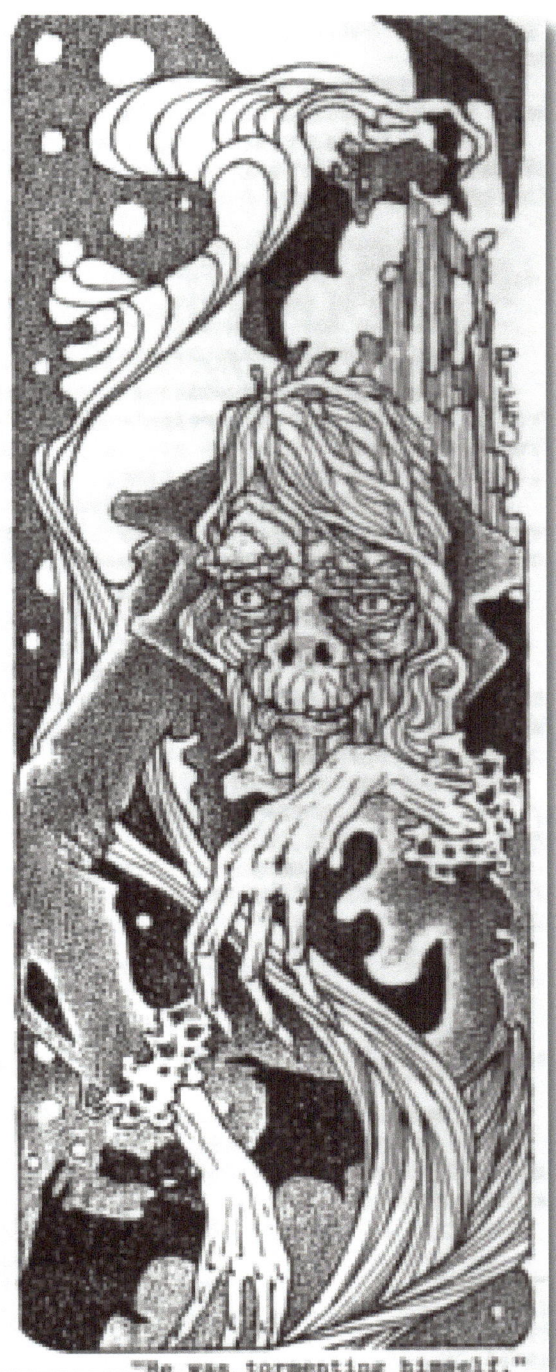

"He was tormenting himself."

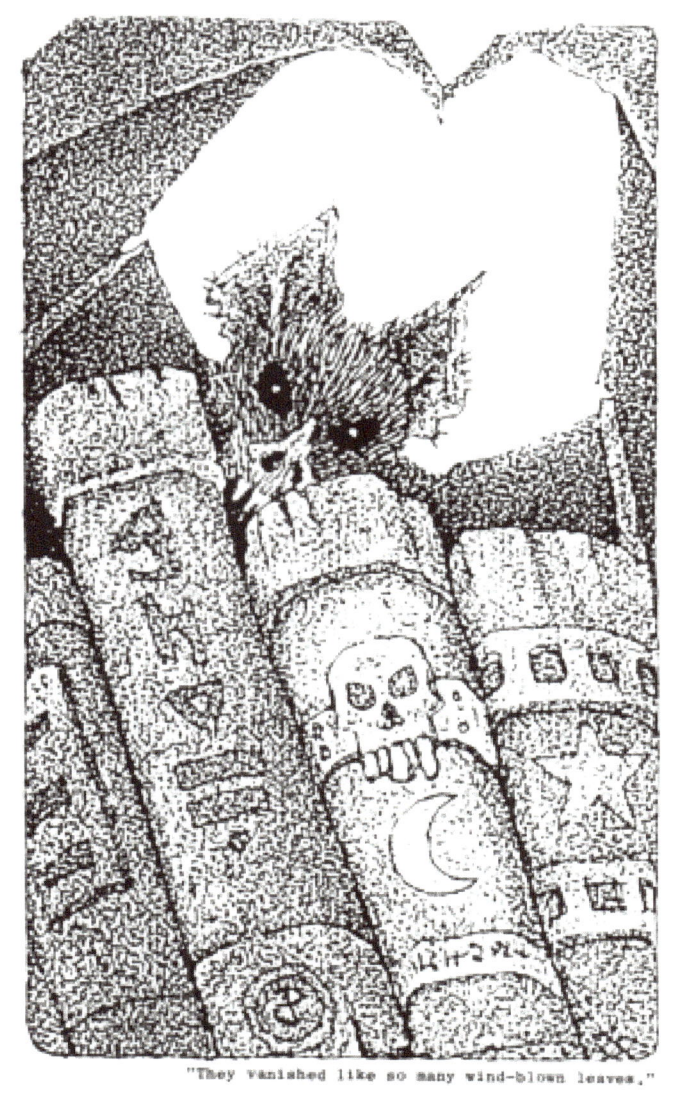

"They vanished like so many wind-blown leaves."

To the left: *After the Funeral* by Hugh B. Cave, *Fantasy Tales* Winter 1986

Below: *Zerail* by Josepha Sherman, *Fantasy Tales* Winter 1986

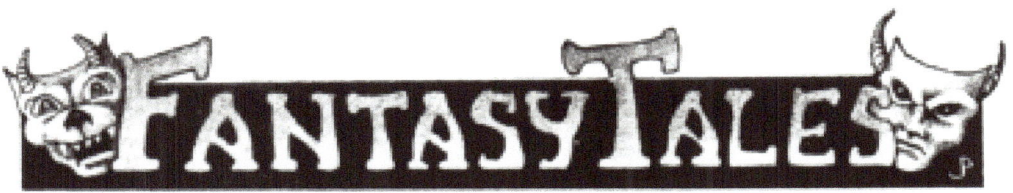

A MAGAZINE OF THE WEIRD AND UNUSUAL

| Volume 7 | CONTENTS FOR WINTER, 1984 | Number 13 |

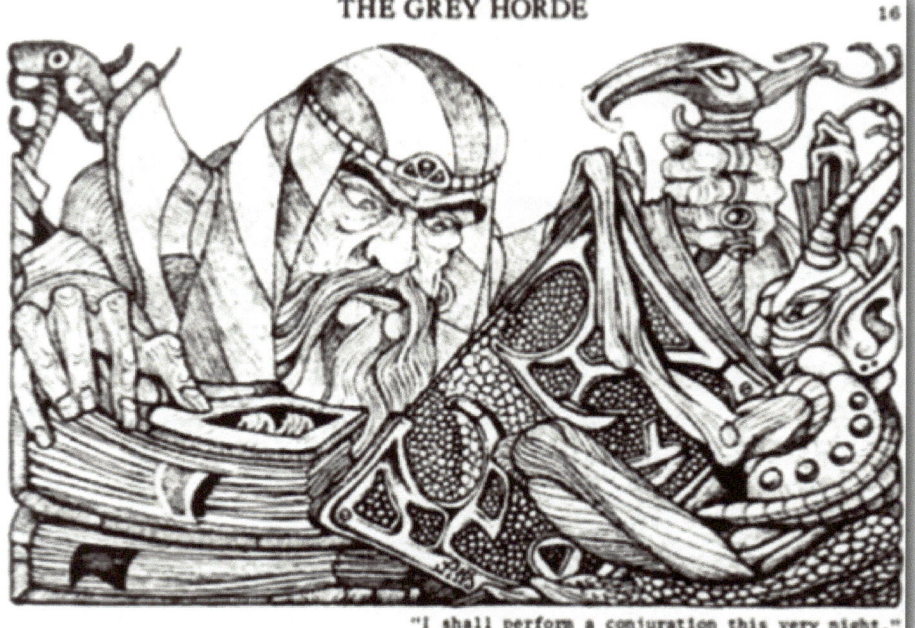

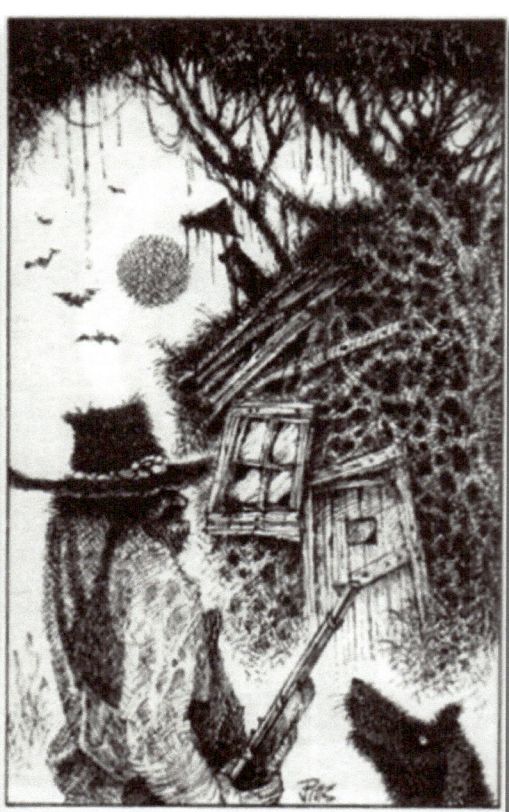

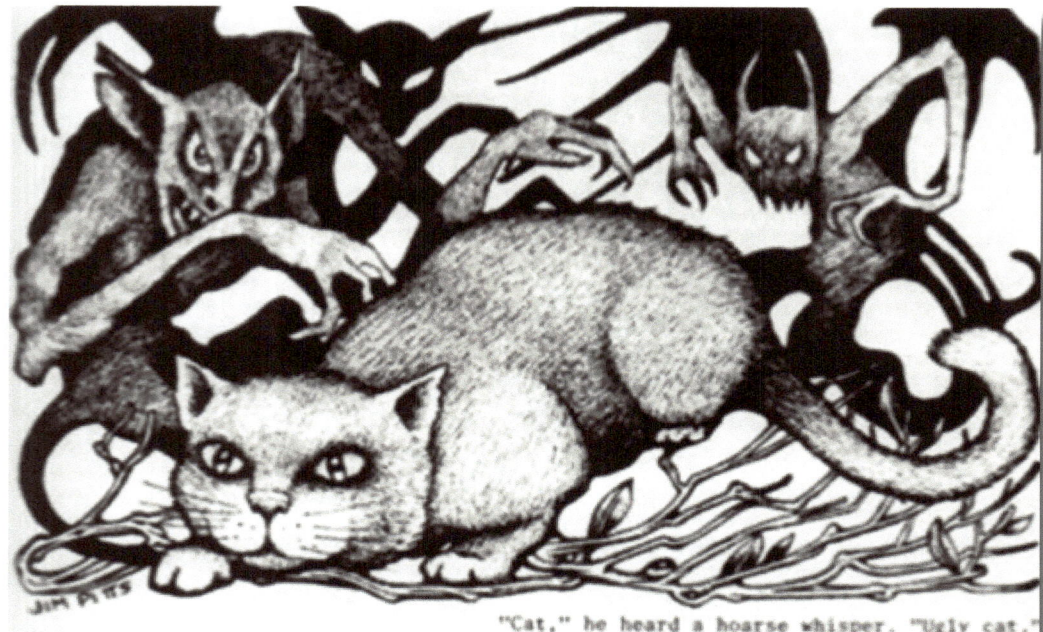

Top left: interior illustration for *The Grey Horde* by David Malpass.

Top right: interior illustration for *John and the Magic Skillet* by Jessica Amanda Salmonson

Bottom left: interior illustration for *The Elementals* by Frances Garfield

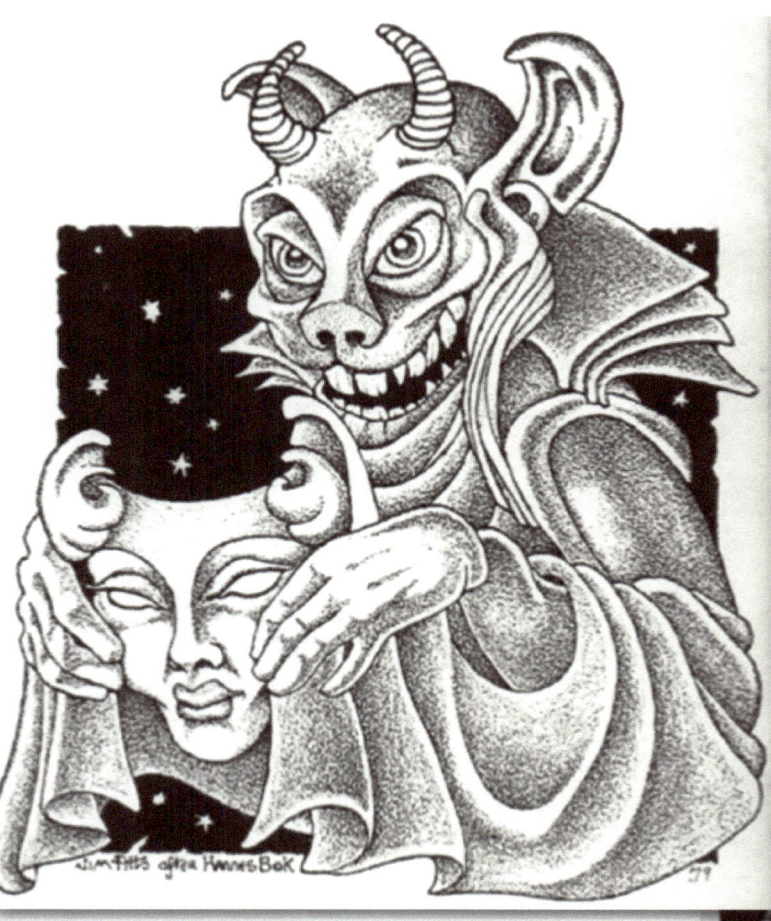

"After Hannes Bok' - Left: based on a sketch by Hannes Bok

Botton left: interior illustration for Adrian Cole's *The Exile of Earthendale*

Bottom right: *The Pit of Wings* by Ramsey Campbell. *Fantasy Tales* Vol 13, No 7, Winter 1991.

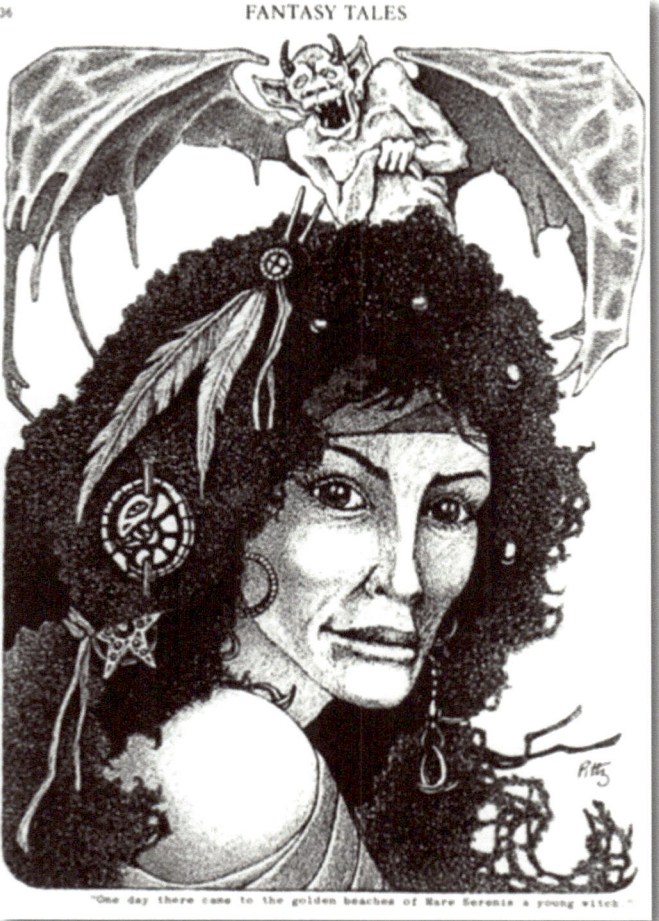

Then the vases swayed, and showed him the figures whose cowled heads he'd glimpsed reflected in the sea. (Art: Jim Pitts).

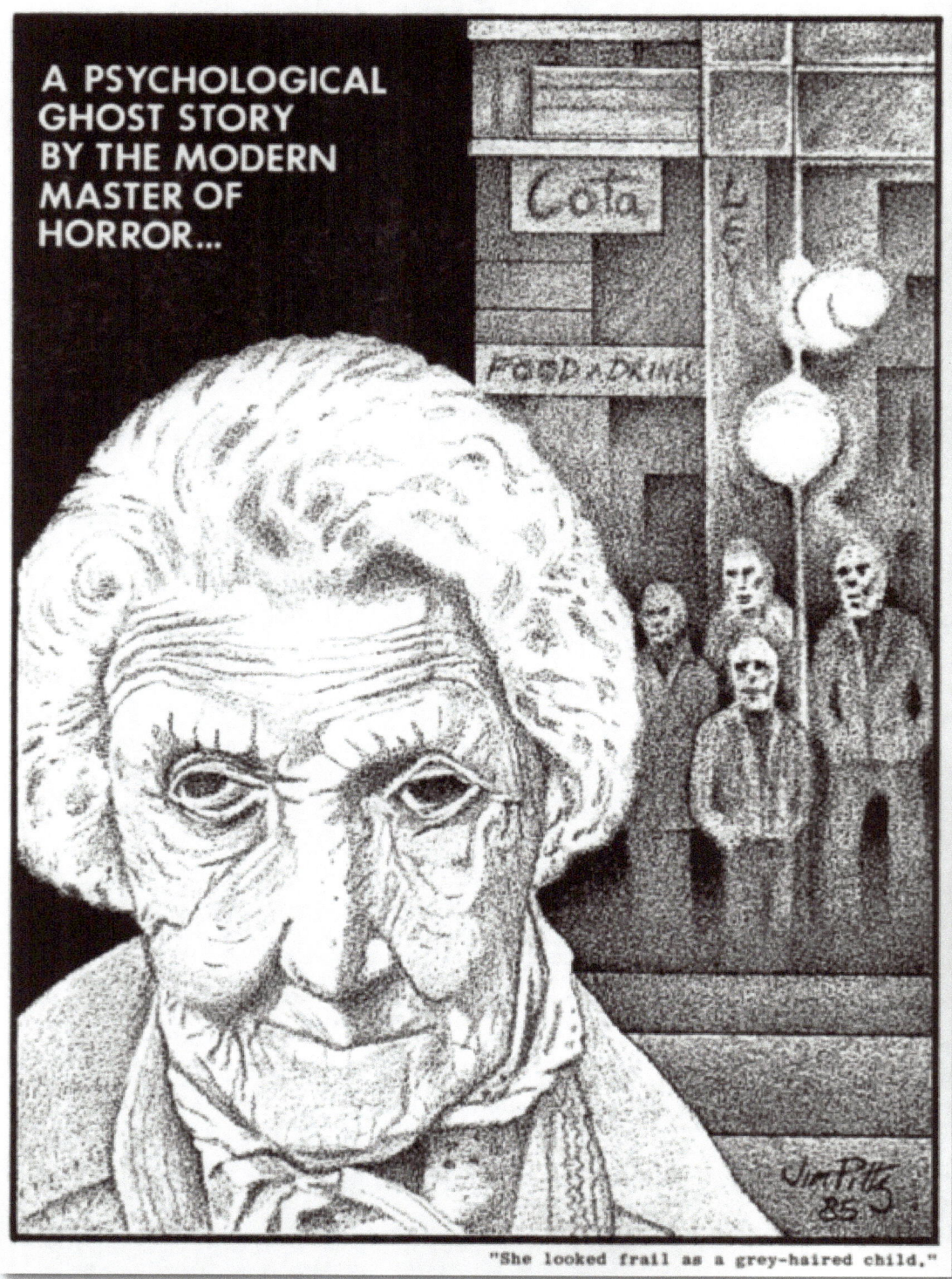

Interior illustration for *The Sneering* by Ramsey Campbell.

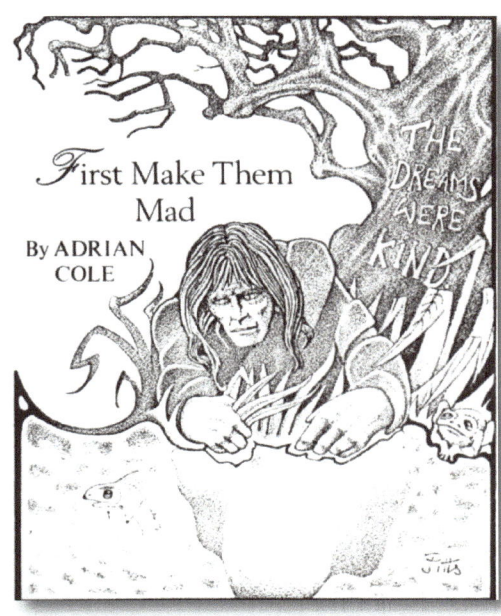

Interior illustrations for Adrian Cole's *First Make Them Mad*.

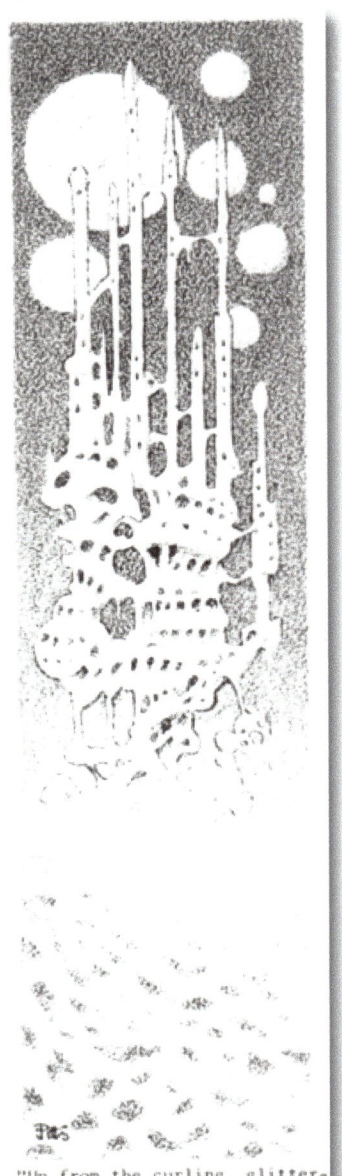

"Up from the curling, glittering glory of the mooncoral city the ragged towers of the sorcerers thrust."

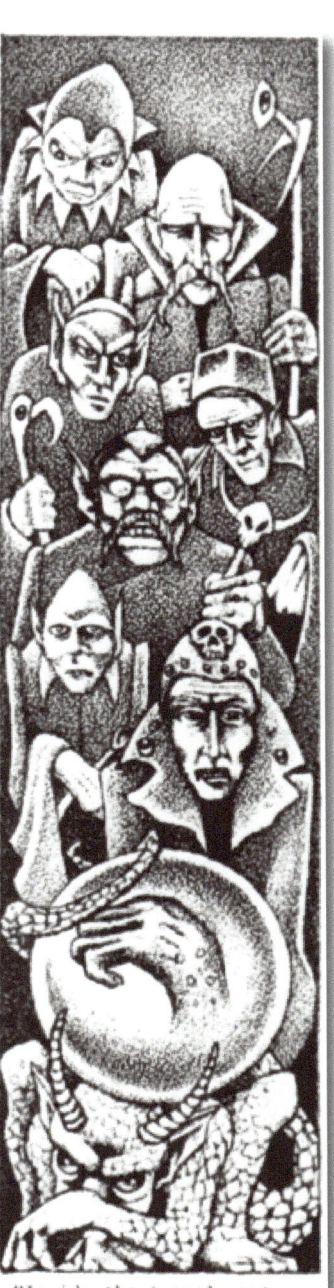

"Inside the translucent globe the deep blue mist swirled ceaselessly like a living cloud."

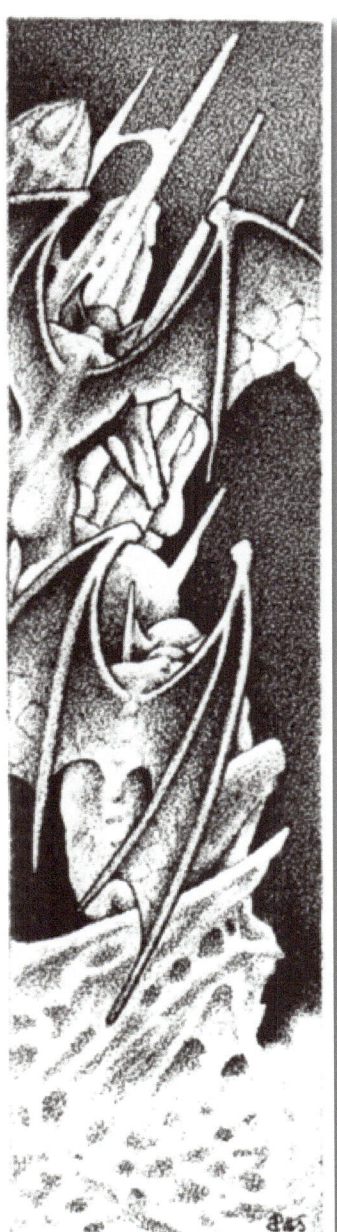

"Owlworm nodded, spitting, then spread his delicate membranous wings and slipped away into the air."

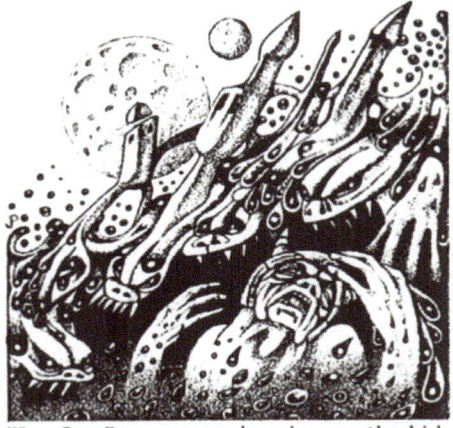

"Dan Zar Enzo screamed as he saw the hideous faces that leered."

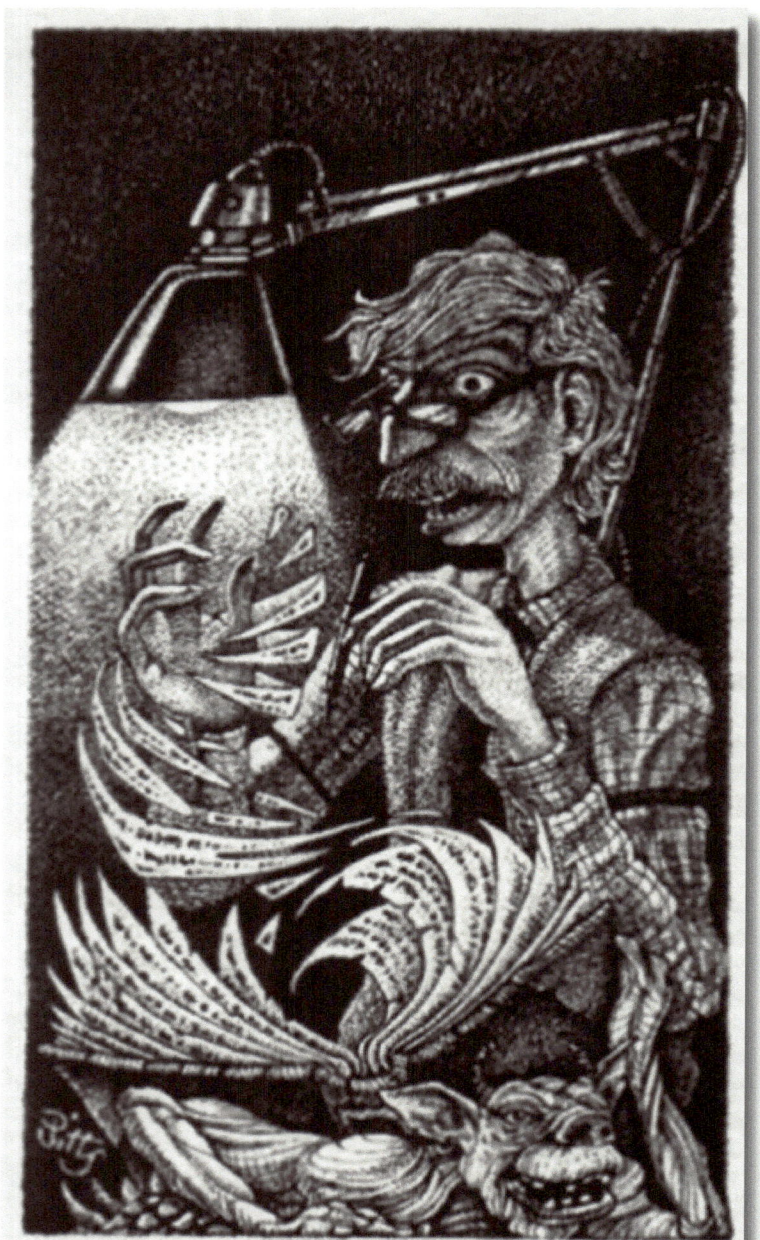

Cartwright-Hughes jerked his hand from the book in revulsion... (Artist: Jim Pitts)

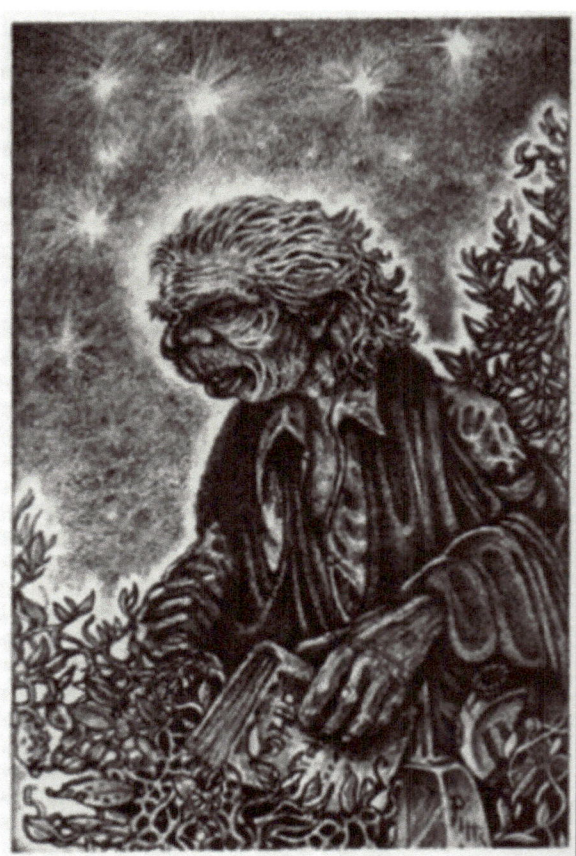

"He uttered his name on a rising note of apology and showed me, in his other hand, a publication, a manual." (Art: Jim Pitts)

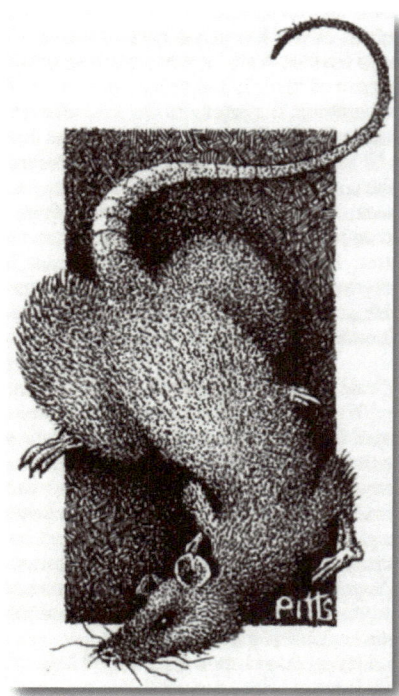

Top left: *Writer's Cramp* by David A. Riley.

Top right: The Bridge People by J. N. Williamson

KADATH

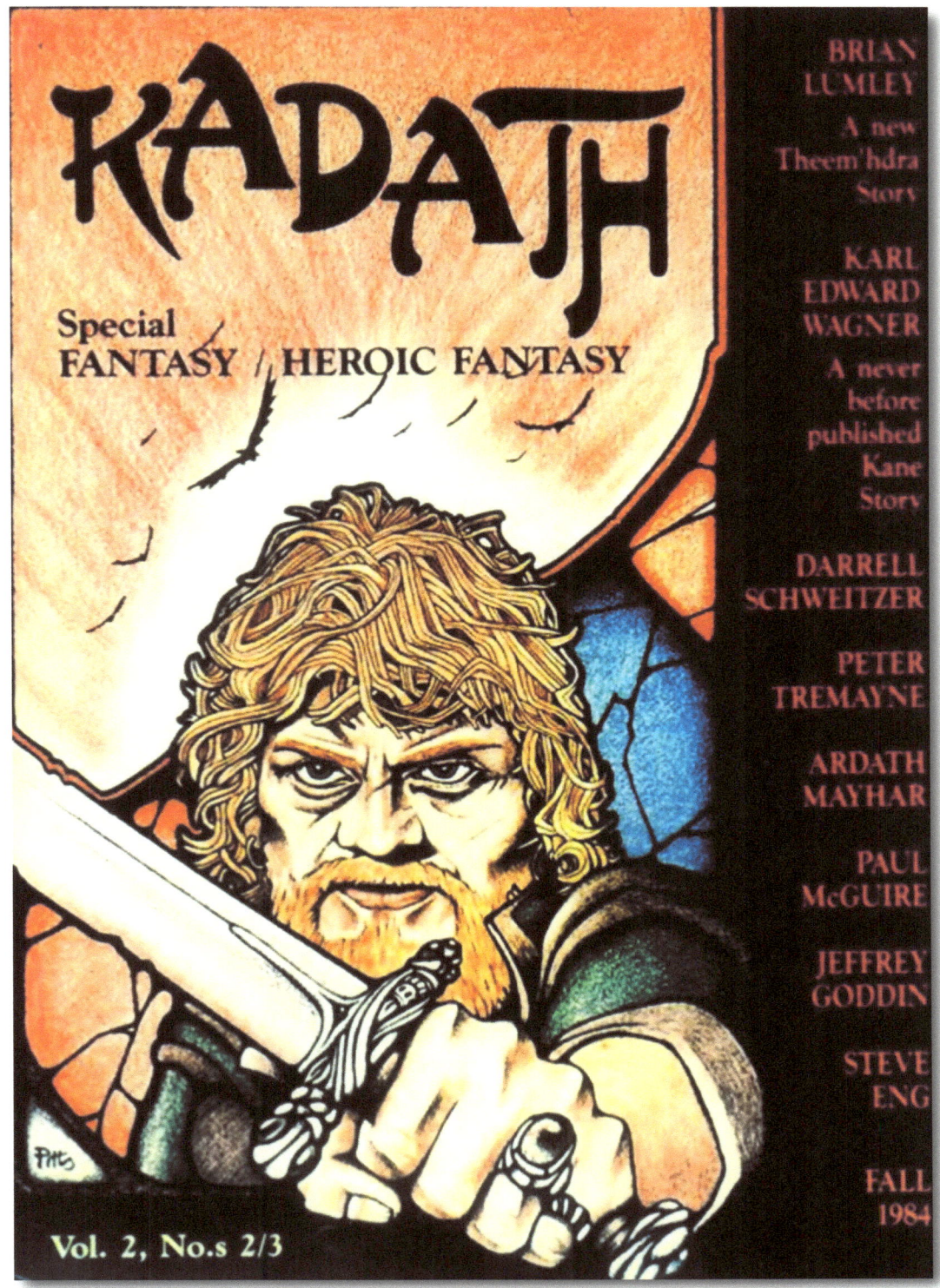

Karl Edward Wagner's Kane

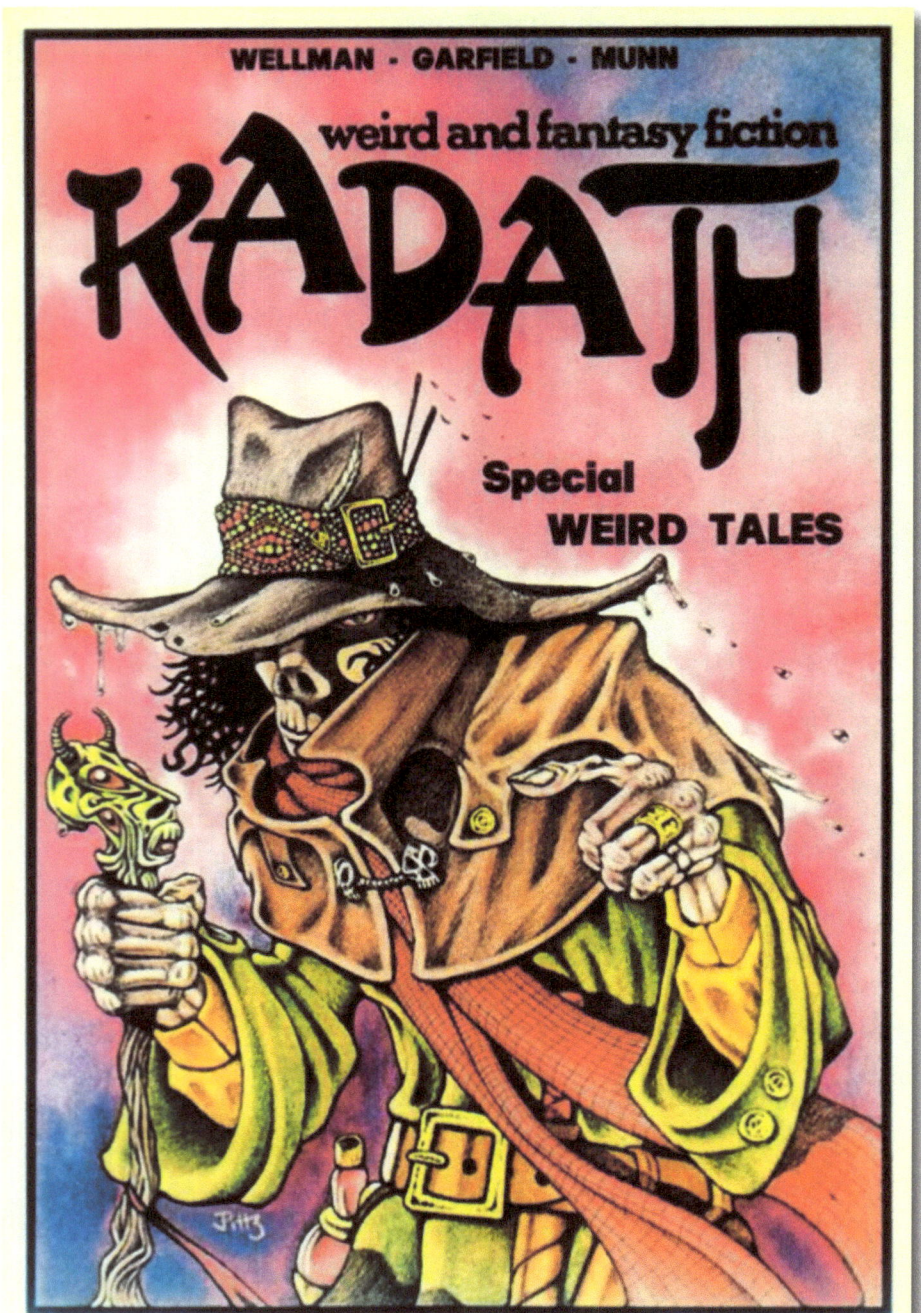

"Magic Man" an original idea by Jim Pitts

"Titus Crow" - back cover of *Kadath* Vol 2, No 1, 1982

During the early 80s Jim's artwork featured on three covers of the Italian fantasy magazine *Kadath*.

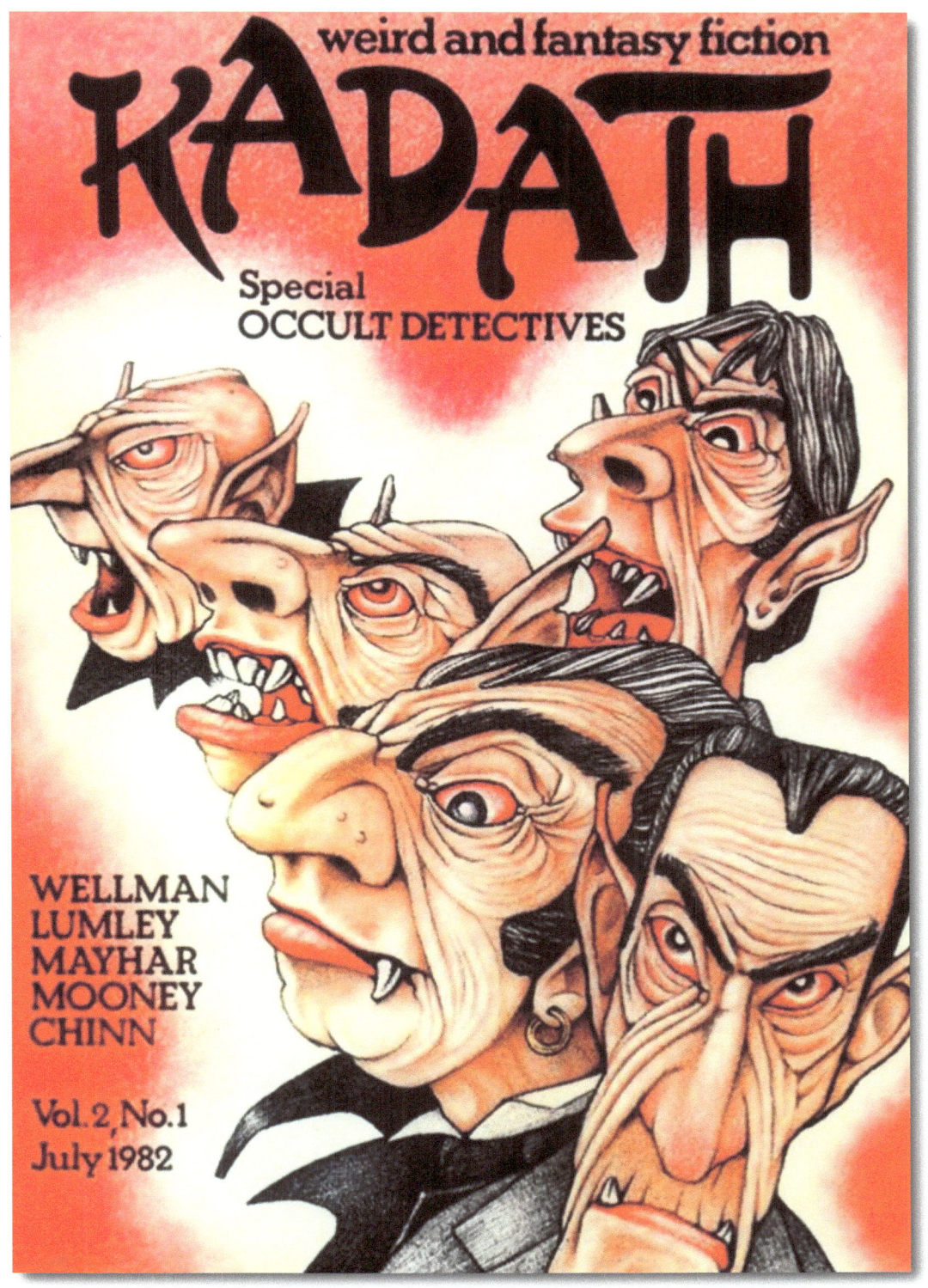

Vampires: "In the Pink"

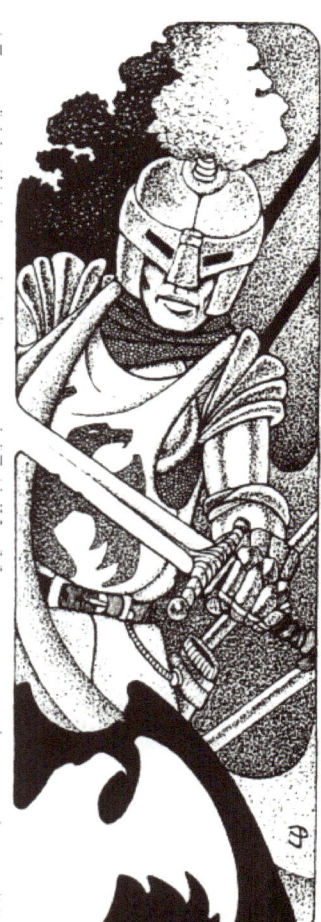

Interior artwork from *Kadath* Vol 2 No 1, 1982   The two illustrations to the left are *Echo of Thunder* by Ardath Mayhar

The Treasure of Abbot Thomas by M. R. James - This illustration was used quite randomly by Francesca in *Kadath*. It was recently placed on the book cover of *Ghosts & Scholars 27*, where Rosemary Pardoe used it more appropriately.

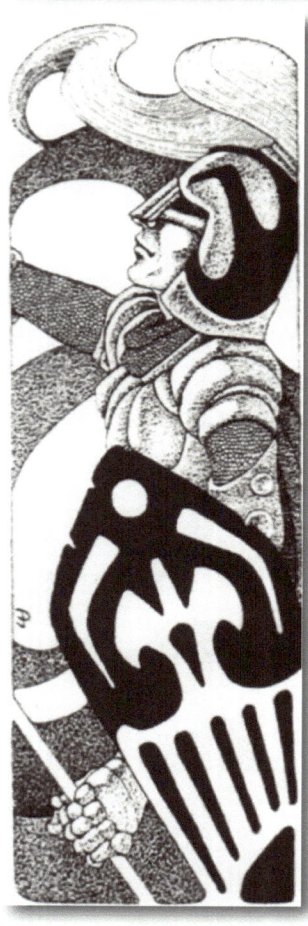

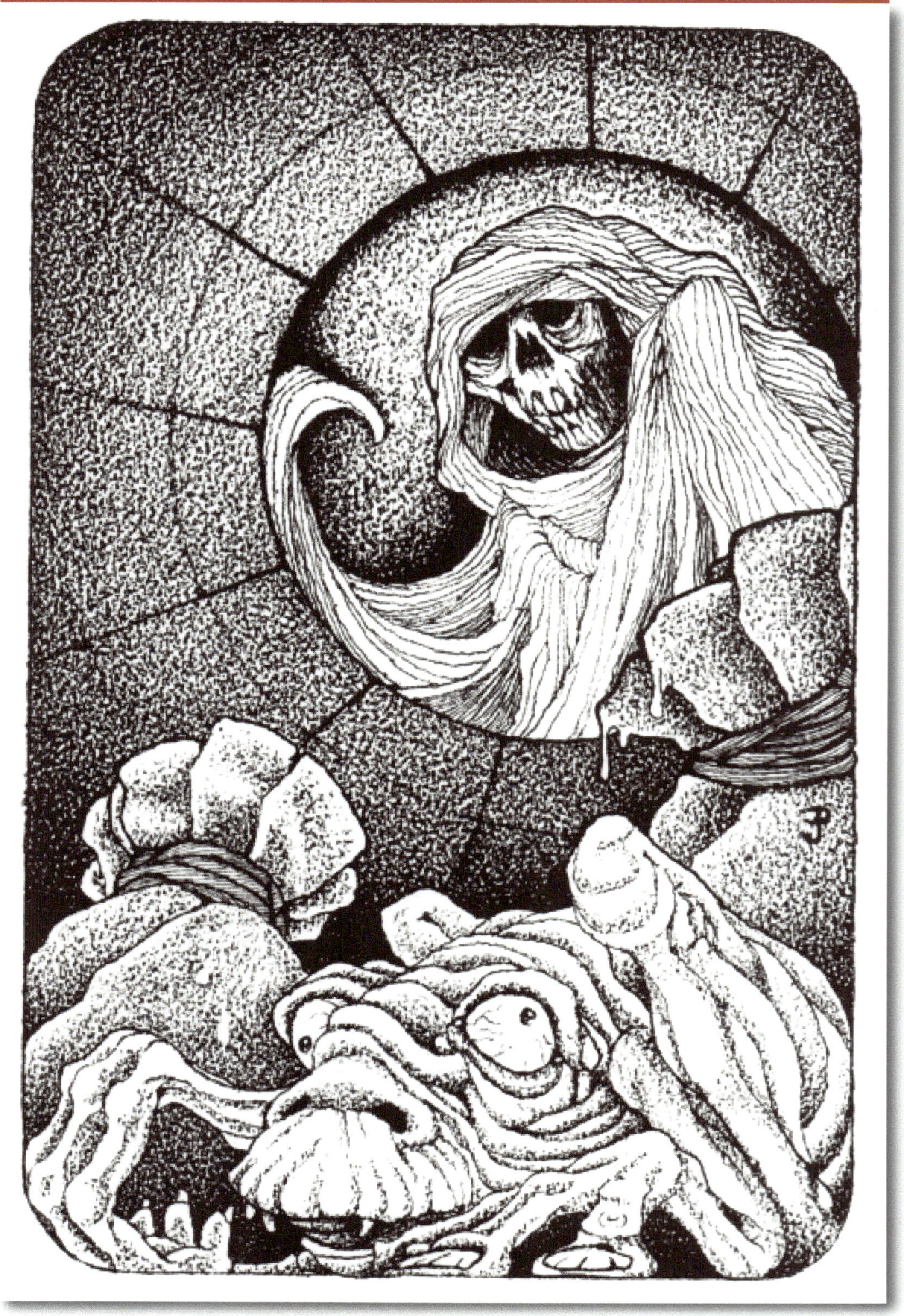

"How Singol Died" by Gordon Larkin, 1975

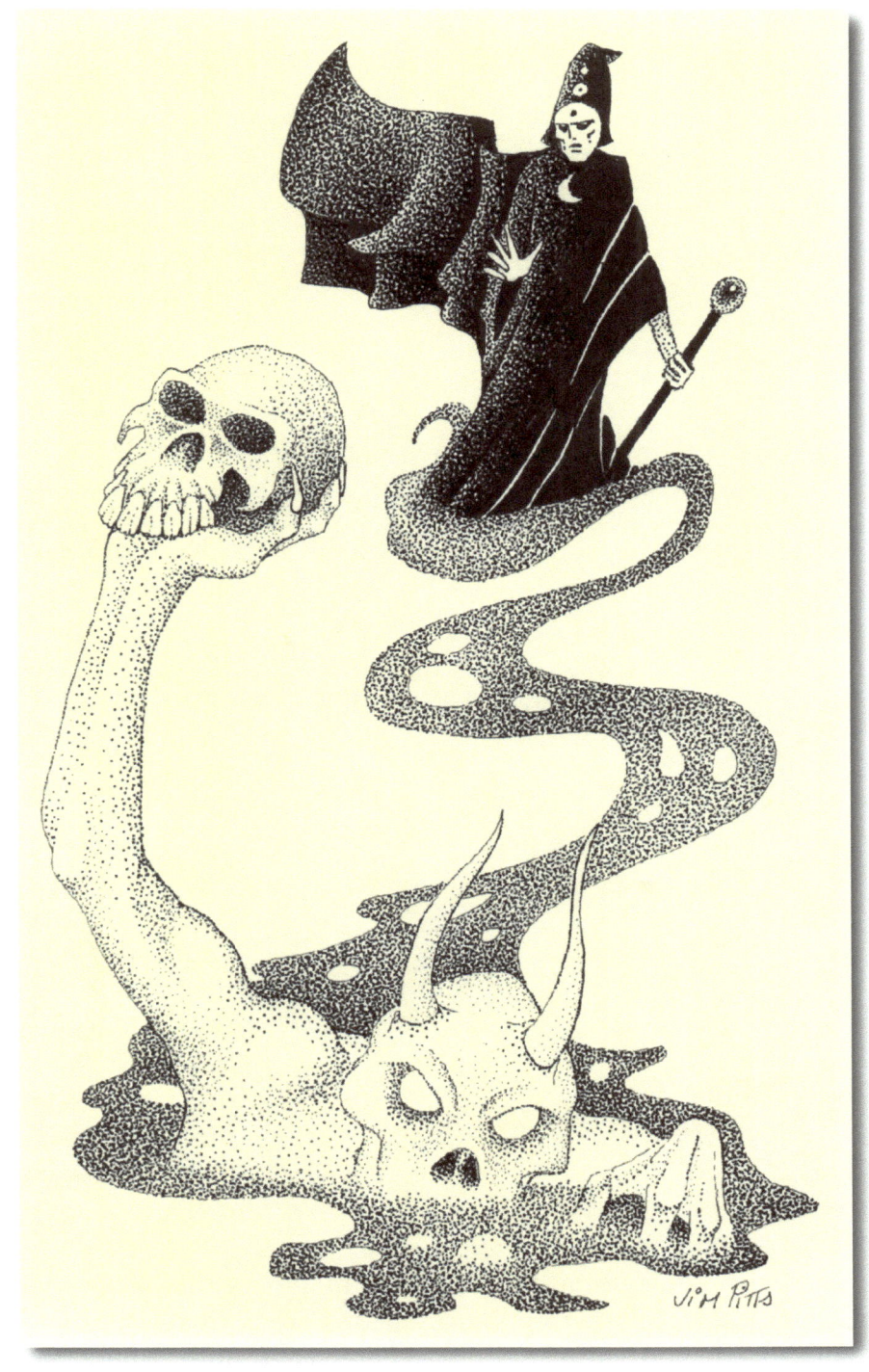

JIM PITTS
by Ramsey Campbell

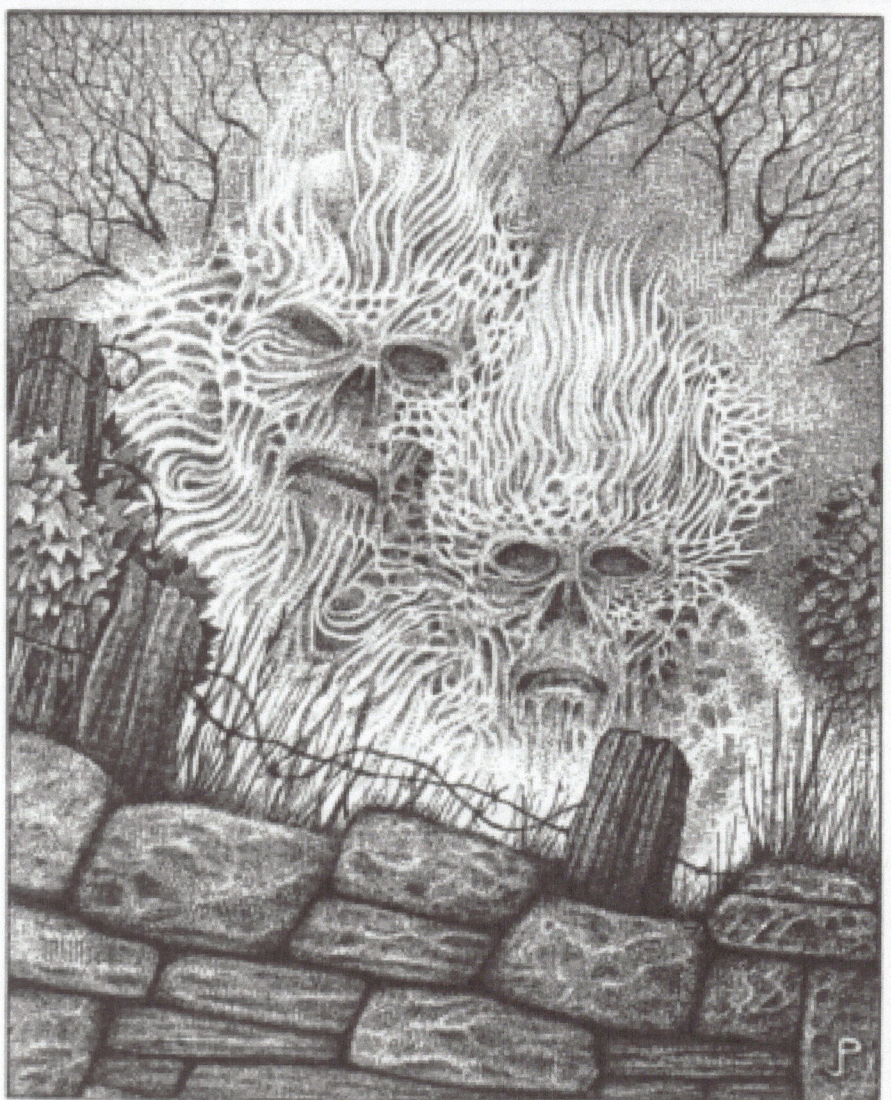

The above illustration was published in *Northern Chills*, edited by Graeme Hurry (Kimota Press) in 1994 for Ramsey Campbell's story *Above the World*.

Though I started reading tales of supernatural horror and the weird at an age so inhumanly precocious it rivalled even Wilbur Whateley, these fields have worked their dark magic on me just as much by visual methods. Rupert Bear's scrawny prancing Christmas tree haunted my infant nights, and soon Arthur Hughes' goblin horrors (illustrating George Macdonald) did. At seven years old – too young to be allowed to buy the magazine – I saw my first *Weird Tales* cover in a shop window, and three years later I began to collect all the issues I could lay my hands on. By then the magazine had gone to its grave, but its ghost retained its legendary power, and for me the covers and interior illustrations lived up to the magazine's name even when the prose they represented sometimes fell short. In my teens I believed I could only enjoy this experience by reaching into the past, as *Weird Tales* roused in me a kind of uncanny nostalgia, all the more poignant because there would be no more issues. I was wrong to feel its qualities were gone, however. A whole generation of enthusiasts who may well have felt as I did – writers, editors, artists – dedicated themselves to keeping the tradition alive, and among the absolutely crucial figures was Jim Pitts.

I first became aware of him in David Sutton's seminal magazine *Shadow* (a little magazine, but only in the best sense). You'll read David's reminiscences elsewhere in this volume, which also reproduces the first Pitts image I enthused about, his *House on the Borderland*. At the time I invoked Hannes Bok, an early influence, but only to praise Jim. Now that I look at the picture again I think it's altogether more individual than my comment at the time suggested. Not just Hodgson's creatures but the house itself live in that image, reinvented by Jim's considerable imagination and technique.

Jim was one of the artists who gave the youthful British Fantasy Society its look – which is to say they celebrated fantasy in all its forms. One of his covers in particular haunted me – the armoured skeletons that display their glowing colours on page 81 of this book. At the time I felt it could almost summon *Weird Tales* from its grave – certainly it could have graced the cover of an issue of The Unique Magazine – and soon, I think, it helped to reincarnate that publication. That was certainly my fancy when the first issuer of *Fantasy Tales* slipped through the letterbox forty years ago. The logo displayed its roots in the best pulp tradition, and so did Jim's cover image, the weathered swordsman and his busty mate behind whom looms a gleeful hooded skeleton. The lady's proud nipple prepares the way for the startlingly explicit hermaphroditic figure that accompanies the cover tale within; Jim is as much of his time as of a tradition. The issue also boasts his witty illustration of a wizard in occult conversation and – alas, now only a nostalgic reference – two little illustrations advertising the Fantasy Centre bookshop.

In time I had the privilege of being illustrated by Jim. His cover for my story "The Sneering" can be found here on page

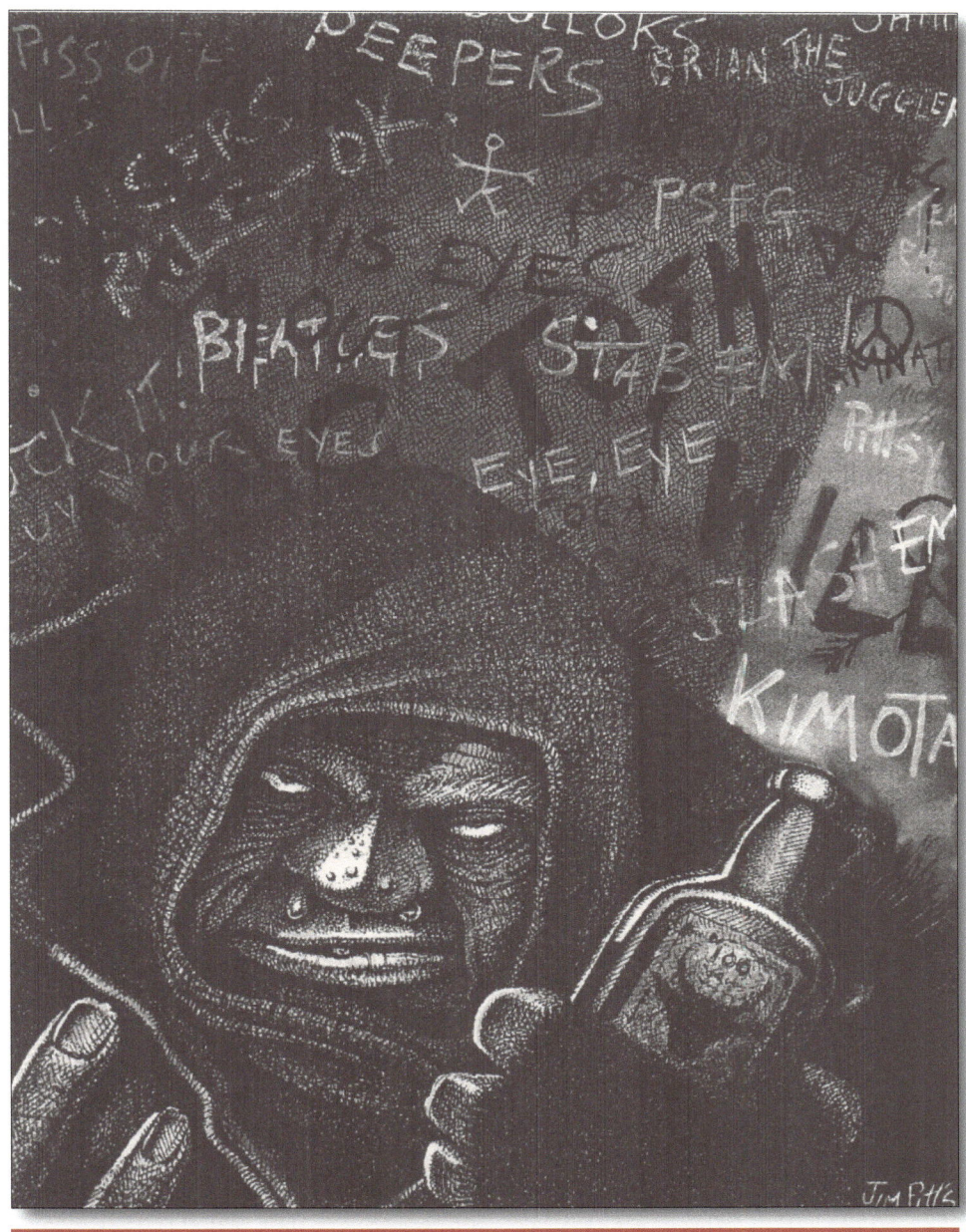

Mackintosh Willy from *Northern Chills*

88. It displays quite a few of his trademark elements – the sureness and economy of line, the expressively restricted palette – but distils many of the emotions the story takes hundreds of words to communicate. He conveys both compassion and threat even more succinctly in the interior illustration for the tale, and the pair of images express a subtle crepuscular menace. We were among the loyal band who continued to contribute when the magazine, having begun as a semi-professional labour of love, turned professional through the offices of Robinson Publishing. Welcome though this development was, I confess that I missed the double columns of prose on each page, a staple of the pulps but now generally abandoned. In this incarnation of the magazine Jim gracefully envisaged one of my fantasies, "The Pit of Wings". His second illustration, and I hope my tale, survived a rogue caption that referred to humber instead of hunger. Leafing through the issues as an aid to writing this appreciation, I experience a pang of nostalgia akin to the feelings *Weird Tales* still prompts. It occurs to me now that the art in both magazines is crucial to the love we feel for them – that it's an essential part of their magic. Just as magical for me is his vision of my tale "Above the World", an illustration that raises ghostly menace to a peak of awe.

Let me not suggest that Jim is simply or even largely about nostalgia. As we see in this collection, his work is highly recognisable as his and continues to develop. I'll end by enthusing about some of my favourites, resisting the urge to celebrate the entire contents one by one. Where are those horribly incomplete voyagers bound in a rowing-boat under the moon? What skull-faced apparition is forming from the clouds above the snowbound house, and what fate awaits the traveller? What welcome has the tentacled denizen of the deep in store for the drowning man? Khash and his equally grim-visaged companion turn the very air crimson with carnage, and the vultures prepare to swoop. In one elemental image, faces appear to explode with the awful pressure of uncanniness. From Lovecraft's tale, have we ever seen an old man more terrible? By contrast, a Deep One prefigures the pathos that recent writers have unearthed in Innsmouth. Cthulhu shows up several times, and an image bejewelled with colour provides him with an altogether grislier Deep One for a worshipper, while elsewhere a greenish moon lends him more malevolence. And let's not forget humour, embodied in (for instance) a splendidly disreputable trio of Irishmen and a bunch of five vampires dis-

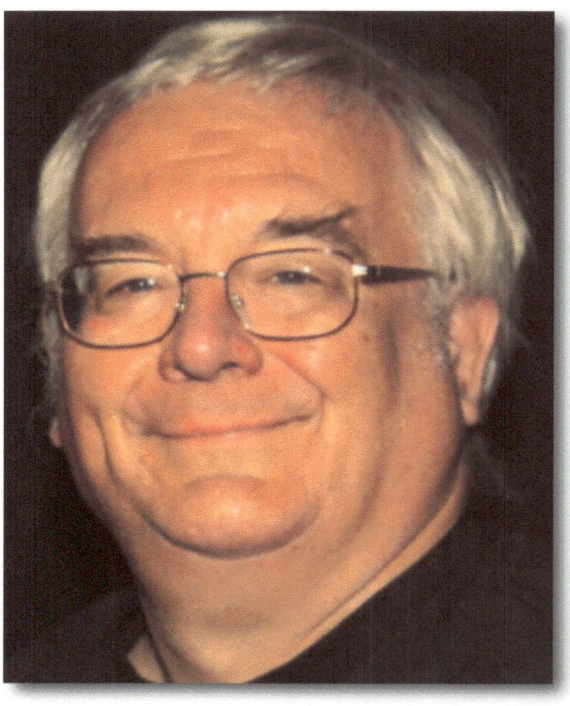

Ramsey Campbell

playing various stages of voraciousness, while a pockmarked crescent-headed creature is a witty product of lunar surrealism. By contrast, Jim's tough guys look as implacable and primitive as monoliths, and the houses by the dead water are delicately spectral. Further on, is that a tentacled sentient tree or something even stranger? Like much of Jim's work, the image suggests whole layers of weirdness – see the drawing where masks and faces appear interchangeable (the King in Yellow would relish it, I imagine), or the scarecrow whose hands are all too human. A final piece among so many that take my fancy: his luminously lyrical cover for *Marianne Dreams* consolidates and develops elements that have always been crucial to his art. May he long continue to surprise and delight us.

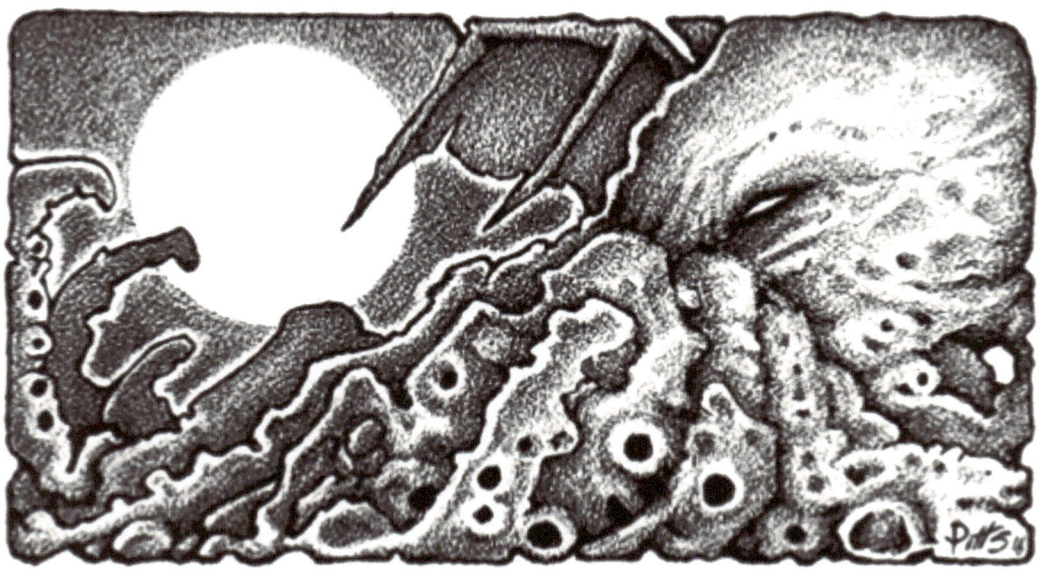

LEGEND HORROR CLASSICS 1975

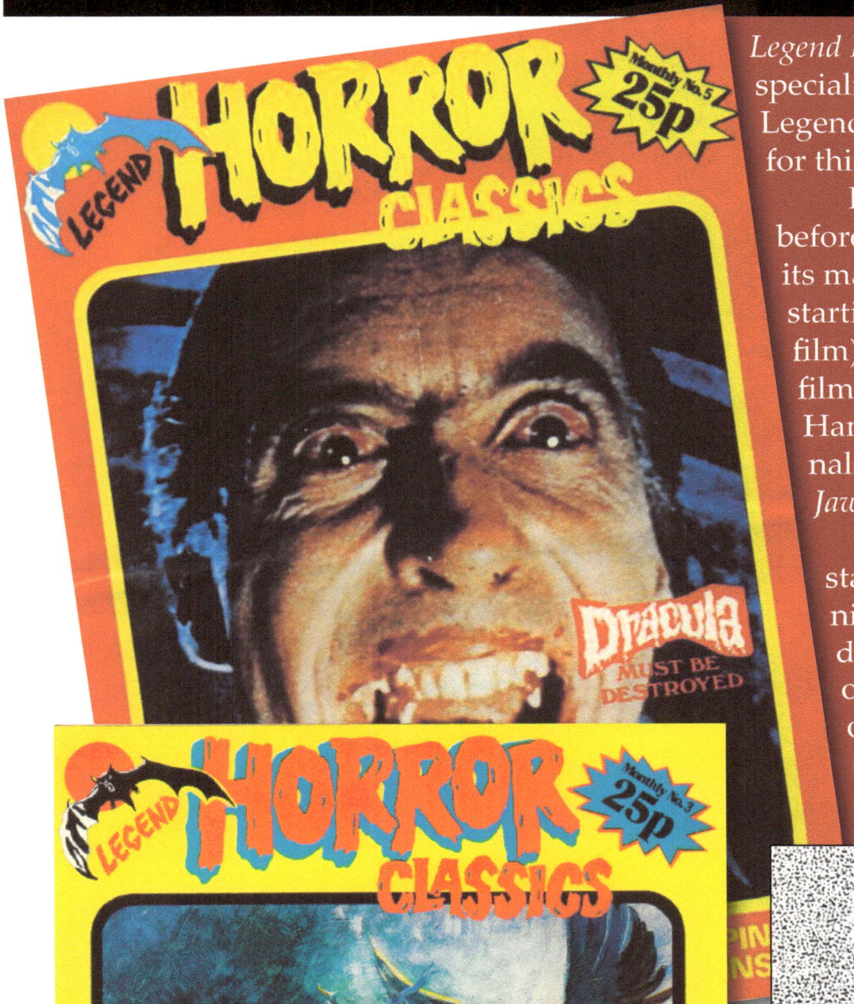

Legend Horror Classics was a British magazine specialising in posters that was published by Legend Publishing during the 1970s. It lasted for thirteen issues before it folded.

Kevin O'Neill was initially its art editor, before becoming its full editor later. One of its main features was a four-page comic strip, starting with *Dracula* (based on the 1973 film), then *Frankenstein* (based on the 1933 film), followed by *The 7th Voyage of Sinbad*, Hammer's *Dracula*, then a series of originals, like *Blood Lust of the Zombies* and *Killer Jaws*.

An odd magazine, even by horror standards, it did at least give an opportunity for Jim to showcase his ability to draw more realistic portraits, such as the one depicting Vincent Price as the notorious Matthew Hopkins from *Witchfinder General* shown below.

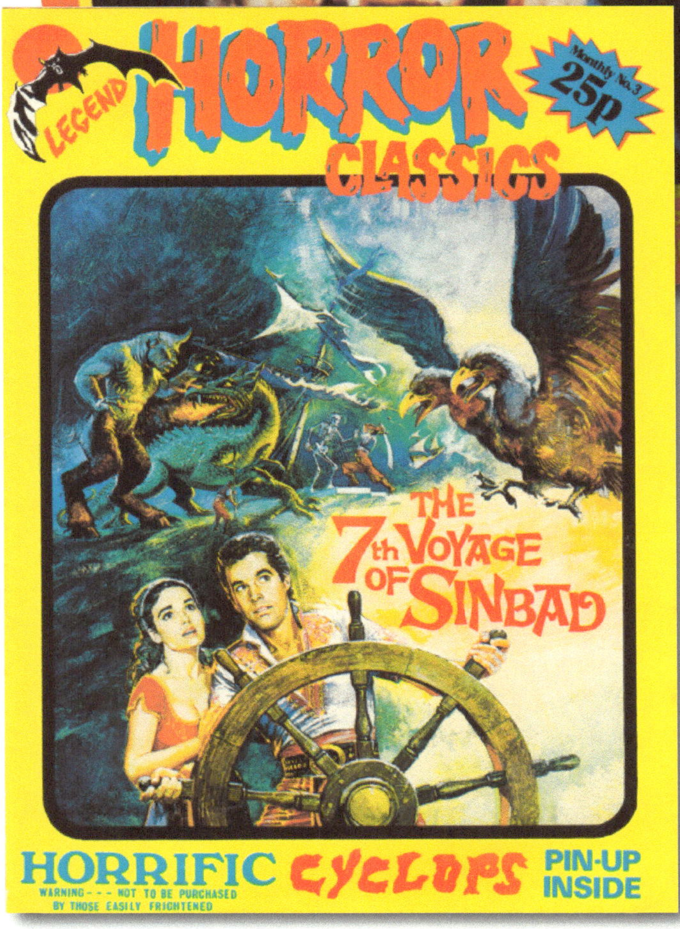

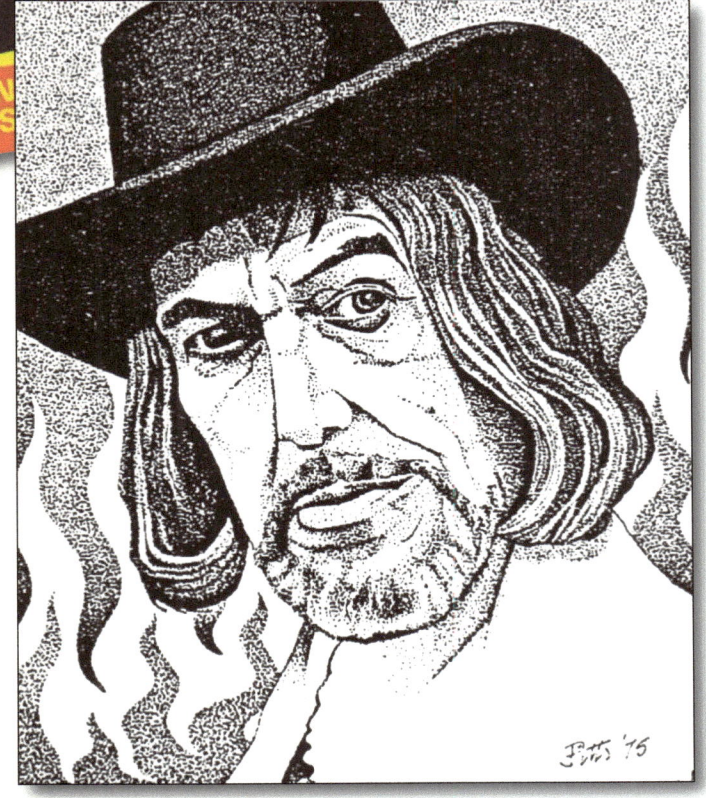

Legend of Horror Classics from 1975 - Jim did three illustrations which were printed full-page on the back covers: Boris Karloff as the Frankenstein creature, Vincent Price as the Witchfinder General, and Boris Karloff as the Mummy.

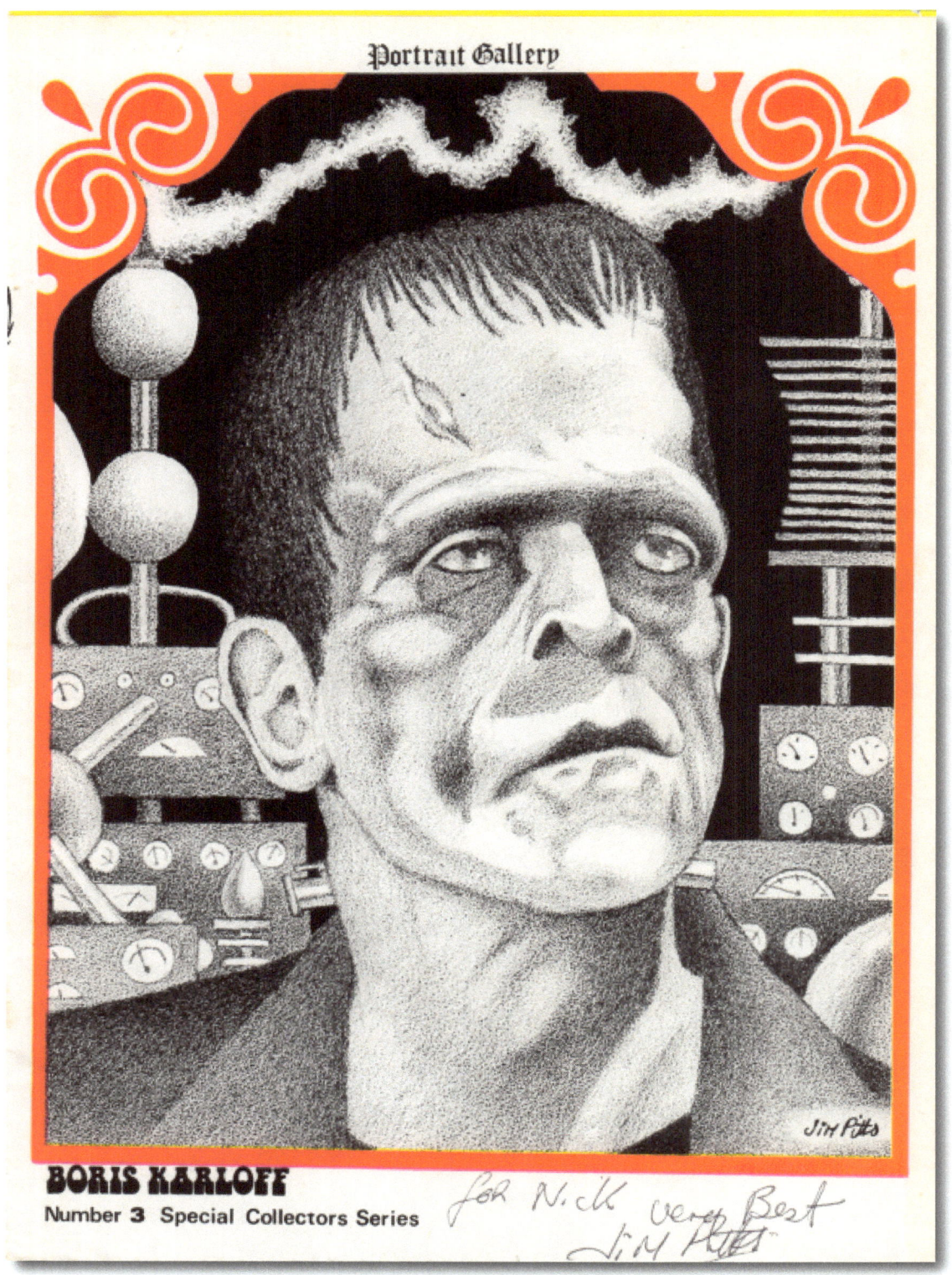

From the collection of Nick Caffrey

This also appeared in *The BFS Bulletin* July/Aug 1980, Volume 8, No 2

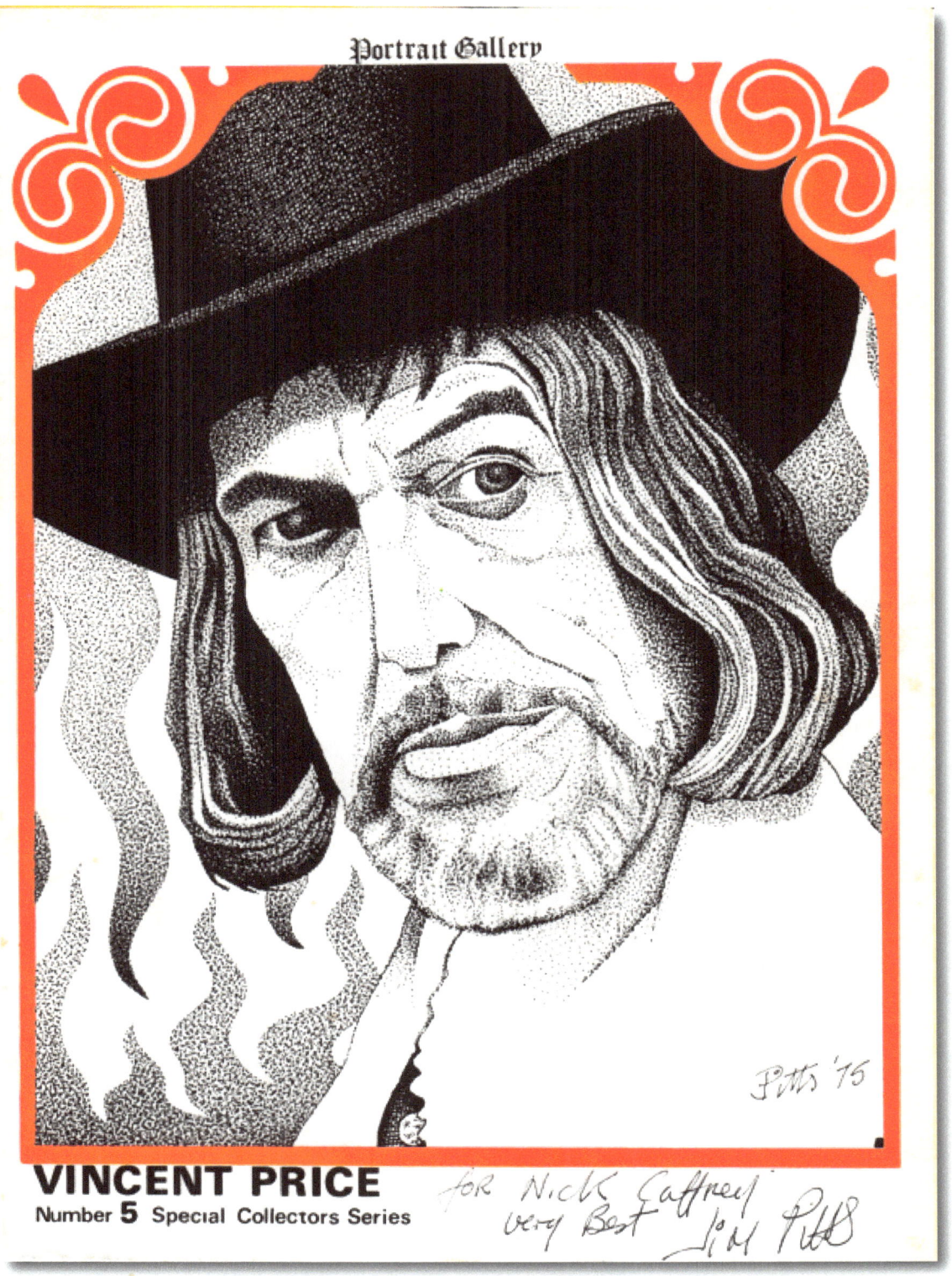

From the collection of Nick Caffrey

The third picture included in *Legend Horror Classics* was Boris Karloff in *The Mummy*. Unfortunately we haven't been able to get hold of the original magazine in which this appeared. This is an enlarged version of the illustration which appeared as a much smaller image in *The BFS Bulletin*, May/June 1981, Volume 9, No 1.

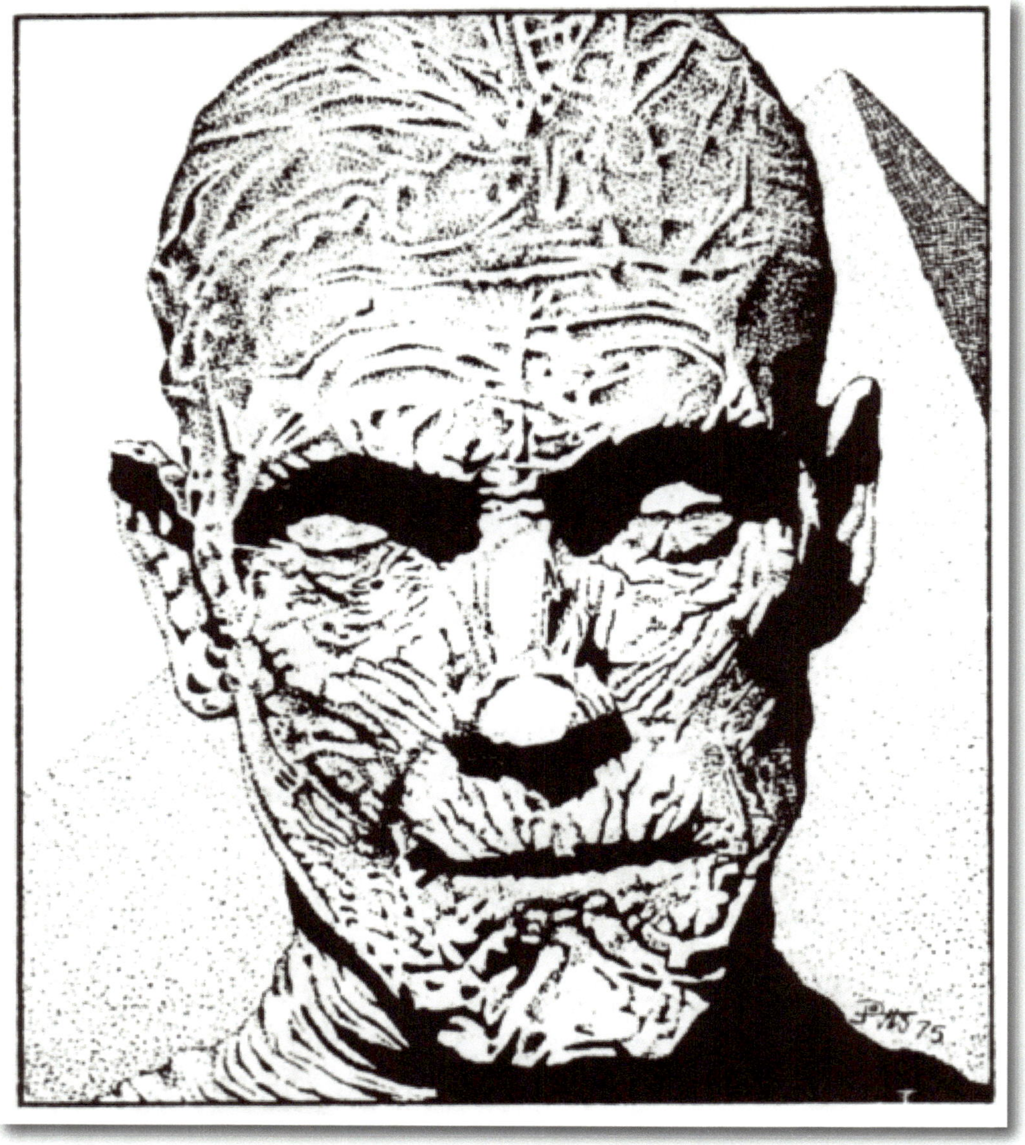

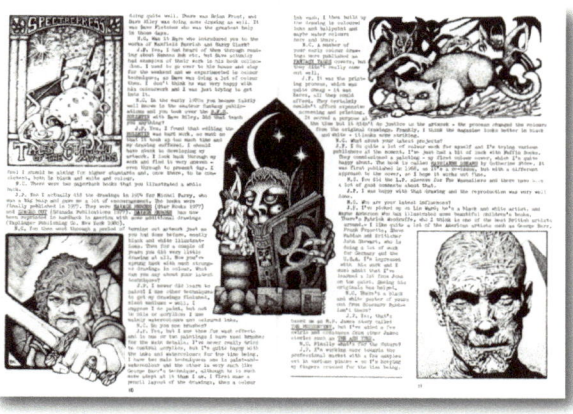

Cthulhu Moon from 1975
(from the collection of Stephen Jones)

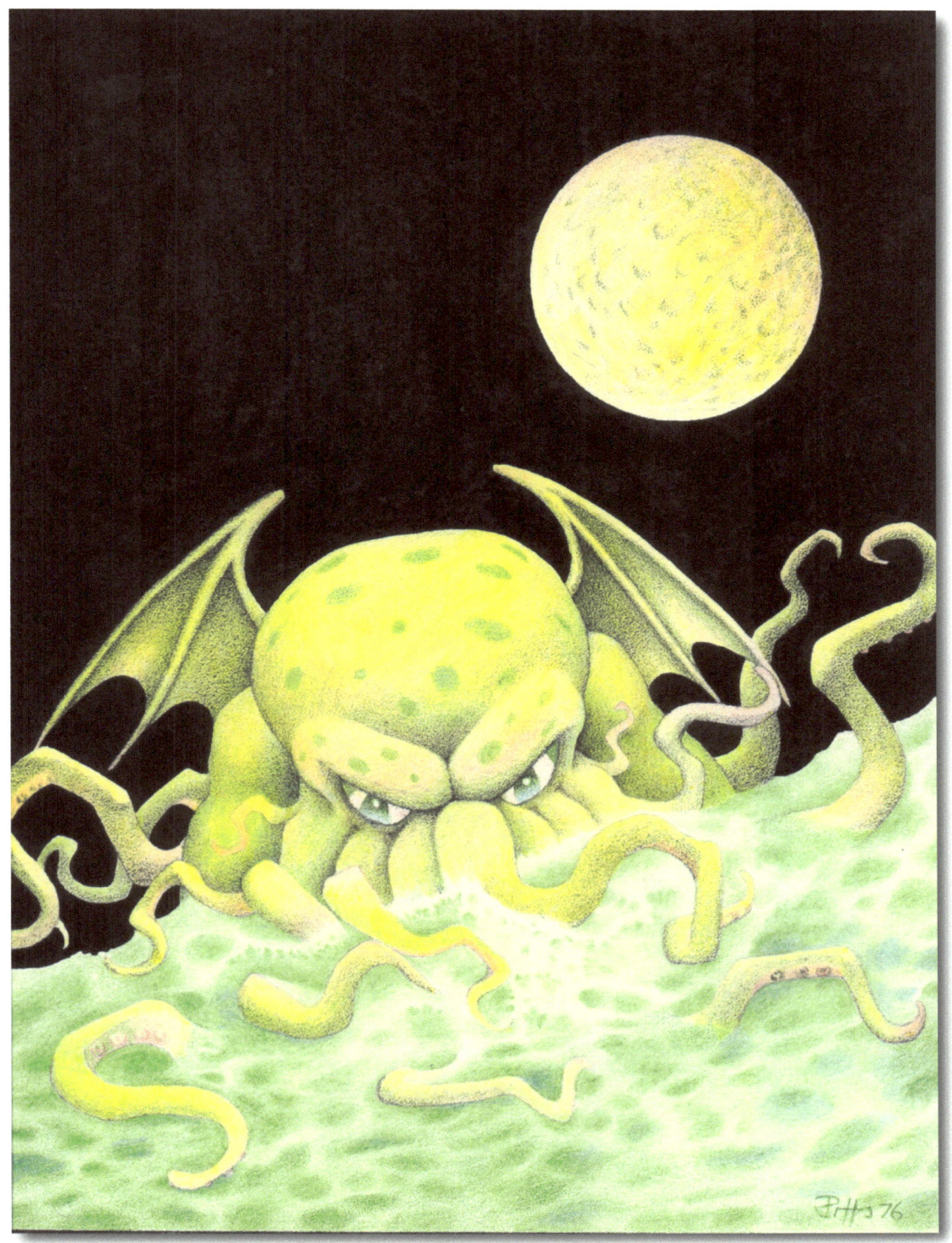

"Vampyre" Hand-tinted print

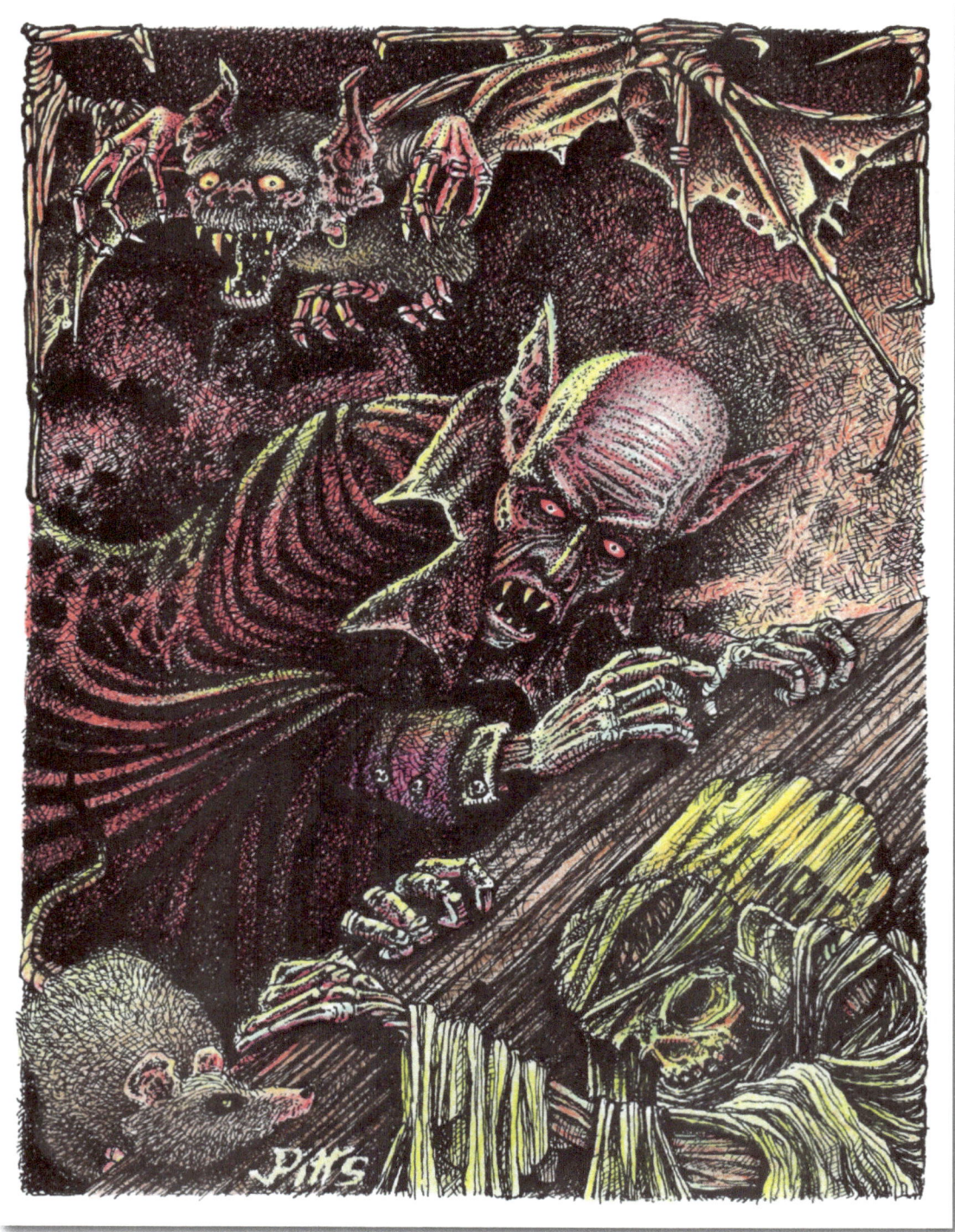

Back in 1970-71 I submitted artwork to David Sutton and Jon Harvey. By 1972 I had gained my first accolade, the Ken McIntyre Award for Best Artist at Eastercon that year. Twenty years later and after the publication of numerous b&w and colour illustrations - in both professional, semi-professional and fan markets - I was awarded the British Fantasy Society Best Artist Award for the consecutive years of 1992 and 1993. Almost fifty years later - after retiring from industry - I am still illustrating magazines and books for various publishers and friends, both here in the UK and America. Without the following people none of this would have been possible. The first four guys are the real reason I was ever published in the first place:

David Riley, David Sutton, Jon Harvey, & Steve Jones

The rest of these ladies and gentlemen also deserve mentioning
for their friendship and help over the years...

Nick Caffrey, Peter Coleborn, Adrian Cole, Stuart Schiff, Brian Lumley, Jo Fletcher, Ramsey Campbell, Dave Carson, John Caffrey, Sylvia Starshine, Les & Val Edwards, Andrew Smith, "Whisperin'" John Carter, Mike Chinn, Rosemary Pardoe, Sandra Sutton,

and finally my thanks and love to **Joyce Tierney**, my partner for the last twenty years!

There are many more. I'm sure they know who they they are! It's been a great ride,
and the years are still rolling on!

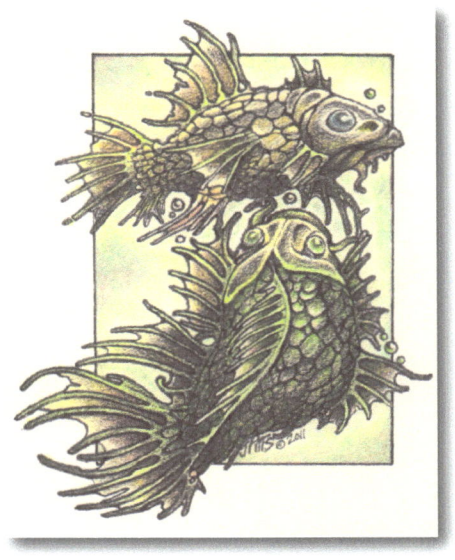

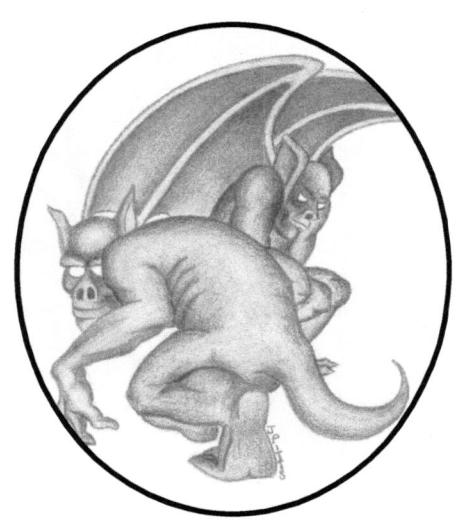

For details of all the books published by Parallel Universe Publications check our website:
paralleluniversepublications.blogspot.co.uk/

www.ingramcontent.com/pod-product-compliance
Lightning Source LLC
Chambersburg PA
CBHW051152220526

45473CB00003B/748